16 Years 2025-2010

ICSE
CHAPTERWISE TOPICWISE
QUESTION BANK

Computer Applications
Class 10

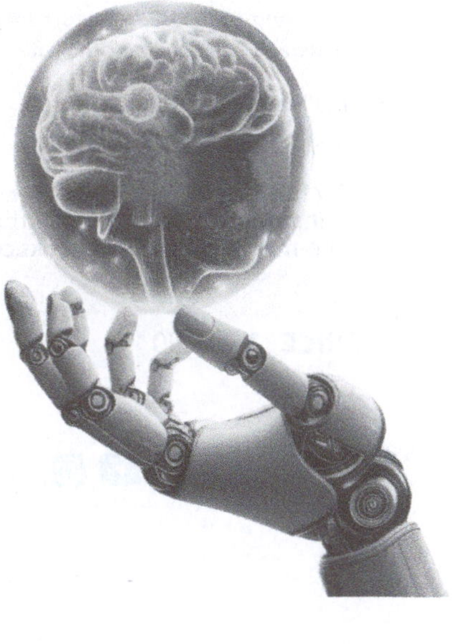

Author
Supriya Patel

arihant
SUCCESS AND NOTHING LESS

arihant
SUCCESS AND NOTHING LESS

ARIHANT PRAKASHAN
(School Division Series)

卐 ADMINISTRATIVE & PRODUCTION OFFICES

Regd. Office
'Ramchhaya' 4577/15, Agarwal Road, Darya Ganj, New Delhi -110002
Tele: 011- 47630600, 43518550

Head Office
Kalindi, TP Nagar, Meerut (UP) - 250002, Tel: 0121-7156203, 7156204

卐 SALES & SUPPORT OFFICES

Agra, Ahmedabad, Bengaluru, Bareilly, Chennai, Delhi, Guwahati, Hyderabad, Jaipur, Jhansi, Kolkata, Lucknow, Nagpur & Pune.

卐 **PO No :** TXT-XX-XXXXXXX-X-XX

Published By Arihant Publications (India) Ltd.

For further information about the books published by Arihant, log on to www.arihantbooks.com or e-mail at info@arihantbooks.com

卐 **PRICE** ₹245.00

Follow us on

Achieving 99+
Marks in Board Exams

Achieving 99+ marks in board exams is definitely an ambitious goal, but with the right approach and these 7 tips from toppers, you can definitely increase your chances of success!

Here are the 7 Topper Tips to ace your board exams:

1. Master the art of consistency

Consistency builds understanding and confidence, both crucial for excelling in exams.

2. Build a winning study strategy

Create a personalised timetable that prioritises subjects based on your strengths and weaknesses.

3. Befriend the syllabus

Focus on high-weightage topics and prioritise mastering core concepts before moving on to advanced ones.

4. Embrace active learning

Explain concepts to yourself or in study groups to solidify understanding.

5. Conquer the past

Solve Past years' papers and Sample Papers under timed conditions to practice time management and understand paper pattern.

6. Seek help, when needed!

Don't hesitate to clarify doubts with teachers, tutors, or study groups. Asking questions strengthens your understanding and prevents confusion.

7. Prioritise well-being

Eat nutritious meals, get enough sleep, have regular exercise practice stress management techniques like meditation to stay calm and focused during exams.

These tips are just a starting point, and you can personalise them to fit your learning style and preferences.

Description of Newly Added Features

01

Revising Basic Java Concepts

TREND ANALYSIS 3 YEARS

Average No. of Questions Across all Sets

	Types of Questions	2023	2019	2018
Revising Basic Java Concepts	1 Mark	11	-	-
	2 Marks	6	12	10
	15 Marks	1	-	-

Trend Analysis

At the start of each chapter, Trend Analysis is given to indicate the types of questions asked from different topics of the chapter. This feature helps students to know the importance of different topics of the given chapter from exam point of view and helps them to prepare accordingly.

39. Write the output for the following *ICSE 2018*

```
System.out.println("Incredible"+"\n"
                              +"world");
```

KEY idea

\n is the escape sequence for newline so Incredible and world are printed on two different lines.

Ans **Output**

Incredible
world

Key Idea

'Key Idea' is given with selected questions with the purpose to help students to get the approach 'to answer the question'. This feature help students to develop the systematic approach to answer difficult/complex questions.

53. Give the output of the following program segment and also mention the number of times the loop is executed *ICSE 2017*

```
int a,b;
for(a=6, b=4; a<=24; a=a+6)
{
    if(a%b==0)
       break;
}
System.out.println(a);
```

Ans **Output** : 12

Number of times the loop is executed = 2

Concept Enhancer In 2nd iteration, as a%b becomes 0 so break statement is executed and the loop exits. Program control comes to the println statement which prints the output as current value.

Concept Enhancer

Concept Enhancer gives the brief description of the concept, which has been used to answer the question. This feature provides revision of important concept along with practice of question solving.

Dream, Believe, Achieve

Insights from ICSE Toppers

"Board exams are way easier than you think. It's easy to score if you study regularly for even an hour. Consistency is key,"

ANONDEE SAHA

ICSE Topper (99.6%)

Before the boards, my school had given all students a month to study and I tried my best to study 8-9 hours every day.

I relied on revising the syllabus of each subject at least twice during this period and went through past years' question papers and extra questions that my teachers had sent.

DIVYANSH AGRAWAL

ICSE Topper (99.40%)

He dedicated time to solving topic-wise papers from the last 10 years, providing valuable practice before his final revision. A planned approach and schedule help to prepare and cover the syllabus better.

For excelling in the boards I would like to advice students to study regularly from DAY 1. They should refer to previous years Board question papers and should always have a positive attitude and should be confident. But not overconfident

MUSKAN PATHAN

ICSE Topper (99.4%)

"I studied everything independently, which gave me a better understanding of what topics I needed to improve. I studied only 1.5 to 2 hours daily but stayed consistent and regular,"

MIHIKA SANJANWALA

ICSE Topper (99%)

NILOTMA SINGH

ICSE Topper (99.6%)

"I had started preparing, chapter by chapter, right from the beginning of the academic session as we had weekly tests on every topic that was covered in class. However, the hard-core preparation started only in late November 2022 which was about three months prior to the board examination.,"

Previous Years Papers guide me to a great extent as they helped me understand the scope and area of the questions that could be asked. The specimen papers were extremely helpful as we had undergone a change in examination pattern this year.

"While my primary schooling in Shanghai (China) taught me to be a global citizen, my higher secondary schooling at Greenwood High (Bannerghatta) elevated my inquisitiveness and curiosity on various subjects,"

"Personally, POMODORO technique, a time-management method based on 25-minute stretches of focused work broken by five-minute breaks, helped me immensely not only to organise myself better but also to cover a vast syllabus with the least fatigue,"

SHIVANI NEELAMRAJU

ICSE Topper (99.40%)

Please Note that all the information is collected from different websites.

Contents

ICSE Chapterwise Question Bank 2025-2010

Latest Syllabus

Class X (2026)

*There will be **one** written paper of **two hours** duration carrying 100 marks and Internal Assessment of 100 marks.*

Theory - 100 Marks

1. Revision of Class IX Syllabus

(i) Introduction to Object Oriented Programming concepts, (ii) Elementary Concept of Objects and Classes, (iii) Values and Data types, (iv) Operators in Java, (v) Input in Java, (vi) Mathematical Library Methods, (vii) Conditional constructs in Java, (viii) Iterative constructs in Java, (ix) Nested for loops.

2. Class as the Basis of all Computation

Objects and Classes

Objects encapsulate state and behaviour – numerous examples; member variables; attributes or features. Variables define state; member methods; Operations/methods/messages/ methods define behaviour.

Classes as abstractions for sets of objects; class as an object factory; primitive data types, composite data types. Variable declarations for both types; difference between the two types. Objects as instances of a class.

Consider real life examples for explaining the concept of class and object.

3. User - defined Methods

Need of methods, syntax of methods, forms of methods, method definition, method calling, method overloading, declaration of methods,

Ways to define a method, ways to invoke the methods – call by value [with programs] and call by reference [only definition with an example], Object creation - invoking the methods with respect to use of multiple methods with different names to implement modular programming, using data members and member methods, Actual parameters and formal parameters, Declaration of methods - static and non-static, method prototype / signature, - Pure and impure methods, - pass by value [with programs] and pass by reference [only definition with an example], Returning values from the methods , use of multiple methods and more than one method with the same name (polymorphism - method overloading).

4. Constructors

Definition of Constructor, characteristics, types of constructors, use of constructors, constructor overloading.

Default constructor, parameterized constructor, constructor overloading, Difference between constructor and method

5. Library classes

Introduction to wrapper classes, methods of wrapper class and their usage with respect to numeric and character data types. Autoboxing and Unboxing in wrapper classes.

Class as a composite type, distinction between primitive data type and composite data type or class types. Class may be considered as a new data type created by the user, that has its own functionality. The distinction between

primitive and composite types should be discussed through examples. Show how classes allow user defined types in programs. All primitive types have corresponding class wrappers. Introduce Autoboxing and Unboxing with their definition and simple examples.

The following methods are to be covered:

int parseInt (String s),

long parse Long (String s),

float parse Float (String s),

double parse Double (String s),

boolean is Digit (char ch),

boolean is Letter (char ch),

boolean is Letter Or Digit (char ch),

boolean is Lower Case (char ch),

boolean is Upper Case (char ch),

boolean is White space (char ch),

char to Lower Case (char ch)

char to Upper Case (char ch)

6. Encapsulation

Access specifiers and its scope and visibility

Access specifiers – private, protected and public. Visibility rules for private, protected and public access specifiers. Scope of variables, class variables, instance variables, argument variables, local variables.

7. Arrays

Definition of an array, types of array, declaration, initialization and accepting data of single and double dimensional arrays, accessing the elements of single dimensional and double dimensional arrays.

Arrays and their uses, sorting technique - selection sort and bubble sort; Search techniques – linear search and binary search, Array as a composite type, length statement to find the size of the array (sorting and searching techniques using single dimensional array only).

Declaration, initialization, accepting data in a double dimensional array, sum of the elements in row, column and diagonal elements [right and left], display the elements of two-dimensional array in a matrix format.

8. String handling

String class, methods of String class, implementation of String class methods, String array

The following String class methods are to be covered:

String trim()

String toLowerCase()

String toUpperCase( )

int length( )

char charAt(int n)

int indexOf(char ch)

int lastIndexOf(char ch)

String concat(String str)

boolean equals(String str)

boolean equalsIgnoreCase(String str)

int compareTo(String str)

int compareToIgnoreCase(String str)

String replace(char old Char, char new Char)

String substring(int begin Index)

String substring(int begin Index, int endIndex)

boolean startsWith(String str)

boolean endsWith(String str)

String valueOf(all types)

Programs based on the above methods, extracting and modifying characters of a string.

Alphabetical order of the strings in an array [Bubble and Selection sort techniques], searching for a string using linear search technique.

Analysis of Pupil Performance: ICSE Computer Applications

TOPICS FOUND DIFFICULT / CONFUSING BY STUDENTS

- Use of Math.max() and Math.abs().
- Extraction of character using substring ().
- Variable declaration with initial value.
- Object creation.
- Type casting
- Extraction of word.
- Loops for sorting elements in an array.
- Constructor concept.
- Program for printing the series (0, 7, 26, 63...).
- Dividing the four-digit number into two halves.
- Principles and features.
- Bits and Bytes.
- Keyword for class variable.
- Name of different tokens.
- Conversion of data type.
- Return type of different functions.
- Continue statement.
- Declaration of instance variables and their initialisation.
- Creation of object and method call.
- Generation of UNICODE characters.
- Sorting technique (inner loop condition).

SUGGESTIONS FOR STUDENTS

- Follow the concepts given in the scope of the syllabus.
- Clarify the concepts and practise them both, on the paper and on the computer.
- Solve a lot of problems based on all the concepts.
- Learn the syntax and working of every construct properly, with suitable examples.
- Comprehend the key terms/definitions and then learn.
- Practice Library class and its various functions.Check its output on the computer to understand their working.
- Develop the habit to do dry run of a program, which you write. This will help in better understanding of concepts and aid in solving questions.
- Apply simple logic in programs to get desired output.
- Complete the assignments and cross check on the computer for their proper working. Get the assignments checked by your teacher.
- Solve previous years' ICSE question papers to understand the types of questions asked and how to attempt an ICSE question paper.
- Check output-based questions on the computer.
- Design your own questions for string functions, math functions, loops - for, while, do while, etc.
- Check for the logic for different variety of numbers-based questions and develop a logic for the same.
- Do not resort to rote learning this subject but understand and practise the concepts learnt regularly.
- Follow a proper study schedule when preparing for the examination.

01

Revising Basic Java Concepts

TREND ANALYSIS 3 YEARS

Average No. of Questions Across all Sets

	Types of Questions	2023	2019	2018
Revising Basic Java Concepts	1 Mark	11	–	–
	2 Marks	6	12	10
	15 Marks	1	–	–

Java is a portable, machine-independent, object oriented and multithreaded, high level programming language. It was developed by James Gosling, Patrick Naughton, Chris Worth, Ed Frank, Mike Sheridan at Sun Microsystems in year 1991. Java was initially called ''**Oak**'' but in 1996, it was renamed as ''Java'', which is now a part of Oracle corporation.

Flow of Java Programming

Java programs are firstly compiled and then interpreted. The flow of Java programming is shown in the following figure:

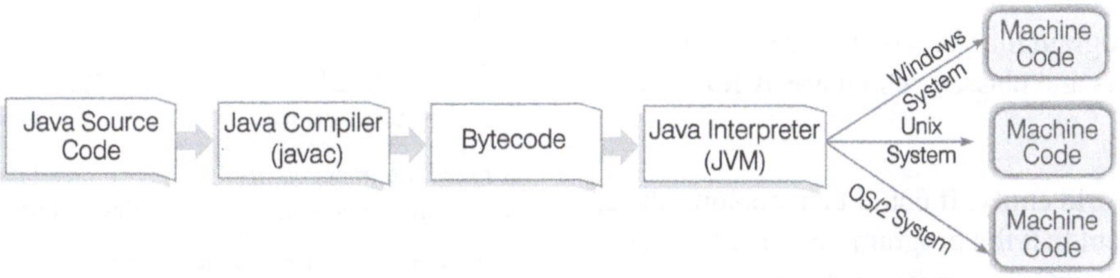

(i) **Java Source Code** It is a collection of computer instructions built by the programmer using Java.

(ii) **Java Compiler** A Java compiler is a set of programs that transforms source code into bytecode.

(iii) **Bytecode** This bytecode is independent of the machine on which the program is to run. This makes a Java compiler highly portable.

(iv) **Java Interpreter** The Java interpreter decodes and executes bytecode for the Java Virtual Machine (JVM). The Java interpreter is actually a part of JVM. JVM is a platform-dependent execution environment that converts Java bytecode into machine code.

(v) **Machine Code** JVM converts bytecode directly into machine code, that is designed to run on a specific microprocessor architecture or operating system such as Windows, UNIX, OS/2, etc.

Object Oriented Programming (OOP)

Object oriented programming is a programming paradigm that represents concepts as **objects** that have data fields and associated procedures known as **methods.** It is a type of programming in which programmers define not only the data types of a data structure, but also define the types of operations (functions), that can be applied to the data structure.

In this way, the data structure becomes an object that includes both data and functions. In addition, programmers can create relationships between two objects.

In other words, OOP is a modular approach, which allows the data to be applied within stipulated program area. It also provides the reusability feature to develop productive logic, which means to give more emphasis on data. e.g. objects can inherit characteristics from other objects.

Features and characteristics of OOP's are as follows:

(i) Emphasis is given on data (objects) rather than function.

(ii) Programs are divided into entities known as objects.

(iii) Objects can communicate with each other through functions.

(iv) Functions that operate on data of an object are tied together.

(v) New data and functions can be easily added whenever necessary.

Elementary Concept of Objects and Classes

In object oriented programming technique, we design a program using objects and classes, which are as follows

Object

An object is a real world entity. It could be a person, place, table, chair or any item that the program may handle. Each object holds data and code to operate on the data.

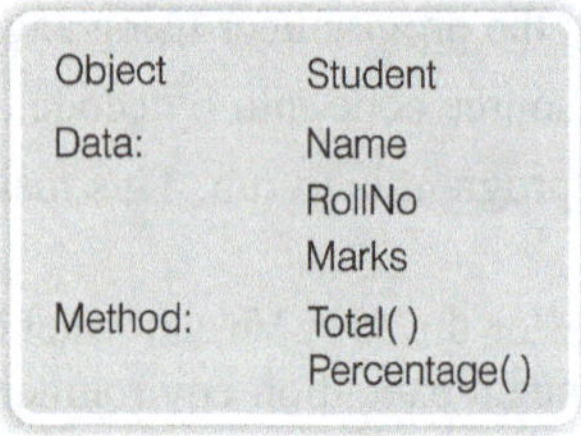

Class

Class is a collection of objects of similar type. Each object of a class possesses same attributes and common behaviour defined within the same class. e.g. **Car, Truck, Bike** and **Cycle** are the objects of class **Vehicle.**

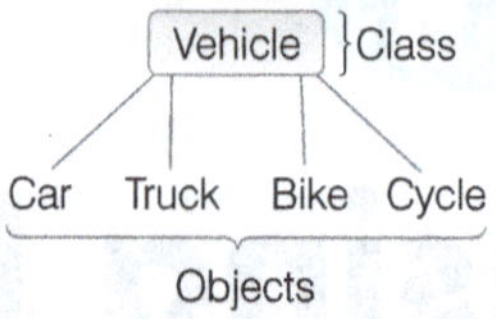

Principles of Object Oriented Programming

OOP works on the principles of encapsulation, abstraction, inheritance and polymorphism, which are as follows

Encapsulation

Process of wrapping up the data and methods in a single unit is known as **encapsulation.** In OOP, data and associated methods are bound together to make a single unit, i.e. class.

Data is not accessible to outside the world and only class methods can get access to it. This isolation of data from direct access by the program is called as **data hiding.**

Data Abstraction

Abstraction is a concept, which is used to represent essential features without including the background details or explanations. It is an essential concept of OOP. The concept of data abstraction can be understood with the help of a simple example of an electric fan.

A user is totally unaware of its internal working, he/she only needs to know how it gets ON/OFF. Thus, the user gets isolated from all the complex circuitry, which is well encapsulated.

Difference between Abstraction and Encapsulation

Abstraction	Encapsulation
It hides the unnecessary details of the object.	It binds data and methods in a single unit.
It implements in Java using interface and abstract class.	It implements in Java using private and protected access modifier.
Abstraction focuses on the outside view of an object (i.e. the interface).	Encapsulation prevents client from seeing it's inside view.
Abstraction is more about 'What' a class can do (Idea).	Encapsulation is more about 'How' to achieve that functionality (Implementation).

Inheritance

The capability of one class to inherit (derive) the properties of any other class completely or partially, is known as inheritance. The class, from which properties are inherited, is known as **super class** (or base class or parent class) and the class, which inherits the properties from superclass is known as **sub class** (or derived or child class).

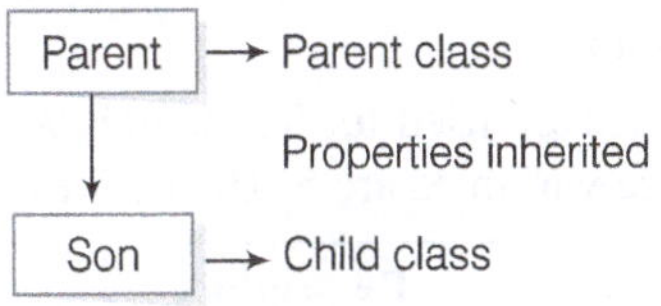

Inheritance

Polymorphism

The term polymorphism literally means the capacity to take 'different forms from one'. It is a feature that allows creating several methods with the same name, which differ from each other in the type.

Polymorphism is broadly used in implementing inheritance. It means that the same operations may behave differently on different classes. It allows us to write generic, reusable code more easily.

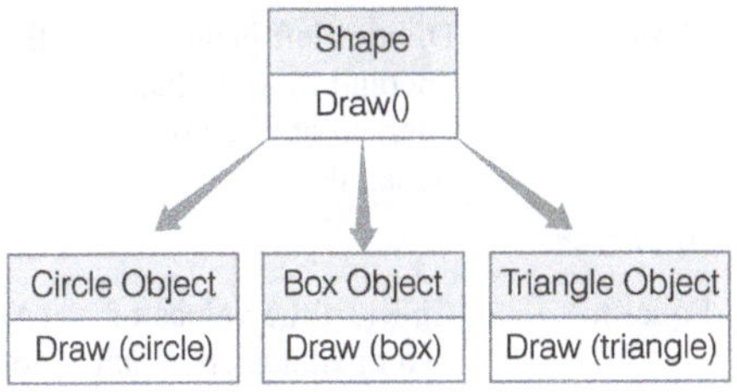

Polymorphism

Suppose that our program uses many kinds of shapes, such as circle, box, triangle etc. So, here we design a super class called **Shape**. In example, all shapes have a method called **Draw**(). In Java, polymorphism is provided by function (or method) overloading.

Tokens

Tokens are the smallest unit or single element of a Java program, which are identified by the compiler. It can also be defined as a individual character used in a Java program. There are five types of tokens, i.e. **literals**, **keywords**, **identifiers**, **operators** and **separators**.

Literals

These are the constants in a Java program. It can be any number, text or other information that represents a value. We can specify any value as a literal such as:

(i) **Integer Literals** It represents positive or negative value without decimal point. e.g. 14, −391, etc.

(ii) **Floating Literals** Java have two kinds of floating point number: float and double. By default, floating literal is double. e.g. 0.01f is floating point literal and 6.5d is double-precision floating point literal.

(iii) **Character Literals** These are constant valued character expressions embedded in a Java program. Character literals are expressed in Java within a pair of single quotes. These characters are termed as **ASCII characters**. e.g. 'A', '3', '*', etc.

(iv) **String Literals** String is a set of alphanumeric characters. String literals are expressed within double quotes. e.g. "Hello", "100 pound", "TAJMAHAL", etc.

(v) **Boolean Literals** Boolean literals represent any one of the two values, either true or false and can be applied in a Java program to verify that whether the given condition is satisfied or not. e.g. boolean chosen = true;

Keywords

These are reserved words used within the program to specify a particular task.
Some keywords are as follows:

boolean	else	long	synchronized
break	extends	native	this
byte	final	new	throw
case	float	package	throws
catch	for	private	transient
char	goto	protected	try
class	if	public	void
const	implements	return	volatile
continue	import	short	while
default	instanceof	static	
do	int	super	
double	interface	switch	

Some Keywords Description

- **break** It is used to resume program execution at the statement immediately following the current enclosing block or statement.
- **catch** Each catch block is an exception handler and handles the type of exception indicated by its argument.
- **continue** It is used to resume program execution at the end of the current loop body.
- **extends** It is used in a class declaration to inherit the property and behaviour of the superclass.
- **final** It defines an entity once that cannot be changed. If a class is declared as final, it cannot be derived later.

- **import** It is used at the beginning of a source file to specify classes or entire Java packages to be referred to later without including their package name in the reference.
- **package** This is a group of similar type of classes. Packages are declared with the package keyword.
- **static** It is used to declare a field, method or inner class as a class field.
- **super** It allows a subclass to access overridden methods and hidden members of its superclass.
- **if** It is used to create an if statement, which tests a boolean expression.
- **new** It is used to create an instance of a class or an array object.
- **return** It is used to finish the execution of a method. It returns control back to the calling function.
- **this** It is used to access class members and as a reference to the current instance.
- **try** It defines a block of statements that might have some cause of exception. A try block must have atleast one catch block or a finally block.
- **void** It is used to declare a method, which does not return any value.

Identifiers

This is a name given to a package, class, interface, method or variable. It allows a programmer to refer to the item from other places in the program. In Java, there are several points to remember about identifiers. They are as follows:

- An identifier can be any combination of alphabets (A to Z or a to z), digits (0 to 9), currency character ($) and underscore (_).
- The first character in identifier must be an alphabet, currency character or underscore.
- No commas or blanks are allowed within an identifier.
- Most importantly identifiers are case sensitive. e.g. foo and Foo are two different identifiers.
- A keyword cannot be used as an identifier.

e.g. **Legal identifiers** are : age, $salary, _value, _1_value

Illegal identifiers are : 123abc, -salary, auto

Operators

These are basically the symbols or tokens, which perform arithmetical or logical operations to yield results. They are used to manipulate primitive data types.

- **Unary Operator** It is used to perform operation on a single operand such as ++, – –, ~, !, etc.
- **Binary Operator** It is used to perform operation between two operand such as +, –, *, >, <, etc.
- **Ternary Operator** It is used to perform operation between three operand such as ?:.

We can also divide all the Java operators into the following groups:

(Three variables are used further namely A, B, and C and values of these variables are 5, 10 and 7 respectively.)

Operator Name		Description	Example
Arithmetic Operator			
+	Addition	It adds the values of operands.	A + B = 15
–	Subtraction	Subtracts the value of right hand operand from left hand operand.	A – B = – 5
*	Multiplication	Multiplies the values of operands.	A * B = 50
/	Division	Divides left hand operand by right hand operand.	B / A = 2
%	Modulus	Divides left hand operand by right hand operand and returns remainder.	B % A = 0
Relational Operator			
= =	Equal to	Check if the values of two operands are equal or not, if yes, then condition becomes true.	(A == B) is not true
! =	Not equal to	Check if the values of two operands are equal or not, if values are not equal, then condition becomes true.	(A ! = B) is true
>	Greater than	Check if the value of left operand is greater than the value of right operand, if yes, then condition becomes true.	(A > B) is not true
<	Less than	Check if the value of left operand is less than the value of right operand, if yes, then condition becomes true.	(A < B) is true
>=	Greater than or equal to	Check if the value of left operand is greater than or equal to the value of right operand, if yes, then condition becomes true.	(A >= B) is not true

Operator	Name	Description	Example
<=	Less than or equal to	Check if the value of left operand is less than or equal to the value of right operand, if yes, then condition becomes true.	(A <= B) is true
Logical Operator			
&&	Logical AND operator	It returns TRUE, if both the condition are true, otherwise returns FALSE.	((A < B)&&(C < B)) returns FALSE
||	Logical OR operator	It returns TRUE, if any of the two conditions is true.	((A < B)||(C < B)) returns TRUE
!	Logical NOT operator	It works on single operand. It is used to reverse the logical state of its operand. If a condition is true, then logical NOT operator will make it false.	!((A < B)&&(C < B)) returns TRUE
Bitwise Operator Here, value of variable a = 44 (00101100) and value of variable b = 10(00001010)			
&	Binary AND	It copies 1 to the result if 1 exists in both operand, otherwise copies 0.	(a & b) will give 8 which is 00001000
|	Binary OR	It copies 1 to the result if 1 exists in either operand, otherwise copies 0.	(a | b) will give 46 which is 00101110
^	Binary XOR	It copies 1 to the result if 1 is in one operand. If it is either in both operand or not in any operand, the operator copies 0.	(a ^ b) will give 38 which is 00100110
~	Binary one's complement	It is unary and has the effect of flipping bits. It is used to change the bits, i.e. 0 to 1 and 1 to 0.	(~a) will give 211 which is 11010011
<<	Binary left shift	The left operand value is moved left by the number of bits specified by the right operand.	(a << 2) will give 176 which is 10110000
>>	Binary right shift	The left operand value is moved right by the number of bits specified by the right operand.	(a >> 2) will give 11 which is 00001011
>>>	Shift right zero fill	The left operand value is moved right by the number of bits specified by right operand and shifted values are filled up with 0.	(a >>> 2) will give 11 which is 00001011

Operator	Name	Description	Example
Increment and Decrement Operator			
A++	Post Increment	Add 1 to the variable after use	int A = 2, B; B= A++; A = 3,B = 2
++A	Pre Increment	Add 1 to the variable before use	int A = 2, B;B= ++A; A = 3, B= 3
A−−	Post Decrement	Subtract 1 from a variable after use	int A = 2, B; B=A−−; A = 1, B= 2
−−A	Pre Decrement	Subtract 1 from a variable before use	int A = 2, B; B= −−A; A = 1,B = 1
Assignment Operator			
=	Assignment	Simple assignment operator, assigns values from right side operands to left side operands.	c = a+b will assign the value of a + b into c

Conditional Operator (?:)

This operator is used to find the condition result, which could be either true or false. The goal of this operator is to decide, which value should be assigned to the variable.

Syntax `variable x = (expression) ? value1 (if true) : value2 (if false);`

Operator Precedence

It shows the order of operators in priority from top to bottom in different rows:

Precedence	Operator	Description	Associativity
1.	( ) [ ] •	Parenthesis Array subscript Access object method	Left to Right
2.	++ −−	Postfix increment Postfix decrement	Left to Right
3.	++ −− +, − ! ~	Prefix increment Prefix decrement Unary plus/minus Logical NOT Bitwise NOT	Right to Left
4.	* / %	Multiplication Division Modulus	Left to Right
5.	+ − +	Addition Subtraction String concatenation	Left to Right
6.	<< >> >>>	Bitwise left shift Bitwise right shift Bitwise right shift with zero extension(zero fill)	Left to Right

Precedence	Operator	Description	Associativity
7.	<, <= >, >=	Less than, less than or equal to Greater than, greater than or equal to	Left to Right
8.	= = ! =	Equal to Not equal to	Left to Right
9.	&	Bitwise AND	Left to Right
10.	^	Bitwise XOR	Left to Right
11.	|	Bitwise OR	Left to Right
12.	&&	Boolean AND	Left to Right
13.	||	Boolean OR	Left to Right
14.	? :	Conditional	Right to Left
15.	=	Assignment	Right to Left

In above table, associativity rules are used to determine the order of evaluation of operators, if the precedence of operators is same.

Separators

It helps to define the structure of a program. Some separators are as follows :

Separator	Symbol	Description
Parenthesis	( )	It holds method definition.
Braces	{ }	It is used to define block/scope of class, code, methods.
Brackets	[ ]	It is used in array declaration.
Period	.	It separates the package name from sub package.
Comma	,	It separates the consecutive variable of same type when declaration.
Semicolon	;	It is used to terminate the statement in Java.

Data Types

It refers to the type of data that can be stored in a variable. Sometimes, Java is called a **strongly typed language** because when you declare a variable, you must specify the variable type. The Java language is rich in its data types.

Data types in Java are classified into two types:

- **Primitive data types** are the data types defined by the language itself. A primitive data type can have only one value at a time and is the simplest built in form of data within Java. byte, short, int, long, float, double, boolean, char are the examples of primitive data types.
- **Non-primitive data types (composite data types)** are referenced data types, which are based on primitive data types. These data types are constructed by using primitive data types, as per user's need.

  Non-primitive data types store the memory address of an object. Class, interface and array are the examples of reference data types.

Note In chapter 2, this topic will be discussed in detail.

Expression

It is a construct mode of variables, operators and method invocations, which are raise according to the syntax of the language, that evaluates to a single value.

e.g. $$a=\frac{2\cdot 34-2x^3}{x+y}$$

In Java, syntax of the above expression will be like:

```
a = (2·34− 2 * x * x * x) / (x+ y);
```

Mathematical Library Functions

Java provides access to a lot of common mathematical functions as well as some of the more common irrational numbers using the Math class.

Function	Format	Description	Example
pow( )	Math.pow(x, y);	Returns double value of x^y.	Math.pow(2, 3) = 8
log( )	Math.log(x);	Returns double value of natural log (base e).	Math. log(3) = 1.0986122886681098
log10( )	Math.log10(x);	Returns the base 10 logarithm of a double value.	Math.log10(1000) = 3
sqrt( )	Math.sqrt(x);	Returns the square root of a positive number. It returns double data type.	Math.sqrt(25) =5
ceil( )	Math.ceil(x);	Returns the whole number greater than equal to the number.	Math.ceil(22.81) = 23 Math.ceil(1.1) = 2 Math.ceil(22.11) = 23
floor( )	Math.floor(x);	Returns the rounded value down to the nearest integer.	Math.floor(11.11) = 11.0 Math.floor(11.97) = 11.0
rint( )	Math.rint(x);	Returns the integer part of the number by removing fractional part (nearest integer value).	Math.rint(14.92) = 15 Math.rint(10.29) = 10

Function	Format	Description	Example
abs( )	Math.abs(a);	Returns absolute value, i.e. only magnitude of the number. It returns int/long/double.	Math.abs(–1.76) = 1.76 Math.abs(1.76) = 1.76
max( )	Math.max(a, b);	Returns the greater number between a and b. It returns int/float/double/long.	Math.max(2, 4) = 4 Math.max(4, 2) = 4
min( )	Math.min(a, b);	Returns the smaller number between a and b. It returns int/float/double/long.	Math.min(2, 4) = 2 Math.min(4, 2) = 2
random( )	Math.random( );	Returns a random number between 0 and 1. It returns a double type value.	
sin( ) cos( ) tan( )	Math.sin(x); Math.cos(x); Math.tan(x);	Returns the sin, cos, tan values respectively of a given angle in radian as an argument.	Math.sin (Math.PI/6) = .499999999 Math.cos (Math.PI/4) = 0.707106781 Math.tan (Math.PI/3) = 1.732050808

Type Casting

It is a term of converting one data type into another. It is necessary because, sometimes data is in a form that is unrecognisable to the program.

In Java, there are two ways of type casting:

(i) **Implicit Type Casting** When the type conversion is performed automatically by the compiler without programmer's intervention, such type of conversion is known as implicit type conversion.

e.g.
```
byte b = 10;
int  i = b;
          //Implicit type casting
long l = i;
          //Implicit type casting
```

(ii) **Explicit Type Casting** A data type of higher size cannot be assigned to a data type of lower size. This is not done implicitly by the compiler and requires explicit conversion; a casting operation to be performed by the programmer.

e.g.
```
double x=10;
int y=(int)x;
          //Explicit type casting
```

Comments

Comments are an integral part of any program for the purpose of documentation or explanation. Comments are non-executable statements that are ignored by the compiler or interpreter. Java has three types of comments: line, block and JavaDoc.

Line Comment is used for a single line of comment. A line comment starts with two forward slashes(`//`).

Block Comment is used for multiple lines comment. A block comment starts with a forward slash and asterisk (`/*`) and ends with asterisk and forward slash (`*/`).

JavaDoc Comment is used specially to document non-private classes, attributes and methods. It starts with one forward slash and two asterisks (`/**`) and ends with one asterisk and one forward slash (`*/`).

Input/Output in Java

Input is any information that is needed by program to complete its execution.

Output is any information that the program must convey to the user.

Stream

A stream can be defined as a sequence of data. The InputStream is used to read data from a source and the OutputStream is used for writing data to a destination.

Byte Streams

Java byte streams are used to perform input and output of 8-bits (bytes) data in the byte format. There are many classes related to byte streams but the most frequently used classes are FileInputStream and FileOutputStream.

Character Streams

Java character streams are used to perform input and output for 16-bit unicode character in the character format. Character stream I/O automatically translates the internal format into the local character set and *vice-versa*.

Different Ways to Take Input in Java

There are two ways by which we can take input from the user as

Using BufferedReader Class

This class is used to read a sequence of characters. InputStreamReader() is a function that converts the input stream of bytes into a stream of characters.

The statement to import java.util package is shown below

```
import java.io.BufferedReader;
```

Or

```
import java.util.*;
```

The syntax to create a BufferedReader object is shown below

```
BufferedReader obj = new BufferedReader
        (new InputStreamReader(System.in));
```

Java BufferedReader Class Methods

Method	Description
int read()	It is used for reading a single character.
int read(char[ ] cbuf, int off, int len)	It is used for reading characters into a portion of an array.
String readLine()	It is used for reading a line of text.
void reset()	It repositions the stream at a position the mark method was last called on this input stream.
void close()	It closes the input stream and releases any of the system resources associated with the stream.

Using Scanner Class

The Scanner class is a class, which allows the user to read values of various types.

Scanner class is available in java.util system package. You must import java.util package to avail the facilities contained in Scanner class. The statement to import java.util package is shown below:

```
import java.util.Scanner;
```

After importing java.util package, create object which can hold a set of values of different types. The syntax to create a Scanner object is shown below:

```
Scanner input = new Scanner(System.in);
```

Methods to Read Tokens from Scanner Object

Methods	Returns
int nextInt( )	Returns the next token as an int.
long nextLong( )	Returns the next token as a long.
float nextFloat( )	Returns the next token as a float.
double nextDouble( )	Returns the next token as a double.
String next( )	Finds and returns the next complete token from the scanner object as a string.
String nextLine( )	Returns the rest part of the current line, excluding any line separator at the end.
void close( )	Closes the Scanner.

Printer Class

Printer classes are required when we need to create a formatted output stream.

There are two kinds of print statements:

- **System.out.print**(argument) prints its argument.
- **System.out.println**(argument) prints its argument and ends the line.

The print method just prints the string but does not move the cursor to a new line, while println( ) prints the string and moves the cursor to a new line.

Control Structure

It determines an order in which the statements used in a program are executed. A Java program contains classes and these classes have some methods, which contain statements that are executed by the compiler.

There are three types of control structure:

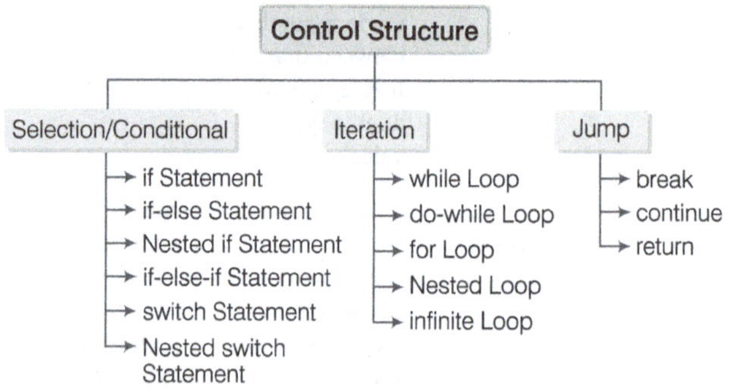

(i) Selection/Conditional

These statements are used in a program to choose different paths of execution based upon the outcome of an expression or the state of a variable.

Some selection statements are as follows:

1. if Statement

It is the most basic form of selection statement, which executes a single block of statements, if the specified condition evaluates to true, otherwise the given set of statements are ignored.

Syntax

```
if(Condition)
{
    Statements;
}
```

2. if-else Statement

It is a type of selection statement in which a single statement or a group of statements enclosed within braces. The if block is executed only when, if condition is true. Otherwise, the else block is executed.

Syntax

```
if(Condition)
{
   Statement 1;
}
else
{
   Statement 2;
}
```

3. Nested if Statement

It is always legal to nested if-else statements, which means you can use if or if-else statements inside another if or if-else block.

Syntax

```
if(Condition 1)
{
   if(Condition 2)
      Statement 1;
   else
      Statement 2;
}
else
{
   Statement 3;
}
```

4. if-else-if Statement

It is a kind of statement, in which a number of logical conditions are checked for executing various statements. It is based upon nested if and is often called the if-else-if ladder.

Syntax

```
if(Condition 1)
   Statement 1;
else if(Condition 2)
   Statement 2;
else if(Condition 3)
   Statement 3;
:
:
else
   Statement;
```

Difference between if and else-if Statement

if Statement	else-if Statement
if statement checks a single condition and executes a set of statements if it evaluates to true.	else-if check is performed when there exist a number of logical conditions.
Flow chart	**Flow chart**

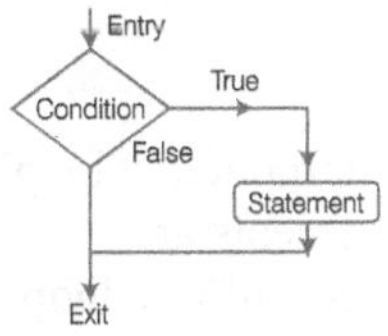

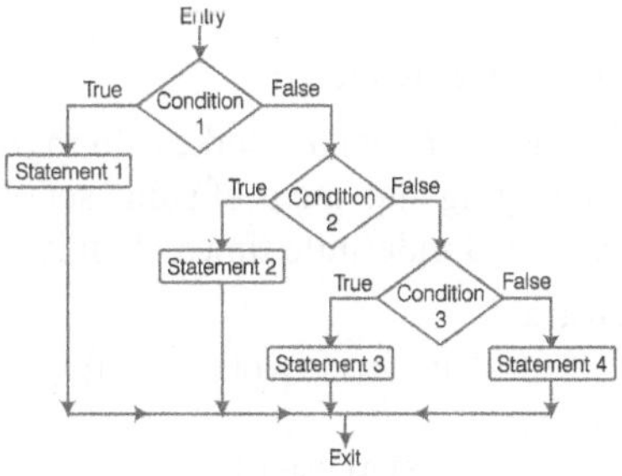

5. switch Statement

It works as a multi way branch statement. It provides an easy way to execute different blocks of a program according to the value of an expression. Instead of using the if-else-if series of statements, using switch statement is a better option.

Syntax

```
switch(expression)
{
   case value 1:
      Statements;
      break;
   case value 2:
      Statements;
      break;
   :
   :
   default:
      Statements;
}
```

6. Nested switch Statement

Switch can also be used as a part of the statement sequence of an outer switch, which is called nested switch and is exactly the same idea as a nested if-else statement.

Syntax

```
switch(Expression 1)
{
   case value 1:
   switch(Expression 2)
   {
      case value A:
         Statements;
         break;
      case value B:
         Statements;
         break;
   }
   case value 2:
      Statements;
      break;
   :
   :
   default:
      Statements;
}
```

Difference between if-else and switch Statement

if-else Statement	switch Statement
if-else can evaluate a relational or logical expression.	switch can test only integer or char expressions. It tests only for the equality condition.
if-else statement encloses mu ltiple statements inside curly braces { }.	switch statement never encloses multiple statements inside curly braces { }.
if-else is used to compare two or more variable.	switch case label value must be constant.

(ii) Iteration

It means repetition of a set of statements, depending upon a condition test. Till the time a condition is true, a set of statements are repeated again and again. Iteration is also known as looping or repetition.

Some iteration statements are as follows:

1. while Loop

This loop is also known as 'entry controlled loop'. While loop checks the condition first before entering in a loop. If the condition evaluates to true, the statements given inside the while loop get executed.

Syntax
```
while(Condition)
{
   Statements
}
```

2. do-while Loop

It is also known as 'exit controlled loop'. This loop ensures that the complete loop is executed atleast once, then it checks whether the given condition is true or false. If the condition is true then the loop will continue but if the condition is false, the loop will be terminated.

Syntax
```
do
{
   Statements
}
while(Condition);
```

Difference between while and do-while Loop

while Loop	do-while Loop
It is a top testing or entry controlled loop.	It is a bottom testing or exit controlled loop.
while loop checks the condition firstly then execute.	do-while loop firstly executes the statement then check the condition.
Syntax `while(Condition) { Statements; }`	Syntax `do { Statements; } while(Condition);`

3. for Loop

It is also an 'entry controlled loop'. It is a short method of looping, which is commonly preferred by programmers. It tests the condition before entering in the loop body, if the condition evaluates to true, the given statements are executed else the loop will not execute.

Syntax
```
for(initialization; condition;
                     increment/decrement)
{
   Statements
}
```

Difference between while and for Loop

while Loop	for Loop
while loop continues while the condition is true.	for loop continues until a certain parameter is met.
It is used when the length of loop is unknown.	It is used when the length of the loop is known.
Syntax `while(Condition) { Statements; }`	Syntax `for(initialization; condition; increment/decrement) { Statements; }`

4. Nested Loop

It is a loop within a loop, i.e. an inner loop within the body of an outer one. The working of the nested loop is that the first pass of the outer loop triggers the inner loop, which executes to completion, then the second pass of the outer loop triggers the inner loop again continue. This process will continue until the outer loop's condition become false.

Syntax

For a nested for loop:
```
for(initialization; condition;
                     increment/decrement)
{
   for(initialization; condition;
                     increment/decrement)
   {
      Statement(s);
   }
   Statement(s);
}
```

For a nested while loop:
```
while(Condition)
{
   while(Condition)
   {
      Statement(s);
   }
   Statement(s);
}
```

5. Infinite Loop

It is also known as 'endless loop' or 'unproductive loop'. In looping statement, if some set of statements are executed indefinite times, then it is called 'infinite loop'.

Syntax
```
for(initialization; ; increment/decrement)
{
   Statement;
}
```

Difference between Entry Control Loop and Exit Control Loop

Entry Control Loop	Exit Control Loop
Entry control loop will check the condition at first.	Exit control loop will check the condition at last.
e.g. while and for loop.	e.g. do-while loop.
Flow chart 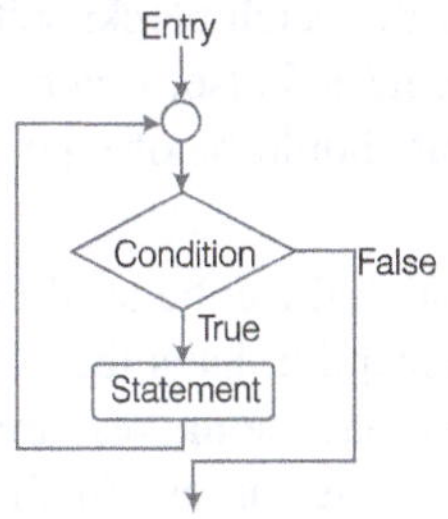	**Flow chart** 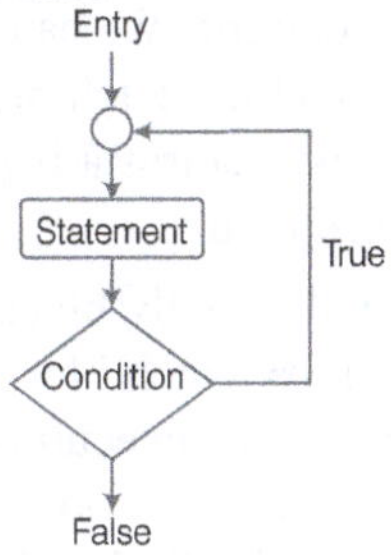

(iii) Jump Statements

These are used to transfer control to other parts of the program. These statements can be used to modify the behaviour of conditional and iterative statements. Jump statements allow you to exit a loop, start the next iteration of a loop or explicitly transfer program control to a specified location in your program.

Some jump statements are as follows:

1. break Statement

It is used to jump out of a loop. On encountering a break statement within a loop, the execution continues with the next statement outside the loop.

Syntax

```
while(Condition)
{
   Statement 1;
   if(Condition)
   {
      break;
   }
   Statement 2;
}
Statement 3;
```

2. continue Statement

It is used only within looping statements. When the continue statement is encountered, the next iteration starts and the remaining statements in the present iteration are skipped.

Syntax

```
do
{
   Statement 1;
   continue;
   :
   :
   :
}
while(Condition);
Statement 2;
```

Difference between break and continue Statement

break Statement	continue Statement
When break is executed, the statements following break are skipped and cause the loop to be terminated.	When continue statement is executed, the statements following continue are skipped and cause the loop to be continued with the next iteration.
It can be used in switch statement to transfer the control outside switch.	It cannot be used inside a switch statement. It is used only with loops.

3. return Statement

It is used to explicitly return from a method. It causes program control to transfer back to the caller of the method. The return statement immediately terminates the method in which it is executed.

Syntax `return(Expression);`

Errors

Errors are those statements or instructions that may be caused to stop the program execution or to stop the compilation process. There are three kinds of errors: syntax errors, runtime errors and logic errors.

(i) **Syntax Errors** These are errors where the compiler finds something wrong with your program and you can not even try to execute it. e.g. you may have incorrect punctuation or may be trying to use a variable that has not been declared.

Syntax errors are the easiest to find and correct. The compiler will tell you, where it got into trouble and its best guess as to what you did wrong ?

(ii) **Runtime Errors** If there are no syntax errors, Java may detect an error while your program is running. You will get an error message telling you the kind of error and a stack trace that tells not only where the error occurred, but also what other method or methods you were in.

e.g. Exception in thread "main"
java.lang.NullPointerException
at Car.placeInCity(Car.java:25)

at City.<init>(City.java:38)
at City.main(City.java:49)

(iii) **Logic Errors** A logic error or bug is when your program compiles and runs, but does the wrong thing. The Java system, of course, has no idea what your program is supposed to do, so it provides no additional information to help you find the error.

Exception Handling Keywords

Java provides specific keywords for exception handling purposes, these are:

- **throw** throw keyword is used to throw exception either user defined or java defined to the runtime to handle it.
- **throws** When we are throwing any exception in a method and not handling it, then we need to use throws keyword in method signature to let caller program know the exceptions that might be thrown by the method. The caller method might handle these exceptions or propagate it using throws keyword.
- **try-catch** We use try-catch block for exception handling in our code. try is the start of the block and catch is at the end of try block to handle the exceptions. We can have multiple catch blocks with a try and try-catch block can be nested also. Catch block requires a parameter that should be of type Exception.
- **finally** finally block is optional and can be used only with try-catch block. Since, exception halts the process of execution, we might have some resources open that will not get closed, so we can use finally block. finally block gets executed always, whether exception occurred or not.

PYQs Previous Years Questions

1 Mark Questions

1. A mechanism where one class acquires the properties of another class *ICSE 2023*

(a) Polymorphism (b) Inheritance
(c) Encapsulation (d) Abstraction

Ans (b) Inheritance

2. The code obtained after compilation is known as *ICSE 2023; ICSE SQP 2022 (Sem I)*

(a) source code (b) object code
(c) machine code (d) java byte code

Ans (d) java byte code

3. The keyword used to call package in the program *ICSE 2023*

(a) extends (b) export
(c) import (d) package

Ans (c) import

4. The Scanner class method used to accept words with space *ICSE 2023*

(a) next() (b) nextLine()
(c) Next() (d) nextString()

Ans (b) nextLine()

5. Identify the type of operator && *ICSE 2023*

(a) ternary (b) unary
(c) logical (d) relational

Ans (c) logical

6. What value will Math.sqrt (Math.ceil (15.3)) return? *ICSE 2023*

(a) 16.0 (b) 16 (c) 4.0 (d) 5.0

Ans (c) 4.0

7. The absence of which statement leads to fall through situation in switch case statement? *ICSE 2023*

(a) continue (b) break
(c) return (d) System.exit(0)

Ans (b) break

8. State the type of loop in the given program segment *ICSE 2023*

```
for(inti=5;i!=0;i-=2)
System.out.println(i);
```

(a) finite (b) infinite (c) null (d) fixed

Ans (b) infinite

9. Consider the following program segment and select the output of the same when n=10 : *ICSE 2023*

```
switch(n)
{
    case 10 : System.out.println(n*2);
    case 4  : System.out.println(n*4);break;
    default : System.out.println(n);
}
```

(a) 20
40 (b) 10
4 (c) 20, 40 (d) 10
10

Ans (a) 20
40

10. int x=(int) 32.8; is an example of .... typecasting. *ICSE 2023*

(a) implicit (b) automatic
(c) explicit (d) coercion

Ans (c) explicit

11. Missing a semicolon in a statement is what type of error? *ICSE 2023*

(a) Logical (b) Syntax
(c) Runtime (d) No error

Ans (b) Syntax

12. The process of binding the data and method together as one unit is called as *ICSE SQP 2023; ICSE 2022 (Sem I)*

(a) encapsulation (b) inheritance
(c) polymorphism (d) dynamic binding

Ans (a) encapsulation

13. Name the type of error that occurs for the following statement *ICSE SQP 2023*

```
System.out.println(Math.sqrt(24-25));
```

(a) Syntax error (b) Runtime error
(c) Logical error (d) No error

Ans (c) Logical error

14. Give the output of the following statement

```
Math.pow(625, ½) + Math.sqrt(144)
```

ICSE SQP 2023

(a) 17.0 (b) 13.0 (c) 37.0 (d) 13

Ans (b) 13.0

15. The logical operator which is an unary operator *ICSE SQP 2023*

(a) && (b) || (c) ! (d) >>

Ans (c) !

16. The correct if statement for the following ternary operation statement is *ICSE SQP 2023*

```
System.out.println(n%2 == 0? "true":"false");
```

(a)
```
if(n%2==0)
   return true;
else
   return false;
```

(b)
```
if(n%2==0)
   return "true";
else
   return "false";
```

(c)
```
if(n%2==0)
   System.out.println("true");
else
   System.out.println("false");
```

(d)
```
if(n%2==0)
   return false;
else
   return false;
```

Ans (c)
```
if(n%2==0)
   System.out.println("true");
else
   System.out.println("false");
```

17. The style of expressing single line comment is *ICSE SQP 2023*

(a) /* comment*/ (b) * comment
(c) //comment (d) /* comment

Ans (c) //comment

18. The number of bytes occupied by the constant 45 are *ICSE SQP 2023*

(a) Four bytes (b) Two bytes
(c) Eight bytes (d) One byte

Ans (a) Four bytes

19. int res= 'A'; What is the value of res? *ICSE SQP 2023*

(a) A (b) 66 (c) 65 (d) 97

Ans (c) 65

20. The datatype which is specified that the method does not return a value is *ICSE SQP 2023*

(a) Void (b) void (c) VOID (d) boolean

Ans (b) void

21. Multiple branching statement of Java is *ICSE SQP 2023*

(a) For (b) while
(c) do ... while (d) switch

Ans (d) switch

22. do..... while loop is an *ICSE SQP 2023*

(a) entry controlled loop (b) infinite loop
(c) exit controlled loop (d) Finite loop

Ans (c) exit controlled loop

23.
```
for(k=1;k<=2;k++)
{ for(m=1;m<=4;m++)
   {
      System.out.println(m*2);
   }
}
```

How many times the inner loop is executed? *ICSE SQP 2023*

(a) 4 times (b) 8 times
(c) 2 times (d) 16 times

Ans (b) 8 times

24. The Scanner class is a .... class. *ICSE SQP 2023*

(a) Primitive (b) Derived
(c) Wrapper (d) Super

Ans (c) Wrapper

25. What is the final value stored in variable x? *ICSE 2022 (Sem I)*

```
double x=Math.ceil(Math.abs(-7.3));
```

(a) 7.0 (b) 8.0 (c) 6.0 (d) 9.0

Ans (b) 8.0

26. Which of the following keyword is used to create symbolic constants in Java? *ICSE 2022 (Sem I)*

(a) final (b) Final (c) Constant (d) Const

Ans (a) final

27. Name the type of error in the statement given below *ICSE 2022 (Sem I)*

```
double x; y; z;
```

(a) Logical error (b) Syntax error
(c) Runtime error (d) No error

Ans (b) Syntax error

28. The operator which acts on one operand is known as ...... *ICSE 2022 (Sem I)*

(a) binary (b) ternary
(c) unary (d) relational

Ans (c) Unary

29. The ASCII code of B is .... *ICSE 2022 (Sem I)*

(a) 67 (b) 66 (c) 98 (d) 99

Ans (b) 66

30. The jump statement that is used inside a switch case construct to terminate a statement sequence. *ICSE 2022 (Sem I)*

(a) continue (b) break
(c) return (d) goto

Ans (b) break

31. The program code written in any high-level language to solve a problem is *ICSE 2022 (Sem I)*

(a) object code (b) source code
(c) machine code (d) bytecode

Ans (b) Source code

32. Multiline comments in Java start with /* and end with */. *ICSE 2022 (Sem I)*

(a) True (b) False

Ans (a) True

33. = = is an assignment operator. *ICSE 2022 (Sem I)*

(a) True (b) False

Ans (b) False

34. System.exit(0) terminates the program from any point. *ICSE 2022 (Sem I)*

(a) True (b) False

Ans (a) True

35. Choose the odd one. *ICSE 2022 (Sem I)*

(a) > = (b) % (c) / (d) *

Ans (a) > =

36. Choose the odd one. *ICSE 2022 (Sem I); ICSE SQP 2022 (Sem I)*

(a) double (b) int (c) char (d) String

Ans (d) String

37. Choose the odd one. *ICSE 2022 (Sem I)*

(a) if else (b) if
(c) switch case (d) while( )

Ans (d) while( )

38. Choose the odd one. *ICSE 2022 (Sem I)*

(a) Robust (b) Platform Independent
(c) Inheritance (d) Multithreading

Ans (c) Inheritance

39. Give the output of the following. *ICSE 2022 (Sem I)*

```
int  x = 2, y = 4, z = 1;
int result = (++z) +y + (++x) + (z++);
```

(a) 11 (b) 12 (c) 10 (d) 9

Ans (a) 11

40. Give the output of the following. *ICSE 2022 (Sem I)*

```
int x;
for ( x =1 ; x <=3; x++ );
System.out.print (x);
```

(a) 1 2 3 (b) 1 2 3 4
(c) 4 (d) 1

Ans (c) 4

41. Give the output of the following. *ICSE 2022 (Sem I)*

```
int f=10,m=9;
String e=(m%f==9)? "YES": "NO";
System.out.print(e);
```

(a) YES (b) NO
(c) YESNO (d) NOYES

Ans (a) YES

42. Give the output of the following. *ICSE 2022 (Sem I)*

```
switch(x)
{
    case 'M':
       System.out.print("Microsoft Teams");
       break;
```

```
    case 'G':
        System.out.print("Google Meet");
    default:
        System.out.print("Any software");
        break;
    case 'W':
        System.out.print("Web Ex");
        break;
}
```

When x='g'

(a) Google Meet (b) Any software
(c) Google Meet Any software (d) WebEx

Ans (b) Any software

43. Give the output of the following. ***ICSE 2022 (Sem I)***

```
int v= 5;
while (--v>=0)
{
    System.out.print(v);
}
```

(a) 43210 (b) 54321 (c) 543210 (d) 4321

Ans (a) 43210

44. What is the final value stored in variable x? ***ICSE SQP 2022 (Sem I)***

```
double a =-8.35;
double x =Math.abs(Math.floor(a));
```

(a) 9.0 (b) 7.0 (c) 6 (d) 7

Ans (a) 9.0

45. Give the output of the following, when x = 5 ***ICSE SQP 2022 (Sem I)***

x + = x++ + ++ x + --x + x;

(a) 29 (b) 28 (c) 26

Ans (a) 29

46. String x = (a >= 90)? "excellent" : "best"; when a = 90 ***ICSE SQP 2022 (Sem I)***

(a) best (b) excellent
(c) excellent best

Ans (b) excellent

47. Which of the following are valid comments? ***ICSE SQP 2022 (Sem I); ICSE 2014***

(i) /* comment */
(ii) /* comment
(iii) // comment
(iv) */ comment */

(a) (i) & (iii) (b) (i) & (ii)
(c) All of these (d) None of these

Ans (a) (i) & (iii)

48. Operators with higher precedence are evaluated before operators with relatively lower precedence. Arrange the operators given below in order of higher precedence to lower precedence. ***ICSE SQP 2022 (Sem I)***

(i) && (ii) %
(iii) >= (iv) ++

(a) (iv), (i), (iii), (ii) (b) (iv), (iii), (ii), (i)
(c) (iv), (ii), (iii), (i) (d) (i), (ii), (iii), (iv)

Ans (d) (i), (ii), (iii), (iv)

49. The assignment operator(=) is left associative. ***ICSE SQP 2022 (Sem I)***

(a) True (b) False

Ans (b) False

50. !(2>3&&4>6) ***ICSE SQP 2022 (Sem I)***

(a) True (b) False

Ans (a) True

51. byte is non-primitive data type. ***ICSE SQP 2022 (Sem I)***

(a) True (b) False

Ans (b) False

52. Choose the odd one. ***ICSE SQP 2022 (Sem I)***

(a) Encapsulation
(b) Data abstraction
(c) Portable
(d) Polymorphism

Ans (c) Portable

53. Choose the odd one. ***ICSE SQP 2022 (Sem I)***

(a) > (b) ==
(c) && (d) <

Ans (c) &&

54. Choose the odd one. ***ICSE SQP 2022 (Sem I)***

(a) + (b) %
(c) / (d) ||

Ans (d) ||

55. Choose the odd one. ***ICSE SQP 2022 (Sem I)***

(a) return (b) break
(c) continue (d) System.exit(0)

Ans (d) System.exit(0)

56. Give the output of the following. When a = 5 and b = 7 ***ICSE 2022 (Sem I)***

```
if(a > b)
System.out.println(a+b);
System.out.println(a*b);
```

(a) 12,35 (b) 35 (c) 35, 12

Ans (b) 35

57. The .... allows a class to use the properties and methods of another class. *ICSE SQP 2022 (Sem I)*

(a) Inheritance (b) Polymorphism
(c) Encapsulation (d) None of these

Ans (a) Inheritance

58. Give the output of the following

```
switch(x)
{
    case 'a' : System.out.println
                        ("Discipline");
    case 'b' : System.out.println
                   ("Dedication"); break;
    case 'c' : System.out.println
                        ("Commitment");
    default : System.out.println("Success");
} when x='A'
```

ICSE SQP 2022 (Sem I)

(a) Discipline (b) Dedication
(c) Success

Ans (c) Success

59.
```
n=1000;
while (n> 10)
{
    n=n/10;
}
System.out.println(n);
```

How many time the loop is executed and what is the output? *ICSE SQP 2022 (Sem I)*

(a) Loop is executed 2 times and the output is 100.
(b) Loop is executed 3 times and the output is 10.
(c) Loop is executed 2 times and the output is 10.

Ans (c) Loop is executed 2 times and the output is 10.

60. The default statement is optional in switch- case. *ICSE SQP 2022 (Sem I)*

(a) True (b) False

Ans (a) True

61. Method that accepts a string without any space is .... *ICSE SQP 2022 (Sem I)*

(a) next() (b) nextLine()
(c) nextInt() (d) None of these

Ans (a) next()

62. Name the type of error in the statement given below *ICSE SQP 2022 (Sem I)*

```
int r=100/0;
```

(a) Syntax (b) Runtime
(c) Logical (d) None of these

Ans (b) Runtime

63. The .... are the words which have special meaning *ICSE SQP 2022 (Sem I)*

(a) Keywords (b) Identifier
(c) Methods (d) Package

Ans (a) Keywords

2 Marks Questions

1. Write the Java expression for $(a+b)^x$. *ICSE 2023*

Ans
```
Math.pow((a + b),x);
```

2. Evaluate the expression when the value of x = 4

```
x * = --x + x++ +x
```

ICSE 2023

Ans The expression can be written as

x = x * – – x + x++ + x
x = 4 * 3 + 3 + 4
x = 12 + 3 + 4
x = 19

3. Convert the following do ... while loop to for loop *ICSE 2023*

```
int x=10;
do
{x- -;
System.out.print(x);
}while (x>=1);
```

Ans
```
int x;
for(x=10; x >= 1; x--);
System.out.println(x);
```

4. Rewrite the following code using the if-else statement. *ICSE 2023*

```
int m=400;
double ch=(m>300) ? (m/10.0)*2:(m/20.0)-2;
```

Ans
```
int m = 400;
if (m > 300)
    double ch = (m / 10.0) * 2;
else
    double ch = (m / 20.0) - 2;
```

5. Give the output of the following program segment. *ICSE 2023*

```
int n = 4279; int d;
while(n>0)
{d=n%10;
    System.out.println(d);
    n=n/100;
}
```

Ans 92

6. Write the value of n after execution. *ICSE 2023*

```
char ch = 'd';
int n = ch + 5;
```

Ans 105

7. Write Java expression for $|x^2 + xy|$. **ICSE SQP 2023**

Ans `Math.abs (Math.pow (x, 2) + x * y);`

8. Evaluate the expression **ICSE SQP 2023**

```
Z += a++ + --b + ++a + --b;
```

where a = 10, b = 5, Z = 10

Ans Z= Z + (a++ + --b + ++a + --b)
Z = 10 + (10 + 4 + 12 + 3)
Z = 10 + 29
Z = 39

Common Mistake Some students were unsure about the pre and post- increment or decrement operator and change of self- value and so miscalculated the value of
Z=10+11+5+12+4=42;
Z=10+10+4+11+3=38;
Z=10+10+5+11+4=40;

9. Rewrite the following using ternary operators **ICSE SQP 2023**

```
if( x > y)
    c= 'A';
else
    c = 'a';
```

Ans c = (x > y)? 'A' : 'a';

10. How many times the following loop will get executed? What is the output of the same? **ICSE SQP 2023**

```
int counter= 1;
do
{
    System.out.println(counter);
} while (counter ++ < 5);
```

Ans The loop is executed 5 times.

Output

1
2
3
4
5

11. Rewrite the following while loop using for loop **ICSE SQP 2023**

```
int x = 5;
while ( x < = 5)
{
    x++;
}
System.out.println(x);
```

Ans

```
int x;
for(x = 5; x <= 5; x++);
System.out.println(x);
```

12. Write a statement in Java for $\sqrt{\frac{(a+b)^3}{|a-b|}}$. **ICSE SQP 2020**

Ans

```
System.out.println (Math.sqrt(Math.pow((a
                + b), 3) / Math.abs(a - b)));
```

13. What is the value of m after evaluating the following expression? **ICSE SQP 2020**

`m - = 9%++n + ++n/2;` when int m=10,n=6

Ans The expression can be written as
m = m – (9 % ++n + ++n / 2)
m = 10 – (9 % 7 + 8 / 2)
m = 10 – (2 + 4)
m = 10 – 6
m = 4

14. Predict output of the following **ICSE SQP 2020**

(i) Math.pow(25, 0.5)+Math.ceil(4.2)
(ii) Math.round (14.7) + Math.floor (7.9)

Ans (i) 10.0
(ii) 22.0

15. Differentiate between = and = = operators. **ICSE SQP 2020; ICSE 2007**

Ans Difference between = and == operator:

= operator	= = operator
It is assignment operator.	It is relational (binary) operator.
It is used to assign a value to any variable. e.g. x = 10;	It compares two object, based on memory reference. e.g. (A = = B)

16. Rewrite the following condition without using logical operators. **ICSE SQP 2020**

```
if( a>b || a>c) .
System.out.println(a);
```

Ans Condition without using logical operators:

```
if (a > b)
    System.out.println(a);
else if (a > c)
    System.out.println(a);
```

17. Explain the purpose of using a 'new' keyword in a Java program. **ICSE SQP 2020; ICSE 2006**

Ans 'new' operator is used to create an instance of an object. It is also used to create an instance of a class. Actually, it dynamically allocates memory in the heap with the reference, we define pointed from the stack.
e.g. `Myclass abc = new Myclass();`
Here, an instance of the class Myclass is created.

18. What are literals? **ICSE SQP 2020; ICSE 2013**

Ans Refer to text on page 3.

19. Differentiate between break and System. exit(0). *ICSE SQP 2020*

Ans

break	System.exit(0)
break statement is used to jump out from the loop or switch-case.	System.exit(0) terminates the entire program.
break is a keyword.	System.exit(0) is a method provided by Java standard library.

20. Rewrite the following loop using for loop. *ICSE SQP 2020*

```
while (true)
System.out.print("*");
```

Ans

```
for (;;)
{
    System.out.print("*");
}
```

21. What is the output of the following *ICSE SQP 2020*

```
String a="Java is programming language \n
developed by \t\'James Gosling\' ";
System.out.println(a);
```

Ans **Output**

Java is programming language
developed by 'James Gosling'

22. State the type of errors if any in the following statements: *ICSE SQP 2020*

(i) switch (n > 2)

(ii) System.out.println(100/0);

Ans (i) **Syntax Error** The expression of switch statement must resolve to byte, short, int, char or String. It cannot resolve to a boolean type so this statement will result in a syntax error.

(ii) **Runtime Error/Exception(Division by Zero)** The program will compile successfully but when this line is executed it will result in "division by zero" error as dividing any number by 0 is an invalid division operation.

23. Name any two basic principles of Object-Oriented Programming. *ICSE 2019*

Ans Encapsulation, Data Abstraction, Polymorphism, Inheritance.

24. Write a difference between unary and binary operators. *ICSE 2019, 2012*

Ans

Unary Operator	Binary Operator
It works/operates on single operand or variables. OR Holds only one operand	It works/operates on two variables or operands. OR Holds more than one operand

25. Name the keyword which

(i) indicates that a method has no return type.

(ii) makes the variable as a class variable. *ICSE 2019*

Ans (i) void (ii) static

26. Write the memory capacity (storage size) of short and float data type in bytes. *ICSE 2019*

Ans Short - 2 bytes

Float - 4 bytes

27. Identify and name the following tokens *ICSE 2019*

(i) public (ii) 'a' (iii) == (iv) { }

Ans (i) Keyword (ii) Variable's value

(iii) Operator (iv) Separator

28. Differentiate between if-else-if and switch case statements. *ICSE 2019*

Ans

if-else-if	switch case
Range of values are checked.	Only one value is compared.
Supports both primitive and composite data types.	Supports only integer (byte, short, int, long), char.
Relational/Logical expressions can be checked.	Only equality can be checked.

29. What are the various types of errors in Java? *ICSE 2019*

Ans Refer to text on pages 11-12.

30. Write a Java expression for the following *ICSE 2019*

$$|x^2 + 2xy|$$

Ans `Math.abs(Math.pow(x, 2) + 2 * x * y);`

31. If the value of basic = 1500, what will be the value of tax after the following statement is executed?

`tax = basic > 1200 ? 200 : 100;` *ICSE 2019*

Ans tax = 200

Concept Enhancer As basic is 1500, the condition of ternary operator - basic > 1200 is true. 200 is returned as the result of ternary operator and it gets assigned to tax.

32. Give the output of the following code and mention how many times the loop will execute? *ICSE 2019*

```
int i;
for (i = 5; i >= 1; i--)
{
    if(i% 2 == 1)
    continue;
    System.out.print(i + '' '');
}
```

Ans **Output** 4 2

loop will execute five times.

33. Evaluate the following expression if the value of x = 2, y = 3 and z = 1. *ICSE 2019*

```
v = x + --z+ y++ +y
```

Ans v = 9

34. Give the output of the following. *ICSE 2019*

```
Math.sqrt(Math.max (9, 16));
```

Ans 4.0

35. Define abstraction. *ICSE 2018*

Or What do you understand by the term data abstraction? Explain with an example. *ICSE 2010*

Ans Refer to text on page 2

36. `int res = 'A';`

What is the value of res? *ICSE 2018*

Ans The value of res is 65.

Concept Enhancer As res is an int variable and we are trying to assign it the character A so through implicit type conversion the ASCII code of A is assigned to res.

37. Write a Java expression for the following *ICSE 2018*

$$\frac{\sqrt{3x + x^2}}{a + b}$$

Ans Java expression for $y = \frac{\sqrt{3x+x^2}}{a+b}$

```
y= (Math.sqrt(3*x+x*x))/(a + b);
```

38. What is the value of y after evaluating the expression given below?

y+ = ++y + y– – + – – y; when int y = 8 *ICSE 2018*

Ans y + = ++y+y – – + – – y

= y+[(++y)+(y– –) + (– –y)]

= 8 + [9 + 9 + 7] = 8 + [25] = 33

39. Write the output for the following *ICSE 2018*

```
System.out.println("Incredible"+"\n"
                        +"world");
```

KEY idea

\n is the escape sequence for newline so Incredible and world are printed on two different lines.

Ans **Output**

Incredible
world

40. Rewrite the following using ternary operator *ICSE 2018*

```
if (bill >10000 )
   discount = bill * 10.0/100;
else
   discount = bill * 5.0/100;
```

Ans Using ternary operator

```
discount =  bill >10000? (bill*10.0/100):
(bill*5.0/100);
```

41. State one similarity and one difference between while and do-while loop. *ICSE 2018, 2005*

Ans One similarity between while and do-while loop

while Loop	do-while Loop
while loop repeats the process as long as user want.	do-while also repeats the process as long as user want.

One difference between while and do-while loop

while Loop	do-while Loop
while checks the condition first, then execute.	In do-while, firstly statement executes and then condition is checked.

42. State the difference between while and do-while loop. *ICSE 2018*

Ans Refer to text on page 10.

43. Give the output of the following program segment and also mention, how many times the loop is executed? *ICSE 2018*

```
int i;
for ( i = 5 ; i > 10; i ++ )
System.out.println( i );
System.out.println( i * 4 );
```

KEY idea

There are no curly braces after the loop which means that the statement System.out.println(i); is inside the loop and the statement System.out.println(i * 4); is outside the loop. Loop is not executed so System.out.println(i); is not executed but System.out. println (i * 4); being outside the loop is executed and prints the output as 20(i*4 ⇒ 5*4 ⇒ 20).

Ans **Output**

20

0 time the loop will be executed.

44. Convert the following if-else-if construct into switch case *ICSE 2018*

```
if( var==1)
   System.out.println("good");
else if(var==2)
   System.out.println("better");
else if(var==3)
   System.out.println("best");
else
   System.out.println("invalid");
```

Ans Program in Switch case

```
switch (var)
```

```
{
    case 1 :
            System.out. println("good");
            break;
    case 2:
            System.out.println("better");
            break;
    case 3:
            System.out.println("best");
            break;
    default:
            System.out.println("invalid");
}
```

45. What is inheritance? **ICSE 2017**

Or What is inheritance and how is it useful in Java? **ICSE 2008**

Ans Inheritance in Java is a cabability of one class (child class) inherit the properties of other class (parent class) in terms of parent class (superclass) and child class (subclass).

It helps in reusability in such a way that it adds some additional features to another class without modifying the contents of a parent class.

46. Name the operators listed below. **ICSE 2017**

(i) < (ii) ++ (iii) && (iv) ? :

Ans (i) < → Less than operator

(ii) ++ → Postfix/Prefix Increment

(iii) && → Logical AND Operator

(iv) ? : → Conditional Operator

47. What is the difference between / and % operator? **ICSE 2017, 11**

Ans Difference between / and % operator are as follows

/ Operator	% Operator
This is a division operator.	This is a modulus operator.
It is used to find the remainder of division of two numbers.	It is used to find the quotient in the division of two numbers.
e.g. int x = 10, y = 5, z; x = x/y; value of z will be 2.	e.g. int x = 10, y = 5, z; z = x%y; value of *z* will be 0.

48. Name the following **ICSE 2017**

(i) A keyword used to call a package in the program.

(ii) Any one reference data type.

Ans (i) import

(ii) class

49. Write the output **ICSE 2017**

```
char ch='F';
int m=ch;
m=m+5;
System.out.println(m+" "+ch);
```

Ans When ch = F [∵ F = 70]

m = ch

m = 70

m = m + 5 = 70 + 5 = 75

Output = 75F

50. Write a Java expression for the following **ICSE 2017**

$ax^5 + bx^3 + c$

Ans Java expression for $ax^5 + bx^3 + c$

= a * x * x * x * x * x + b * x * x * x + c

51. What is the value of x1 if x= 5? **ICSE 2017**

x1= ++x− x++ + −−x

Ans If x = 5

x1 = ++x − x ++ + − − x

= 6 − 6 + 6

x1 = 6

52. Write difference between entry control loop and exit control loop. **ICSE 2017**

Ans Refer to text on page 11.

53. Give the output of the following program segment and also mention the number of times the loop is executed **ICSE 2017**

```
int a,b;
for(a=6, b=4; a<=24; a=a+6)
{
    if(a%b==0)
        break;
}
System.out.println(a);
```

Ans **Output** : 12

Number of times the loop is executed = 2

Concept Enhancer In 2nd iteration, as a%b becomes 0 so break statement is executed and the loop exits. Program control comes to the println statement which prints the output as current value.

54. Convert following do-while loop into for loop. **ICSE 2017**

```
int i=1;
int d=5;
do {
    d=d*2;
    System.out.println(d);
    i++; } while(i<=5);
```

Ans

```
int d=5;
int i;
for(i=1; i<=5; i++)
```

```
    {
        d=d*2;
        System.out.println(d);
    }
```

55. Analyze the given program segment and answer the following questions:

```
for(int i=3; i<=4; i++)
{
   for(int j=2; j<i; j++)
   {
      System.out.print(" ");
   }
   System.out.println("WIN");
}
```

(i) How many times does the inner loop execute?

(ii) Write the output of the program segment. **ICSE 2017**

Ans (i) The inner loop will execute 3 times.

(ii) **Output**

WIN

WIN

56. What is the difference between the Scanner class functions next() and nextLine()? **ICSE 2017**

Ans Differences between the Scanner class functions next() and nextLine() are as follows

next( )	nextLine( )
next( ) can read the input only till the space.	nextLine( ) reads input including space between the words.
next( ) only gets up to the next space.	nextLine( ) gets to the line break.

57. Name any four tokens of Java. **ICSE SQP 2017**

Ans Four tokens in Java are

1. Keywords
2. Literals
3. Identifiers
4. Operators

58. What is an identifier? **ICSE SQP 2017; ICSE 2015**

Ans Refer to text on page 4.

59. Write an expression in Java for $\cos x + \sqrt{a^2 + b^2}$. **ICSE SQP 2017**

Ans
```
Math.cos (x) + Math.sqrt(Math.pow (a,2) +
Math.pow (b,2));
```

60. What is the result produced by $2 - 10 * 3 + 100 / 11$? Show the steps. **ICSE SQP 2017**

Ans 2 – 10 * 3 + 100/11

⇒ 2.0 – 10.0 * 3.0 + 100.0/11.0

⇒ 2.0 – 10.0 * 3.0 + 9.09090909

⇒ 2.0 – 30.0 + 9.09090909

⇒ 37.09090909

61. int x=20, y=10, z; **ICSE SQP 2017**

What is the value of z in

z = ++x * (y– –) – y?

Show the steps.

Ans z = ++x * (y - -) - y

⇒ z = 21 * 10 - y (given x=21, y=9)

⇒ z = 210 - 9

⇒ z = 201

62. What will be the output of the following code? **ICSE SQP 2017**

```
int a=5, b=2, c;
if (a>b || a ! = b)
c = ++a+--b;
System.out.print(c+" "+a+" "+b);
```

Ans **Output** 7 6 1

Common Mistake One common mistake in the given code is the syntax error in the if statement condition. The condition is a > b || a ! = b, which contains a space between ! and = in the inequality operator ! =. This will cause a syntax error, and the code will not compile.

63. What will be the output of the following code? **ICSE SQP 2017**

```
int a = 0;
if(a>0 && a <20)
    a++;
else a-- ;
    System.out.println(a);
```

Ans Output: – 1

64. What is the purpose of default in a switch? **ICSE SQP 2017**

Or

Explain, with the help of an example, the purpose of default in a switch statement. **ICSE 2005**

Ans The purpose of default in a switch statement, is that, if no case value matches the switch expression value, then the default clause is executed.

e.g.
```
int ch=10;
switch(ch)
{
   case1:
     System.out.println("Its one");
     break;
   case2:
     System.out.println("Its two");
     break;
   default:
     System.out.println("Not working");
}
```

Output Not working

65. State the difference between if-else if ladder and switch … case. ***ICSE SQP 2017***

Ans In the if-else if ladder, if the condition of an if clause is found true, the statements in the complete if block are executed and the corresponding else and remaining if's are not checked is not executed, but in switch...case, if a case matches, then fall-through occurs and all the remaining statements in the switch statements are executed until a break is encountered or the statement ends.

66.
```
int i=1;
while(i++<=1)
{
    i++;
    System.out.print(i+" ");
}
System.out.print(i);
```
What will be the output of the following code? ***ICSE SQP 2017***

Ans Output: 3 4

67. What will be the output of the following code? ***ICSE SQP 2017***
```
float x = 7.87;
System.out.println(Math.ceil(x));
System.out.println(Math.floor(x));
```
Ans Output: 8.00000000
7.00000000

68. Define encapsulation. ***ICSE 2016, 06***

Ans Refer to text on page 2.

69. What are the types of casting shown by the following examples? ***ICSE 2016***

(i) `char c =(char) 120;`

(ii) `int x = 't';`

Ans (i) Explicit Type Casting
(ii) Implicit Type Casting

70. Write down Java expression for ***ICSE 2016***

$$T=\sqrt{A^2+B^2+C^2}$$

Ans Java expression for $T=\sqrt{A^2+B^2+C^2}$ is
```
T = Math.sqrt ((Math.pow (A,2)) +
(Math.pow (B,2)) + (Math.pow (C,2)));
```

71. Rewrite the following using ternary operator ***ICSE 2016***
```
if (x% 2 = = 0)
   System.out.print("EVEN");
else
   System.out.print("ODD");
```

Ans Using ternary operator
```
(x % 2 = = 0) ? System.out.print (''EVEN'')
: System.out.print ("ODD");
```

72. Give the output of the following expression ***ICSE 2016***

a+ = a ++ + ++ a + -- a +a--; when a =7

Ans When a = 7

$$\begin{aligned} a+ &= a++ ++ +a + -- a + a -- \\ &= a+[(a++] + (++a) + (--a) + (a--)] \\ &= 7+[7+9+8+8] \\ &= 7+32 \\ &= 39 \end{aligned}$$

73. Convert the following while loop of the corresponding for loop ***ICSE 2016***
```
int m = 5, n = 10;
while(n>=1)
{
   System.out.println(m*n);
   n - - ;
}
```

Ans
```
int m= 5;
for (int n= 10; n>= 1; n--)
{
   System.out.println (m * n);
}
```

74. Analyse the given program segment and answer the following questions ***ICSE 2016***
```
for(int m=5; m<=20; m+ =5)
{
   if(m%3= =0)
      break;
   else
      if(m%5==0)
      System.out.println(m);
   continue;
}
```
(i) Write the output of the program segment

(ii) How many times does the body of the loop get executed?

Ans (i) **Output**
5
10

(ii) Three times the body of the loop will be executed.

Common Mistake A common mistake for this question is that some students might think that the program will output the numbers that are divisible by 5 between 5 and 20. However, the program will not output any numbers since the break statement inside the loop will terminate the loop as soon as 'm' becomes divisible by 3.

75. What are keywords? Give an example. ***ICSE 2016***

Or

What does the token 'keyword' refer to, in the context of Java? Give an example for keyword. ***ICSE 2011***

Ans Keywords are special tokens which have reserved use in the language. It can not be used as identifier in Java and you can not declare a field whose name is keyword, for instance.

e.g. if, new, case, goto, int, etc.

76. Identify the literals listed below ***ICSE 2015***

(i) 0.5 (ii) 'A'

(iii) false (iv) "a"

Ans (i) **0.5** is a double precision floating point literal.

(ii) **'A'** is a character literal.

(iii) **false** is a boolean literal.

(iv) **"a"** is a string literal.

77. Evaluate the value of n if value of p = 5, q = 19 ***ICSE 2015***

```
int n=(q-p)>(p-q)? (q-p):(p-q);
```

Ans The value of n is 14.

78. Write the Java expression for $\frac{a^2+b^2}{2ab}$ ***ICSE 2015***

Ans Java expression for $\frac{a^2+b^2}{2ab}$

```
y = (a*a + b*b)/(2*a*b);
```

79. If int y = 10, then find int z = (+ +y * (y+ + +5)); ***ICSE 2015***

Ans int y = 10;

z = (++y * (y++ + 5));

= 11 * (11 + 5)

= 11 * 16 = 176

80. What is the function of catch block in exception handling? Where does it appear in a program? ***ICSE 2015***

Ans The main function of catch block is to handle the exception that is thrown by try block. It catches the exception into the object of same type that is specified in the argument of catch function definition. It is also used to represent the notification and causes during which exception raises. It appears after try block in the program.

81. Write the output of the following program code: ***ICSE 2015***

```
char ch;
int x = 97;
do
{
   ch = (char)x;
   System.out.print(ch+" ");
   if (x%10==0)
    break;
   --x;
}
while(x<=100);
```

Ans **Output** a b c d

82. Operators with higher precedence are evaluated before operators with relatively lower precedence. Arrange the operators given below in order of higher precedence to lower precedence.

(i) && (ii) %

(iii) >= (iv) ++ ***ICSE 2014***

Ans The operators are arranged in order of higher to lower precedence.

(iv) ++ (ii) % (iii) >= (i) &&

83. State one difference between the floating point literals float and double. ***ICSE 2014***

Ans Difference between floating point literals float and double

Float Literals	Double Literals
The float literal has a limited range to store decimal data item. It can hold 32-bit data.	The double literal has a wider range as compared to float, to store decimal data items. It can hold 64-bit data.

84. List the variables from those given below that are composite data types

(i) `static int x;`

(ii) `arr [i] = 10;`

(iii) `obj.display( );`

(iv) `boolean b;`

(v) `private char chr;`

(vi) `String str;` ***ICSE 2014***

Ans Composite data types are as:

(i) arr[i] = 10;

(ii) obj.display( );

(vi) String str;

85. Give two differences between the switch statement and the if-else statement. ***ICSE 2014***

Ans Refer to text on page 9.

86. What is an infinite loop? Write an infinite loop statement. ***ICSE 2014, 08***

Ans Infinite loop is that in which iteration never stops. This is because, condition output is always true, loop continues for an infinite number of times. e.g. entry control loop.

Statement

```
int a=0;
for(a=10; a>0; a++)
{
 System.out.println("The value of a="+a);
}
```

In the above example, the 'for' loop will check condition first and as the initial values of a (i.e. 10) is greater than 0 so it will execute once.

Next time, the loop will increase the value of a by 1 and the condition will again evaluated.

This process will be repeated again and again and the loop will execute infinite times.

87. Rewrite the following program segment using if-else statements instead of the ternary operator. ***ICSE 2014***

```
String
grade=(mark>=90)?"A":(mark>=80)?"B":"C";
```

Ans Program segment using if-else statements

```
if(mark>=90)
{
    String grade="A";
}
else
{
    if(mark>=80)
    {
       String grade="B";
    }
    else
    {
       String grade="C";
    }
}
```

88. Find the errors in the given program segment and rewrite the statements correctly to assign values to an integer array. ***ICSE 2014***

```
int a = new int(5);
for(int i=0; i<=5; i++) a[i]=i;
```

Ans The corrected code is

```
int[] a=new int[5];
for(int i=0; i<5; i++)
{
    a[i]=i;
}
```

89. State the Java concept that is implemented through

(i) a super class and a sub class.

(ii) the act of representing essential features without including background details. ***ICSE 2013***

Ans (i) The sub class just use the items inherited from its super class as it is, or the sub class can modify or override it, this process is known as inheritance. In inheritance, super class is called as parent class and sub class is called as child class.

(ii) Abstraction

90. What is meant by precedence of operators? ***ICSE 2013***

Ans Refer to text on page 5.

91. Name the Java keyword that

(i) indicates a method has no return type.

(ii) stores the address of the currently calling object. ***ICSE 2013***

Ans (i) The void keyword, it allows us to create functions that either do not require any parameters or do not return a value.

(ii) In Java, this keyword is a reference variable that refers to the current object.

92. Write a Java expression for $ut + \frac{1}{2}ft^2$. ***ICSE 2013***

Ans Expression for $ut + \frac{1}{2}ft^2 = u * t + (1/2) * f * t * t$

93. What are the types of casting shown by the following examples? ***ICSE 2013***

(i)
```
double x = 15.2;
   int y = (int)x;
```

(ii)
```
int x  = 12;
long y = x;
```

Ans (i) Explicit type casting, because here we want to assign x value into y, but x is double type variable and y is int type, so int is unable to hold the variable of double and when we required downcasting.

(ii) Implicit type casting, because we require upcasting here as int type is to be convert into long type.

94. What is the difference between a break statement and a continue statement when they occur in a loop? ***ICSE 2013***

Ans Difference between break and continue statement

break Statement	continue Statement
When break is executed, the statements following break are skipped and cause the loop to be terminated.	When continue statement is executed, the statements following continue are skipped and cause the loop to be continued with the next iteration.

e.g.`for(i=1; i<=5; i++)`
`{`
`if(i%2==0) break;`
`System.out.print(i);`
`}`
Output 1
	e.g.`for(i=1; i<=5; i++)`
	`{`
	`if(i%2==0) continue;`
	`System.out.print(i);`
	`}`
	Output 1 3 5

95. Rewrite the following program segment using the if-else statement. ***ICSE 2013***

```
comm=(sale>15000) ? sale*5/100:0;
```

Ans Program segment using the if-else statement

```
if(sale>15000)
{
    comm=(sale*5)/100;
}
else
{
    comm=0;
}
```

96. How many times will the following loop execute? What value will be returned? **ICSE 2013**

```
int x=2, y=50;
do
{
   ++x;
   y -= x++;
}
while(x <= 10);
return y;
```

Ans Initially, x=2, y=50

x	y	++x	y – = x++ ⇒ y = y - x++	x <= 10	return y
2	50	3	y = 50 – 3 = 47 Now, x = 4	4 <= 10	47
4	47	5	y = 47 – 5 = 42 Now, x = 6	6 <= 10	42
6	42	7	y = 42 – 7 = 35 Now, x = 8	8 <= 10	35
8	35	9	y = 35 – 9 = 26 Now, x = 10	10 <= 10	26
10	26	11	y = 26 – 11 = 15 Now, x = 12	12 <= 10 (false)	15

Loop will execute 5 times and return the value of y = 15.

Concept Enhancer This program initializes two integer variables x and y with the values 2 and 50, respectively. It then enters a do-while loop that increments x by 1 and subtracts the original value of x + 1 from y in each iteration until x is greater than 10.

97. What is the final value of ctr where the iteration process given below, executes? **ICSE 2013**

```
int ctr=0;
for(int i=1; i<=5; i++)
for(int j=1; j<=5; j+=2)
++ctr;
```

Ans The final value of ctr = 15

98. Name the methods of Scanner class that

(i) is used to input an integer data from the standard input stream.

(ii) is used to input a string data from the standard input stream. **ICSE 2013**

Ans (i) int nextInt()

(ii) String nextLine()

99. Give one example each of primitive data type and composite data type. **ICSE 2012**

Ans Primitive data type : char
Composite data type : class

100. What are the value of x and y when the following statements are executed?

```
int a=63, b=36;
boolean x=(a>b)?true:false;
int y=(a<b)?a:b;
```

ICSE 2012

Ans The value of x = true, and
The value of y = 36

101. State the value of n and ch.

```
char c='A';
int n=c+1;
char ch=(char) n;
```

ICSE 2012

Ans Given, c = 'A'

∴ 'A' = 65

n = c + 1 = 65 + 1 = 66

The value of n = 66

ch = n

The value of ch = B [∵ B = 66]

102. What will be the result stored in x after evaluating the following expression?

```
int x=4;
x+=(x++)+(++x)+x;
```

ICSE 2012

Ans

```
int x = 4;
 x + = (x++) + (++x) + x;      [∴ left to right]
     = 4 + (4 + 6 + 6)
     = 4 + 16
     = 20
```

103. Name the type of errors (syntax, runtime or logical error) in each case given below: **ICSE 2012**

(i) Division by a variable that contains a value of zero.

(ii) Multiplication operator used when the operation should be division.

(iii) Missing semicolon.

Ans (i) runtime error

(ii) logical error

(iii) syntax error

104. Rewrite the following program segment using while instead of for statement **ICSE 2012**

```
int f=1, i;
for(i=1; i<=5; i++)
```

```
{
   f*=i;
   System.out.println(f);
}
```

Ans
```
int f=1, i;
while(i<=5)
{
    f*=i;
    System.out.println(f);
    i++;
}
```

105. Complete the code below to create an object of Scanner class.

```
Scanner sc = ____ Scanner(____)
```
ICSE 2012

Ans `Scanner sc = new Scanner(System.in);`

106. What will be the output of the following code?

```
int k = 5, j = 9;
k+=k++ - ++j+k;
System.out.println("k ="+k);
System.out.println("j ="+j);
```
ICSE 2011

Ans k += (k++) − (++j) + k;

= k + (k++ − ++j + k); [∴ left to right]

= 5 + (5 − 10 + 6);

k = 6

Hence, k = 6, j = 10

107. Analyse the following program segment and determine how many times the loop will be executed and what will be the output of the program segment? **ICSE 2011**

```
int p = 200;
while(true)
{
   if(p<100)
      break;
   p = p-20;
}
System.out.println(p);
```

> **KEY idea**
>
> The code initializes an integer variable "p" to 200, and then enters a while loop that runs indefinitely. Within the loop, there is an "if" statement that checks whether "p" is less than 100; if it is, the loop is terminated using the "break" statement. Otherwise, the value of "p" is decremented by 20. After the loop, the value of "p" is printed to the console, which will be 80 in this case.

Ans

p	p < 100	p = p − 20	System.out.println(p)
200	200 < 100 false	p = 200 − 20 = 180	—
180	180 < 100 false	p = 180 − 20 = 160	—
160	160 < 100 false	p = 160 − 20 = 140	—
140	140 < 100 false	p = 140 − 20 = 120	—
120	120 < 100 false	p = 120 − 20 = 100	—
100	100 < 100 false	p = 100 − 20 = 80	—
80	80 < 100 true	break;	80 (print)

The loop will be executed 7 times and output of the program segment = 80.

108. Define the term bytecode. **ICSE 2010**

Ans Refer to text on page 1.

109. What is the result stored in x, after evaluating the following expression

```
int x = 5;
x=x++*2+3*--x;
```
ICSE 2010

Ans The value of x is

x = x++ * 2 + 3 * −−x;

We know the value of x = 5,

So, = 5 * 2 + 3 * 5

= 10 + 15 = 25

Hence, x = 25

110. What do you mean by type conversion? How is implicit conversion different from explicit conversion? **ICSE 2010**

Or

Explain the terms of type casting. **ICSE 2007**

Ans Type conversion is changing a value from one data type to another type. Data type conversions are either implicit or explicit, it depends on the data capacities of the data type involved.

Difference between implicit and explicit conversion:

Implicit Conversion	Explicit Conversion
It is automatically type conversion.	It is completely defined within a program.
This method is used when upcasting is required like: int to long.	This method is used when downcasting is required like : double to byte.

111. Name two jump statements and their use. **ICSE 2010**

Or

Explain the function of each of the following with an example. **ICSE 2008**

(i) break; (ii) continue;

Or

Explain the meaning of break and continue statement. **ICSE 2005**

Ans Two jump statements :

(i) A **break statement** terminates the current loop and proceeds to the first statement that follows the loop.

e.g.
```
for(int i=2; i<n; i++)
{
   if=(n%1==0)
   System.out.println(n);
   break;
}
```

(ii) A **continue statement** transfers the control to the next iteration leaving all the other statement unexecuted that follows after the continue statement.

e.g.
```
for(int i=1; i<20; i++)
{
   if(i%2==0)
      continue;
   System.out.println(i);
}
```

The above loop will print all the odd numbers.

112. Analyse the following program segment and determine how many times the loop will be executed and what will be the output of the program segment?

```
int k=1, i=2;
while(++i<6)
{ k* = i; }
System.out.println(k);
```

ICSE 2010

Ans int k=1, i=2

++i < 6	k *= i	k
3 < 6 (True)	k = k × i = 1 × 3 = 3	3
4 < 6 (True)	k = 3 × 4 = 12	12
5 < 6 (True)	k = 12 × 5 = 60	60

The value of k=60

The loop will be executed 3 times.

113. State the difference between a boolean literal and character literal. ***ICSE 2009***

Ans Difference between boolean literal and character literal are as follows

Boolean Literal	Character Literal
Boolean literal consists of the keyword true and false.	Character literal is expressed by a single character.
Boolean literal are never enclosed within quotes. e.g. true, false	A character literal constant enclosed within single quotes. e.g. 'A' ,'d', '*', etc.

114. What is the use and syntax of a ternary operator? ***ICSE 2009***

Ans Ternary operator deals with three operands. It is also called conditional assignment statement because the value assigned to a variable depends upon the logical expression. The common use of ternary operator is in checking the condition.

Syntax

```
Variable = (test expression)?
Value 1: Value 2
```

115. What is the use of the this keyword? ***ICSE 2009***

Ans Refer to text on page 4.

116. State one similarity and one difference between while and for loop. ***ICSE 2009***

Ans One difference between while loop and for loop

while Loop	for Loop
In while loop, number of iteration are not known in advance.	In for loop, number of iteration are known in advance.

One similarity between while loop and for loop:

while Loop	for Loop
while loop is entry controlled loop.	for loop is also the entry controlled loop.

117. The following is a segment of program ***ICSE 2009***

```
x=1; y=1;
if(n>0)
{
   x=x+1;
   y=y-1;
}
```

What will be the value of x and y, if n assumes a value (i) 1 (ii) 0?

Ans (i) If, n assume as a value 1

```
x=1; y=1;
if(n>0)
{
   x=x+1;
   y=y-1;
}
```

Then, value of x=2, y=0

(ii) If, n assume as a value 0

```
x=1; y=1;
if(n>0)
{
   x=x+1;
   y=y-1;
}
```

Then, value of x=1 and y=1

118. Analyse the following program segment and determine how many times the body of loop will be executed (show the working). ***ICSE 2009***

```
x=5; y=50;
while(x<=y)
{
   y = y/x;
   System.out.println(y);
}
```

Ans

Value of x and y	(x <= y)	y = y/x;
5 and 50	5 <= 50 (True)	y = 50/5; y = 10
5 and 10	5 <= 10 (True)	y = 10/5; y = 2
5 and 2	5 <= 2 (False)	Exit the loop

Thus, loop will execute 2 times and now value of y = 2.

119. Differentiate between base class and derived class. **ICSE 2008**

Ans Difference between base class and derived class are as follows :

Base Class	Derived Class
A base class facilitates the creation of other class.	Derived classes use the functionality of base class.
It is also known as parent/super class.	It is also known as child/sub class.

120. State the difference between token and identifier. **ICSE 2008**

Ans Difference between token and identifier:

Token	Identifier
It is the smallest element in a program that is meaningful to the compiler.	These are the names of variable, method, class, package, interface, etc.
These define the structure of the language. e.g. keyword, literal etc.	These are used to uniquely identify them to the compiler. e.g. 123ab, __ salary etc.

121. If a = 5, b = 9 calculate the value of

a+=a++ − ++b+a; **ICSE 2008**

Ans a+ = a++ − ++b + a (∵ left to right)

= a + (a++ − ++b + a)

= 5 + (5 − 10 + 6)

= 5 + 1 = 6

The value of a after execution will be 6.

122. Convert the following segment into equivalent for loop **ICSE 2008**

```
int i=0;
while(i<=20)
{
   System.out.print(i+ " ");
   i++;
}
```

Ans Program in for loop

```
for(int i=0; i<=20; i++)
{
   System.out.print(i+ " ");
}
```

123. Name two types of Java programs. **ICSE 2007**

Ans Two types of Java programs are:

(i) Applets

(ii) Stand-alone applications

124. Assign the value of pie (i.e. 3.142) to a variable with requisite data type. **ICSE 2007**

Ans double pie = 3.142;

Here, for pie (3.142) the suitable data type is double because it can hold 64-bit floating point.

125. Write an equivalent Java syntax for the following expression.

$$a = \frac{0.05 - 2y^3}{x - y}$$ **ICSE 2007**

Ans $a = \frac{0.05 - 2y^3}{x - y}$

We can write this statement in Java like,

```
a = (0.05-2*y*y*y)/(x-y);
```

126. Rewrite the following using ternary operator

```
if(income<=10000)
   tax=0;
else
   tax=12;
```

ICSE 2007

Ans tax=income < = 10000 ? 0 : 12;

127. Write a statement for each of the following

(i) Store a number 275 as a string.

(ii) Convert the string to a numeric value.

(iii) Add it to the existing total of 1000 to update the total. **ICSE 2007**

Ans Statement for each of the followings are:

(i) String s = "275";

(ii) int a = Integer.parseInt(s);

(iii) total = 1000 + a;

128. Evaluate the following expressions, if the values of the variables are a = 2, b = 3 and c = 9

(i) a − (b++) * (−−c)

(ii) a * (++b) % c **ICSE 2007**

Ans (i) 2 − 3 × 8 = 2 − 24 = − 22

(ii) 2 * 4 % 9 = 8 % 9 = 8

129. Explain, with an example, if-else-if construct. **ICSE 2007**

Ans if-else-if statement is a kind of statement, in which a number of logical conditions are checked for executing various statements.

e.g.

```
int x=30;
if(x==10)
```

```
{
   System.out.print("value of x is 10");
}
else if(x==20)
{
   System.out.print("value of x is 20");
}
else if(x==30)
{
   System.out.print("value of x is 30");
}
else
{
   System.out.print("This is else
                                statement");
}
```

130. Find the output of the following program segment, when

(i) val= 500

(ii) val=1600

```
int val, sum, n = 550;
sum = n +val>1750?400:200;
System.out.println(sum);
```

ICSE 2006

Ans (i) When, val = 500, n = 550

Sum = n+val > 1750 ? 400 : 200;

= 550+ 500> 1750? 400 : 200;

= 1050 > 1750 ? 400 : 200;

Sum = 200

(ii) When, val = 1600, n = 550

Sum = n + val > 1750 ? 400 : 200;

= 550 + 1600> 1750? 400 : 200;

= 2150 > 1750 ? 400 : 200;

Sum = 400

131. What will be the output for the following program segment? **ICSE 2006**

```
int a=0, b=30,c=40;
a=--b + c + ++b;
System.out.println("a ="+ a);
```

Ans int a = 0, b = 30, c = 40;

a = --b + c + ++b (∵ left to right)

= 29 + 40 + 30 = 99

132. Differentiate between if and switch statements. **ICSE 2006**

Ans Difference between if and switch statement

if Statement	switch Statement
It works under the boolean literals.	It works under the integer/character literals.
It uses relational operator for check conditions.	It uses 'case' for check conditions.

133. Mention two different styles of expressing a comment in a program. **ICSE 2005**

Ans In Java, two different styles of expressing a comment in a program:

(i) // for single line comment

(ii) /* comment */ for multiline comment.

134. Differentiate between operator and expression. **ICSE 2005**

Ans Differences between operator and expression:

Operator	Expression
Operators are special symbols used for mathematical or logical function.	An expression is a statement that can convey a value.
Generally, these are used between two operands.	It may be any combination of variables, literals, operators.
e.g. x + y here + is an operator.	e.g. a = b + c is an expression.

135. If m = 5 and n = 2, output the values of m and n after execution in (i) and (ii)

(i) m −= n;

(ii) $n = m + \frac{m}{n}$; **ICSE 2005**

Ans Given, m = 5, n = 2

(i) m−= n; m = m − n = 5 − 2 ⇒ m = 3

(ii) $n = m + \frac{m}{n} = 5 + \frac{5}{2} = 5 + 2.5$

n = 7.5

Hence, m = 3, n = 7.5

136. What will be the output of the following, if x = 5 initially?

(i) 5 * ++x;

(ii) 5 * x++; **ICSE 2005**

Ans Given, x = 5

(i) 5 * ++x;
5 * 6 = 30

(ii) 5 * x++;
5 * 5 = 25

137. What is the output of the following?

```
char c='A';
short m=26;
int n=c+m;
System.out.println(n);
```

ICSE 2005

Ans char c = 'A' (∴ We know 'A' = 65)

short m = 26

int n = c + m = 65 + 26 = 91

Output 91

138. Explain the term for loop with an example. **ICSE 2005**

Ans A for loop is "entry controlled" loop. It is a short method of looping, which is commonly preferred by programmers. It test the condition before entering in the loop body.
e.g.

```
for(int x=5; x<20; x++)
{
   System.out.println("value of x:" +x);
}
```

3/4 Marks Questions

1. Read the following case study and answer the questions given below by choosing the correct option.

Java compilation is different from the compilation of other high-level languages. Other high-level languages use interpreter or compiler but in Java, the source code is first compiled to produce an intermediate code called the byte code, this byte code is platform independent and is a highly optimized set of instructions designed to be executed by Java in the run time system called JVM (Java Virtual Machine). JVM is a Java interpreter loaded in the computer memory as soon as Java is loaded. JVM is different for different platforms. ***ICSE 2022 (Sem I)***

(i) Full form of JVM is
 (a) Java Visual Machine
 (b) Joint Vision Mechanism
 (c) Java Virtual Machine
 (d) Java Virtual Mechanism

(ii) JAVA code is
 (a) compiled and interpreted
 (b) only compiled
 (c) only interpreted
 (d) translated

(iii) JAVA source code is compiled to produce
 (a) object code (b) byte code
 (c) final code (d) machine code

(iv) JVM is an / a
 (a) interpreter (b) compiler
 (c) intermediate code (d) high level language

Ans (i) (c) Full form of JVM is Java Virtual Machine.
(ii) (a) Java code first compiled and produces byte code and then byte code is interpreted by JVM.
(iii) (b) It produce byte code.
(iv) (a) JVM is an interpreter.

2. The following program segment calculates the norm of a number, norm of a number is square root of sum of squares of all digits of the number.

Example:

The norm of 68 is 10

$6 \times 6 + 8 \times 8 = 36 + 64 = 100$ square root of 100 is 10.

Fill in the blanks with appropriate Java statements.

```
void norm ( int n)
{
    int d, s =(i) _____ ;
    while ( (ii) ____')
    {
       d = n%10;
       s = (iii) _____ ;
       n=n/10;
    }
    System.out.println("Norm ="+(iv) ____);
}
```

ICSE SQP 2022 (Sem I)

(i) (a) 0 (b) 0.0 (c) 1
(ii) (a) n>0 (b) n<0 (c) n>1
(iii) (a) s+d*d (b) s*d+d (c) s*s+d
(iv) (a) Math.sqrt(s) (b) Math.SQRT(s)
 (c) Math.sqrt(n)

Ans (i) (a) 0 (ii) (a) n > 0
(iii) (a) s + d * d (iv) (a) Math.sqrt(s)

3. Read the paragraph given below and answer the questions given below ***ICSE SQP 2022 (Sem I)***

Decision control statements are used to check for condition and execute the statements based on the condition. The two decision control statements in Java are if and switch, switch is also called as multiple branching statement.

An if statement within another if statement is termed as Nested if Statement. Repetitive execution of a set of statements is termed as looping. The two types of looping statements are entry controlled and exit controlled loops. Both while and for are termed as entry-controlled loops. A for loop is used when the number of iterations is known. A while is used when the set of statements are executed as long as the condition is true, it is executed when the number of iterations are not known.

(i) What are the two decision control statements in Java?
 (a) if and switch (b) for and while
 (c) ternary and logical

(ii) An if statement within another if statement is termed as
 (a) Nested
 (b) Nested while
 (c) Nested if

(iii) Name given for repetitive execution of set of statements.
 (a) Looping
 (b) Decision Control
 (c) Assignment

(iv) Which one of the following does not execute even once?

(a) for(k = 1; k<=100;k++);

(b) for(k= 10;k< 1;k++);

(c) for k=l; k>=1;k,++);

Ans (i) (a) if and switch

(ii) (c) Nested if

(iii) (a) Looping

(iv) (b) for (k = 10; k < 1; k ++);

4. What will be the output of the following code? **ICSE 2010**

(i)
```
int m = 2;
int n = 15;
for(int i=1;i<5; i++)
  m++;
--n;
System.out.println("m ="+m);
System.out.println("n ="+n);
```

(ii)
```
char x='A'
int m;
m = (x=='aa'?'A':'a');
System.out.println("m ="+m);
```

Ans (i) m = 6, n = 14

(ii) m = 97

5. Convert the following segment into an equivalent do-while loop **ICSE 2009**

```
int x, c;
for(x=10, c=20; c>=10; c=c-2)
x++;
```

Ans do-while loop segment

```
int x, c;
x=10; c=20;
do
{
    x++;
    c = c-2;
}
while(c >= 10);
```

6. Give the output of the following code fragment **ICSE 2009**

when (i) opn = 'b' (ii) opn = 'x' (iii) opn = 'a'

```
switch(opn)
{
   case 'a':
      System.out.println("Platform
                          Independent");
      break;
   case 'b':
      System.out.println("Object
                          Oriented");
   case 'c':
      System.out.println("Robust and
                          Secure");
      break;
   default:
      System.out.println("Wrong Input");
}
```

Ans (i) opn='b'

When opn = 'b' it reach on case 'b'. Then print the value:

Object Oriented

Robust and Secure

(ii) opn='x'

When opn = 'x' it check all case but no one is equivalent to x, so it reach in default segment and print the value :

Wrong Input

(iii) opn='a'

When opn = 'a' it found case 'a'. Then enter in that case and print value:

Platform Independent

6 Marks Questions

1. Given below is a class with the following specifications

Class name	overload
Member Methods	
void print (int n)	to print the first 'n' natural numbers
boolean print (int m, int n)	to check whether n is a multiple of m or not

Fill in the blanks of the given program with appropriate Java statements. **ICSE SQP 2022 (Sem I)**

```
class (i) ________
{
   void print (int n)
   {
      int k;
      for ((ii)____; (iii)____; (iv)___)
      {
         System.out.println(k);
      }
   }
   boolean print( int m,(v) ______)
   {
      if ( (vi) _________ )
         return true;
      else
         return false
   }
}
```

(i) (a) OVERLOAD (b) overload

(c) class

(ii) (a) k = 1; (b) k = n;

(c) k = 0

(iii) (a) k<=n; (b) k>=n;
(c) k+n;
(iv) (a) k+=2 (b) k+=5
(c) k++
(v) (a) int n (b) double n
(c) char n
(vi) (a) if (n%m = = 0) (b) if (m%n==0)
(c) if (m/n= =0)

Ans (i) (a) OVERLOAD
(ii) (a) k = 1;
(iii) (a) k < = n;
(iv) (c) k ++
(v) (a) int n
(vi) (a) if (n % m = = 0)

2. The following program is based on the specification given below. ***ICSE SQP 2022 (Sem I)***

Class name	telephone
Member variables	
int noc	[number of calls]
double bill	[telephone bill to be paid]
String n	[name of the customer]
Member methods	
void input ( )	to accept the data using the scanner class
void print ()	to print the details
void calculate()	to calculate the telephone bill as per the following criteria based on number of calls
	Number of calls / **Rate per call**
	First 100 calls / free
	Above 100 calls / ₹ 2.50
void main ( )	to create an object of the class and invoke the functions of the class

Fill in the blanks with appropriate Java statements.

```
class (i) ______
{
    int noc; double bill; String n;
    Scanner ob = (ii)___ Scanner(System.in);
    void input( )
    {
        System.out.println("Enter Number of
                                    calls");
        noc = (iii) __________ ;
        System.out.println("Enter name");
        n=ob.next();
    }
    void calculate()
    {
        if ( (iv)________)
            bill =0;
        else
            bill = (v) __________;
    }
    void print()
    {
        System.out.println("Name = "+ n);
        System.out.println("Amount to be
                                  paid="+bill);
    }
    void main ()
    {
        telephone t = new telephone();
        t.input();
        (vi) ____________ ;
        t.print();
    }
}
```

(i) (a) telephone (b) class
(c) object
(ii) (a) old (b) new
(c) void
(iii) (a) ob.nextDouble() (b) ob.nextLine()
(c) ob.nextInt()
(iv) (a) noc<100 (b) noc < = 100
(c) noc> 100
(v) (a) bill=0+(noc-l00)*2.50
(b) bill = (noc-l00)*3.50
(c) bill = noc*2.50
(vi) (a) t.input() (b) t.calculate()
(c) t.print()

Ans (i) (a) telephone
(ii) (b) new
(iii) (c) ob.nextInt()
(iv) (b) noc < = 100
(v) (a) bill = 0 + (noc – 100) * 2.50
(vi) (b) t.calculate()

15 Marks Questions

1. Design a class with the following specifications

Class name	Student
Member variables	
name	name of student
age	age of student
mks	marks obtained
stream	stream allocated (Declare the variables using appropriate data types)

Member methods	
void accept()	Accept name, age and marks using methods of Scanner class.
void allocation()	Allocate the stream as per following criteria
	mks — **stream**
	>=300 — Science and Computer
	>=200 and <300 — Commerce and Computer
	>=75 and 200 — Arts and Animation
	<75 — Try Again
void print ()	Display students name, age, mks and stream allocated.

Call all the above methods in main method using an object. ***ICSE 2023***

Ans

```
import java.util.Scanner;
public class Student
{
    private String name;
    private int age;
    private int mks;
    private String stream;
    public void accept()
    {
        Scanner in = new Scanner(System.in);
        System.out.print("Enter name of
                                 student:");
        name = in.nextLine();
        System.out.print("Enter age of student:");
        age = in.nextInt();
        System.out.print("Enter marks obtained
                           by the student:");
        mks = in.nextInt();
    }
    public void allocation()
    {
        if (mks > 300)
        {
            System.out.print("stream allocated to
             the student: Science and Computer");
        }
        else if (mks >= 200 && mks < 300)
        {
            System.out.print("stream allocated to
            the student: Commerce and Computer");
        }
        else if (mks >= 75 && mks < 200)
        {
            System.out.print("stream allocated to
              the student: Arts and Animation");
        }
        else
        {
            System.out.print("stream allocated to
                      the student: Try Again");
        }
    }
    public void print()
    {
        System.out.println("Name: " + name);
        System.out.println("age: " + age);
        System.out.println("mks: " + mks);
    }
    public static void main(String args[])
    {
        Student obj = new Student();
        obj.accept();
        obj.allocation();
        obj.print();
    }
}
```

2. Using the switch statement, write a menu driven program to perform following operations ***ICSE SQP 2020***

(i) To print the value of Z, where $Z = \frac{x^3 + 0.5x}{Y}$, where x ranges from – 10 to 10 with an increment of 2 and Y remains constant at 5.5.

(ii) To print the Floyds triangle with N rows

Example: If N = 5,

Output:

```
1
2   3
4   5   6
7   8   9   10
11  12  13  14  15
```

Ans

```
import java.util.Scanner;
public class SwitchMenu
{
    public static void main(String args[])
    {
        Scanner in = new Scanner(System.in);
        System.out.println("Type 1 for Value
                                      of Z");
        System.out.println("Type 2 for Floyd\'s
                                  triangle");
        System.out.print("Enter your choice:");
        int choice = in.nextInt();
        switch (choice)
        {
            case 1:
            double Z, Y = 5.5;
            for (int x = -10; x <= 10; x+= 2)
```

```
            {
                Z=(Math.pow(x,3)+0.5 * x) / Y;
                System.out.println("Value of Z
                    when x is "+ x + " = " + Z);
            }
            break;
            case 2:
            System.out.print("Enter number of
                                        rows: ");
            int N = in.nextInt();
            int k = 1;
            for (int i = 1; i <= N; i++)
            {
                for (int j = 1; j <= i; j++)
                {
                    System.out.print(k + " ");
                    k++;
                }
                System.out.println();
            }
            break;
            default:
            System.out.println("Incorrect Choice");
            break;
        }
    }
}
```

3. Write a menu driven program to find the sum of the following series depending on the user choosing 1 or 2 ***ICSE SQP 2017***

   1. S=1/4+1/8+1/12 .... upto *n* terms
   2. S=1/1!-2/2!+3/3! ...... upto *n* terms

where ! stands for factorial of the number and the factorial value of a number is the product of all integers from 1 to that number, e.g. $5! = 1\times 2\times 3\times 4\times 5$.
(use switch-case)

Ans

```
import java.io. *;
class Main
{
    int n,choice;
    BufferedReader br=new BufferedReader(new
                InputStreamReader(System.in));
    public void series() throws Exception
    {
        System.out.println("Enter value of n:");
        n=Integer.parseInt(br.readLine());
        System.out.println("Enter choice (1 or
                                        2):");
        choice=Integer.parseInt(br.readLine());
        switch(choice)
        {
            case 1:
            series_first(n);
            break;
            case 2:
            series_second(n);
            break;
            default:
            System.out.println("Invalid number!!!");
        }
    }
    void series_first(int n)
    {
        int i,x=4;
        double s=0;
        for(i=0;i<n;i++)
        {
            s=s+(double)1/x;
            x=x+4;
        }
        System.out.println("Result="+s);
    }
    void series_second(int n)
    {
        int i;
        double s=0;
        int j, f;
        for (i=1;i<=n;i++)
        {
            f=1;
            for (j=2;j<=i;j++)
            f=f*j;
            s=s+(double)1/f;
        }
        System.out.println("Sum of the series
                                        ="+s);
    }
    public static void main(String args[])
                                throws Exception
    {
        Main se=new Main();
        se.series();
    }
}
```

4. Write a program to calculate the sum of all the prime numbers between the range of 1 and 100.

ICSE SQP 2017

Ans
```
import java.io. *;
class abc
{
    public static boolean checkPrime(int a)
    {
        for(int b=2; b<=a/2; b++)
        if(a%b==0) //a divisor of 'a' has been
                found except for 1 and 'a' itself
        return false;
        return true; //no divisor of 'a' was
                found except 1 and 'a' itself
    }
    public static void main(String arg[])
    {
        int sum=0;
        for(int i=1; i<=100; i++)
        if(checkPrime(i)==true)
        sum+=i;
        System.out.println(sum);
    }
}
```

CHAPTER TEST

1 Mark Questions

1. The ..... can only have a value of true or false.
(a) Boolean (b) Int (c) String (d) None of these

2. What is the extension of a byte code file?
(a) .java (b) .javac (c) .class (d) .doc

3. How many bytes does float and double requires?
(a) 2, 4 (b) 4, 8 (c) 8, 16 (d) None of these

2 Marks Questions

4. How is data hiding related to data abstraction?

5. What do you mean by type conversion? How is implicit conversion different from explicit conversion?

6. Predict the output of the following code, if p = 1.

```
int a= 1, b=2, c=3;
switch(p)
{
    case 1: a++;
    case 2: ++b;
      break;
    case 3: c--;
}
System.out.println(a + " , " + b + " , " + c);
```

15 Marks Questions

7. Write a program to input three numbers (positive or negative). If they are unequal then display the greatest number otherwise, display they are equal. The program also displays whether the numbers entered by the user are 'All positive', 'All negative' or 'Mixed numbers'. Sample Input: 56, -15, 12 Sample Output: The greatest number is 56 Entered numbers are mixed numbers.

8. A prime number is said to be 'Twisted Prime', if the new number obtained after reversing the digits is also a prime number. Write a program to accept a number and check whether the number is 'Twisted Prime' or not.
Sample Input: 167
Sample Output: 761
167 is a 'Twisted Prime'.

02

Class As Basis of All Computation

TREND ANALYSIS 3 YEARS

Average No. of Questions Across all Sets

	Types of Questions	2023	2019	2018
Class As Basis of All Computation	1 Mark	2	–	–
	2 Marks	–	–	2
	15 Marks	–	2	1

Class

A class can be defined as a template/blue print that describes the state and behaviour of its object. A class can contain fields and methods to describe the state and behaviour of an object.

Class as Composite Types

Composite types are reference type, which holds the reference id of a memory location.

A class is a composite data type because it requires a reference to use its attributes. The class binds various primitive types together for using them as a unit. These primitive types can be member variables (primitive type variables) or member methods (primitive type methods).

e.g. A class Abc has two values x and y and the value of these variable cannot be assigned directly. They can be assigned with the help of reference

```
Abc obj1; //Creating an object of Abc class
obj1.x = 5;    //Referencing the variables
obj1.y = 10;
```

Declaration of Class

In general, class declarations can include these components in order:

(i) Modifiers such as public, private and a number of others that you will encounter later.

(ii) The class name with the initial letter **capitalised** by convention.

(iii) The name of the class's parent (superclass), if any preceded by the keyword extends.

(iv) The class body, surrounded by braces {}.

e.g.

```
class MyFirstClass
{
    public int gear;
    public int speed;
      //Field
    public MyFirstClass(int speedup,
      int startgear)  // Constructor
    {
      gear = startgear;
      speed = speedup;
    }
```

```
        public void setGear(int newValue)
                                    // Method
        {
            gear = newValue;
        }
    }
```

In this example, we have created MyFirstClass class which has two member variables gear and speed one constructor and member method setGear().

Member Variables and Member Functions

In Java, member functions are the functions within the class, while a member variable is a variable, which is associated with a specific object and accessible for all its member functions. In a class, body of the class is enclosed between curlybraces {}. The data or variables, defined within a class are called instance variables. The code is contained within methods. Collectively the methods and variables defined within a class are called members of the class.

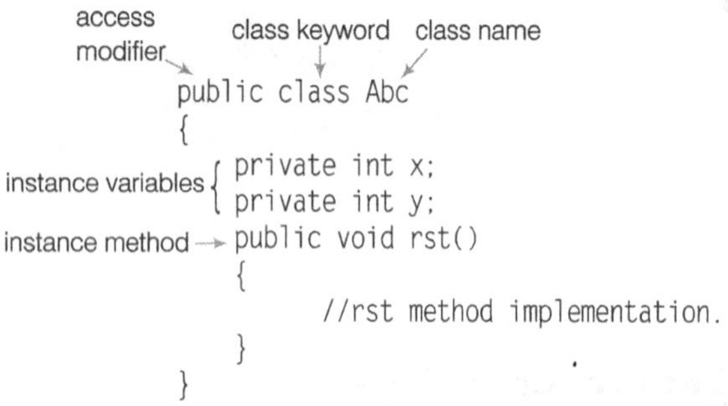

Initialization of Class

Class initialization is the explicit initialization of class fields to values. Each class field explicitly initializes to a value *via* a class field initializer.

e.g.
```
class Once
{
    static boolean b;
    public static void main(String[] args)
    {
        System.out.println("b=" +b);
    }
}
```

Output b = False

Object as Instance of a Class

An object is an instance of class or a class type variable that holds individual copy of data. An object can access all fields and methods of class.

The data type of an object is the class itself.

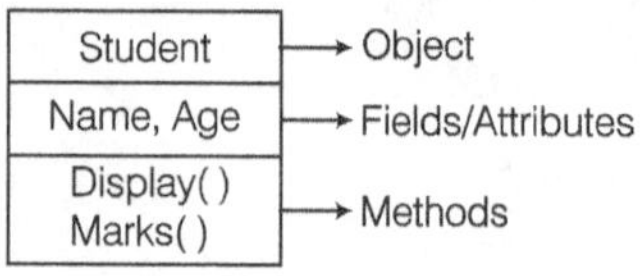

Creating Objects of a Class

An object is created from a class. In Java, the 'new' keyword is used to create a new object. There are three steps to create an object of a class:

Declaration An object is declared with an object name as class type.

Instantiation The 'new' keyword is used to create the object.

Initialization The new keyword is followed by a call to a constructor. This call initializes the new object (i.e. to set the initial value of instance variable).

e.g.

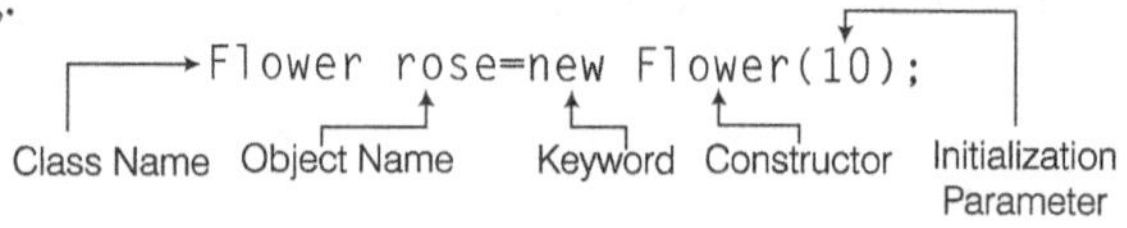

Class as an Object Factory

The factory of object means a factory that produces the objects. Class is known as object factory, because a single class generates a lot of objects. It also contains the statements that describe the operation that the object is going to perform or which operation is to be performed on object. e.g. in a class "company", there are different objects for different employee as and when required and thus can contain the different value of different employee.

Classes as Abstraction for Sets of Objects

A class is an abstract description of a set of objects and thus it contains the description of all the behaviours of the objects that it represents. A class may, but not always, contain description of the internal data held by the objects, called its fields, as well as implementation details about its methods and fields. Thus, we can say that a class is a template or recipe for the creation of a particular type of objects.

Objects Encapsulate State (attributes) and Behaviours (functions)

An objects encapsulates both state and behaviour, where the behaviour is defined by the actual state. Each object has its own attributes. e.g. consider a "door" as object. It has four states: close, open, opening, closing. Also, it has its own behaviours (functions) like-open and close.

Depending on state, behaviour will behave differently. Thus, its state (attributes) and the behaviour is bound in one unit that is ''object''.

Main Function

The main function is so special because it is implicitly invoked to execute a program.

Before a Java application runs, Java's class loader loads its starting main class (the class with main method) and Java's byte code verifier verify that class. Then, the class initializes.

Syntax

```
public static void main(String args[])
throws IOException
```

Here,

- **public** is a access modifier. It is applied here so that, JVM (Java Virtual Machine) can call main method easily outside the class.
- **static** is a reserved keyword, which means that a method is accessible and usable even though, no objects of the class exist.
- **void** is a keyword declares nothing would be returned from method.
- **main** It is the first function of a program or in other words, it is an entry point from, where control enters in a program.
- **String[ ]** It is an array of string.
- **args** is the name of the String[ ] (within main( )). You can change the name of args and the program would work the same.
- **IOException** An exception is a problem that arises during the execution of a program. In Java, for exceptions produced by failed or interrupted I/O operations, we have IOException class.

```
java.io.IOException;
```

Data Types

It refers to the type of data that can be stored in a variable. Sometimes, Java is called a **strongly typed language** because when you declare a variable, you must specify the variable type.

Data types in Java are classified into two types:

Primitive Data Types

These are the data types defined by the language itself. A primitive data type can have only one value at a time and is the simplest built in form of data within Java. Java supports eight primitive data types, they are as follows :

Type	Size	Range	Default Value	Example
byte	8-bit	–128 to +127	0	byte x = 90;
short	16-bit	–32,768 to +32,767	0	short s = 20000;
int	32-bit	–2,147,483,648 to +2,147,483,647	0	int a = 50000;
long	64-bit	-2^{63} to $+2^{63}-1$	0L	int a = 100000L;
float	32-bit	–3.4e-38 to +3.4e+38	0.0f	float fl = 234.5f;
double	64-bit	–1.7e-308 to +1.7e+308	0.0d	double d = 123.4d;
boolean	1-bit	True/False	False	Boolean one = true;
char	16-bit	0 to 65,535	'\u0000' or 0	char letter = 'n';

Non-Primitive Data Types (Composite Data Types)

These are **referenced** data types, which are based on primitive data types. These data types are constructed by using primitive data types, as per user's need.

Non-primitive data types store the memory address of an object. Class, interface and array are the examples of reference data types.

Note (i) The default value of any reference variable is null.

(ii) Whenever we are passing a non-primitive data type to a method, we are passing the address of that object where the data is stored.

There are five types of non-primitive data types in Java, which are as follows:

1. A **class** in Java is a user-defined data type, i.e. it is created by the user. It acts a template to the data which consists of member variables and methods.
2. An **object** is the variable of the class, which can access the elements of class, i.e. methods and variables.
3. An **interface** is similar to a class however the only difference is that its methods are abstract by default i.e. they do not have body. An interface has only the final variables and method declarations. It is also called a fully abstract class.
4. A **string** represents a sequence of characters for example "Javatpoint", "Hello world", etc. String is the class of Java.

One of the ways to create a string and store a value in it is shown below:

```
String str = "You're the best";
```

Here, String type variable str has the value "You're the best".

5. An **array** is a data type which can store multiple homogenous variables i.e., variables of same type in a sequence.

   They are stored in an indexed manner starting with index 0. The variables can be either primitive or non-primitive data types.

   Following example shows how to declare array of primitive data type

```
int [ ] marks;
```

   Following example shows how to declare array of non-primitive data type

```
Student[] students;
```

Difference between Primitive and Non-Primitive Data Types

Primitive Data Type	Non-Primitive Data Type
Primitive types are pre-defined in Java.	Non-primitive types are created by the programmer and is not defined by Java.
A primitive type always has a value.	Non-primitive types can be null.
A primitive type starts with a lowercase letter.	Non-primitive types start with an uppercase letter.
The size of a primitive type depends on the data type.	Non-primitive types have all the same size.
Examples of primitive data type are int, char, float, etc.	Examples of non-primitive data type are array, class, interface, etc.

Variable

It is a container that holds values that are used in a Java programming language. It can possess any combination of letter without space. Each variable in Java has a specific type, which determines the size and layout of the variable's memory.

Declaration of Variable

A declaration of a variable refers to the following:

(i) Specify the name of the variable.

(ii) Specify the data type of the variable.

(iii) Specify the scope of usage of the variable.

Syntax `datatype variablename;`

e.g. `int age;`

Initialising the Variables

We can combine a declaration with an assignment statement to provide an initial value for the variable.

Syntax `datatype variablename = value;`

e.g. `int val = 10`

Types of Variable

The Java programming language defines the following kinds of variables:

(i) **Instance Variable** Non-static variables are called instance variables. Instance variables are used to store the state of an object. Every object created from a class definition would have its own copy of variable.

Syntax `ObjectReference.VariableName`

(ii) **Class Variable** It is any field declared with the static modifier. It is a special type of class attribute (or class property, field, or data member). Class variable is created when the program starts and destroyed when the program stops. It can be accessed by calling with the class name. Static keyword to make a variable as a class variable.

Syntax `ClassName.VariableName`

(iii) **Local Variable** These variables are declared in method, constructors or blocks. These are implemented at stack level internally. There is no default value for local variable, so when local variable is declared, an initial value should be assigned to it before the first use.

Syntax `VariableName`

Note A method that takes variable number of arguments is called a method argument or argument variable.

PYQs Previous Years Questions

1 Mark Questions

1. What is an instance of the class called? *ICSE 2023*

Ans Object

2. The number of bits occupied by the value a are *ICSE 2023*

(a) 1 bit (b) 2 bits
(c) 4 bits (d) 16 bits

Ans (d) 16 bits

3. The blueprint that defines the variables and the methods common to all of a certain kind is termed as *ICSE 2022 (Sem I)*

(a) class (b) object
(c) package (d) method

Ans (a) class

4. A data type which contains integer as well as fractional part and occupies 32 bits space is *ICSE 2022 (Sem I)*

(a) float (b) char
(c) double (d) byte

Ans (a) float

5. The keyword to create an object of a class is .... *ICSE 2022 (Sem I)*

(a) create (b) new
(c) New (d) NEW

Ans (b) new

6. char is a non-primitive data type. *ICSE 2022 (Sem I)*

(a) True (b) False

Ans (b) False

7. A variable that is bounded to the object itself is called as *ICSE SQP 2022 (Sem I)*

(a) Instance variable (b) class variable
(c) Local variable (d) Argument variable

Ans (a) Instance variable

8. Variable that is declared with in the body of a method is termed as *ICSE SQP 2022 (Sem I)*

(a) Instance variable (b) class variable
(c) Local variable (d) Argument variable

Ans (c) Local variable

9. The keyword to make a variable as a class variable *ICSE SQP 2022 (Sem I)*

(a) static (b) Static (c) final

Ans (a) static

10. The number of bytes occupied by char data type is .... byte/s. *ICSE SQP 2022 (Sem I)*

(a) 4 (b) 8
(c) 2 (d) None

Ans (c) 2

11. Which of the following keyword is used to create an instance of a class? *ICSE SQP 2022 (Sem I)*

(a) new (b) public
(c) class (d) None of these

Ans (a) new

12. The .... is called an instance of a class *ICSE SQP 2022 (Sem I)*

(a) Object (b) Attributes
(c) State (d) None

Ans (a) Object

13. Scope of local variable is within a class. *ICSE SQP 2022 (Sem I)*

(a) True (b) False

Ans (b) False

2 Marks Questions

1. Consider the following program and answer the questions given below *ICSE SQP 2023*

```
class sample
{
    int a,b;
    sample(int x,int y)
    {
        a=x;b=y;
    }
    void calculate()
    {
        int z;
        z= a+b;
        System.out.println(z);
    }
}
```

(i) Name the global variables.
(ii) What are the method variables?

Ans (i) a and b (ii) x, y, z

2. Classify the following as primitive or non-primitive datatypes *ICSE 2018*

(i) char (ii) arrays
(iii) int (iv) classes

Ans Primitive datatypes

(i) char (iii) int

Non-primitive datatypes

(ii) arrays (iv) classes

3.
```
System.out.print("BEST ");
System.out.println("OF LUCK");
```
ICSE 2018

Choose the correct option for the output of the above statements

(i) BEST OF LUCK (ii) BEST
OF LUCK

Ans The correct option for the output of the given statements

(i) BEST OF LUCK

4. Why is an object called an instance of a class? **ICSE 2017, 10**

Ans An object is an instance of class or a class type variable that holds individual copy of data. An object can access all fields and methods of class. The data type of an object is the class itself.

5. State the number of bytes occupied by char and int data types. **ICSE 2017**

Ans Number of bytes occupied by

char → 16-bit

Number of bytes occupied by

int → 32-bit

6. Arrange the following primitive data types in an ascending order of their size: **ICSE 2015**

(i) char (ii) byte
(iii) double (iv) int

Ans Ascending order of primitive data types with their size

byte < char < int < double

7. Name the primitive data type in Java that is

(i) a 64-bit integer and is used when you need a range of values under than those provided by int.

(ii) a single 16-bit unicode character whose default value is '\u0000'. **ICSE 2014**

Ans (i) long, because it contain eight byte (64-bit) and it belongs to the int data type.

(ii) char, because firstly it assume a size of 2 byte (16-bits) and another is that unicode characters are of char data type.

8. Identify the statements listed below as assignment, increment, method invocation or object creation statements.

(i) System.out.println("Java");
(ii) costPrice = 457.50;
(iii) Car hybrid = new Car( );
(iv) petrolPrice++; **ICSE 2014**

Ans (i) Method invocation statement.

(ii) Assignment statement.

(iii) Object creation statement.

(iv) Increment statement.

9. Write a Java statement to create an object "mp4" of class "digital". **ICSE 2013**

Ans Class name is "digital" and object name is "mp4"

```
digital mp4 = new digital();
```

10. In the program given below, state the name and the value of the **ICSE 2012**

(i) method argument or argument variable.
(ii) class variable.
(iii) local variable.
(iv) instance variable.

```
class myClass
{
   static int x=7;
   int y=2;
   public static void main(String args[])
   {
      myClass obj=new myClass();
      System.out.println(x);
      obj.sampleMethod(5);
      int a=6;
      System.out.println(a);
   }
   void sampleMethod(int x)
   {
      System.out.println(x);
      System.out.println(y);
   }
}
```

Ans (i) method argument or argument variable= x

(ii) class variable = x

(iii) local variable = a

(iv) instance variable = y

11. Name the keyword. **ICSE 2011**

(i) Informs that an error has occurred in an input/output operation.

(ii) Distinguishes between instance variable and class variable.

Ans (i) throws IOException

(ii) static keyword

12. What is the difference between an object and a class? **ICSE 2011**

Ans Difference between object and class are as follows

Object	Class
Object is instance of class or variable of class.	Class is mechanism of binding data members and associated methods in a single unit.

Object	Class
It is physical existence.	It is logical existence.
Memory space is allocated, when it is created.	Memory space is not allocated, when it is created.

13. Why is class called a factory of objects? **ICSE 2009**

Ans Class is called a factory of objects, because the class contains a collection of objects and all the attributes to create an object.

14. Why is class known as composite data type? **ICSE 2009**

Ans A class is known as composite data type because it binds both member variables and functions as a single identity. Composite data type holds reference of any variable, it is assigned with the help of reference. e.g. A class abc has two value *x* and *y* and the value of these variable cannot be assigned directly. They can be assigned with the help of reference

```
abc obj1;  //Creating an object of abc class
obj1.x = 5;//Referencing the variables
obj1.y = 10;
```

Thus a class is a composite data type because it requires a reference to use its attributes.

15. Mention any two attributes required for class declaration. **ICSE 2008**

Ans Two attributes required for class declaration

(i) Modifiers such as public, private.

(ii) The class name with the initial letter capitalised by convention.

16. What does the following mean? **ICSE 2008**

```
Employee staff = new Employee();
```

Ans In given statement, Employee is a class and it creates a object whose name is staff.

17. Explain instance variable. Give an example. **ICSE 2008**

Or

Define instance variable. Give an example of the same. **ICSE 2007**

Ans Instance variables are any variables, without "static" field modifier, that are defined within the class body and outside any class's methods body. It can be declared in class level before or after use. For numbers, the default value is 0 and for boolean, it is false.

e.g.

```
class Book
{
   int sub;
     //instance variable
   int price;
     //instance variable
}
```

18. Explain the term object using an example. **ICSE 2006**

Ans Object is an instance of a class. The relationship is such that many objects can be created by using only one class. Each object has its own data but its underlying structure (i.e. the type of data it stores, its behaviour) is defined by the class.

e.g. Class Book, in which objects are created

```
Book buk=new Book("The short books");
Book lbuk=new Book("Long books");
Book opt=new Book("Objective type");
Book All=new Book("All in one");
```

19. Define a variable. **ICSE 2006**

Ans A variable provides us with named storage that our programs can manipulate. Each variable in Java has a specific type, which determines the size and layout of the variable's memory; range of values that can be stored within memory and the set of operations that can be applied to the variable.

20. State the two kinds of data types. **ICSE 2006**

Ans Data types are used within type system, which means to identify the type of data and associated operations for handling it.

There are two types of data type:

(i) **Primitive Data Types** byte, float, char, boolean, int.

(ii) **Composite Data Types** class, array, interface.

15 Marks Questions

1. Using the **switch case** statement, write a menu driven program to do the following: **ICSE 2019**

(i) To generate and print Letters from A to Z and their Unicode

Letters	Unicode
A	65
B	66
-	-
-	-
-	-
Z	90

(ii) Display the following pattern using **iteration** (looping) statement:

```
1
1 2
1 2 3
1 2 3 4
1 2 3 4 5
```

Ans (i)
```
import java.util.Scanner;
public class Patterns
{
  public static void main(String args[])
  {
    Scanner in =new Scanner(System.in);
    System.out.println("Enter 1 for letters and
                                              Unicode");
    System.out.println("Enter 2 to display the
                                              pattern");
    System.out.print("Enter your choice: ");
    int ch=in.nextInt();
    switch(ch)
    {
      case 1:
      System.out.println("Letters\tUnicode");
      for (int i=65; i<=90; i++)
      System.out.println((char)i+"\t"+i);
      break;
      case 2:
      for (int i=1; i<=5; i++)
      {
        for (int j =1; j <=i; j++)
        System.out.print(j +" ");
        System.out.println();
      }
      break;
      default:
      System.out.println("Wrong choice");
      break;
    }
  }
}
```

(ii)
```
import java.util.Scanner;
public class MainClass
{
    public static void main(String[] args)
    {
      Scanner sc = new Scanner(System.in);
      System.out.println("How many rows you want
                                   in this pattern?");
      int rows = sc.nextInt();
      System.out.println("Here is your pattern
                                         ....!!!");
      for (int i = 1; i <= rows; i++)
      {
        for (int j = 1; j <= i; j++)
        {
          System.out.print(j+" ");
        }
        System.out.println();
      }
    }
}
```

2. A tech number has even number of digits. If the number is split in two equal halves, then the square of sum of these halves is equal to the number itself. Write a program to generate and print all four digits tech numbers. ***ICSE 2019***

Example:

Consider the number 3025

Square of sum of the halves of 3025 $= (30+25)^2$

$= (55)^2 = 3025$ is a tech number.

Ans
```
import java.io.*;
import java.util.Scanner;
public class TechNum
{
  public static void main(String args[]) throws
                                        IOException
  {
    int num;
    double s;
    InputStreamReader IR=new InputStreamReader
                                      (System.in);
    BufferedReader br=new BufferedReader(IR);
    System.out.println("Enter four digits number");
    num=Integer.parseInt(br.readLine());
    int len=String.valueOf(num).length();
    if(len%2==0)
    {
      System.out.println("Valid String");
      int R1=num/100;
      int R2=num%100;
      int a=Integer.valueOf(R1)+Integer.valueOf
                                            (R2);
      s=Integer.valueOf(a)*Integer.valueOf(a);
      if(s==num)
      {
        System.out.println("Entered number
                                is Tech number");
      }
      else
      {
        System.out.println("Entered number is
                             not a Tech number");
      }
    }
    else
    {
      System.out.println("Invalid String");
    }
  }
}
```

3. Write a menu driven program to display the pattern as per user's choice. ***ICSE 2018***

Pattern 1	**Pattern 2**
ABCDE	B
ABCD	LL
ABC	UUU
AB	EEEE
A	

For an incorrect option, an appropriate error message should be displayed.

Ans
```
import java.io.*;
import java.util.Scanner;
public class Pattern
{
  public static void main (String[] args)
                               throws IOException
  {
    InputStreamReader IR=new
                 InputStreamReader(System.in);
    BufferedReader br=new BufferedReader(IR);
    int ch;
    System.out.println ("Enter 1 for Pattern 1
                       and 2 for Pattern 2");
    ch=Integer.parseInt (br.readLine());
    System.out.println("Enter a String:");
    Scanner sc = new Scanner(System.in);
    String S = sc.nextLine();
    sc.close();
    int length=S.length();
    char []a=S.toCharArray();
    System.out.println("\nPrinting the
                                  pattern:");
    switch(ch)
    {
      case 1:
        for(int i = length-1; i > = 0;i—)
      {
        for(int j = 0; j <= i; j++)
        {
          System.out.print(a[j]);
        }
          System.out.println();
      }
      break;
      case 2:
        for(int i = 1; i<=length;i++)
      {
        for(int j=1;j<=i;j++)
        {
          System.out.print(S.charAt(i));
        }
        System.out.println();
      }
      break;
      default:
      System.out.println("Invalid option");
    }
  }
}
```

4. Using switch statement, write a menu driven program for the following **ICSE 2017**

(i) To find and display the sum of the series given below

$$S= x^1 - x^2 + x^3 - x^4 + x^5 - ... - x^{20}$$

(where x= 2)

(ii) To display the following series:

1 11 111 1111 11111

For an incorrect option, an appropriate error message should be displayed.

Ans
```
import java.io.*;
class Series
{
  public static void main(String args[])
                              throws IOException
  {
    int ch;
    InputStreamReader IR=new
              InputStreamReader(System.in);
    BufferedReader br=new BufferedReader(IR);
    System.out.println("1. To display sum of
                                a series");
    System.out.println("2. To display a
                                  series");
    System.out.println("Enter the choice");
    ch=Integer.parseInt(br.readLine());
    switch(ch)
    {
      case 1:
        int x=2, S=0,P;
        for(int i=1;i<=20;i++)
      {
        P=1;
        for(int j=1;j<=i;j++)
          P=P*x;
        if(i%2==0)
          S=S-P;
        else
          S=S+P;
      }
      System.out.println("Sum of series:"+S);
      break;
      case 2:
      int T=1;
      for(int i=1;i<=5;i++)
      {
        System.out.print(T+" ");
          T=T*10+1;
      }
      break;
      default:
      System.out.println("Your choice is
                                 wrong");
    }
  }
}
```

5. Using the switch statement, write a menu driven program for the following **ICSE 2016**

(i) To print the Floyd's triangle

```
1
2   3
4   5   6
7   8   9   10
11  12  13  14  15
```

(ii) To display the following pattern

```
I
I C
I C S
I C S E
```

For an incorrect option, an appropriate error message should be displayed.

KEY idea

To print Floyd's triangle, a loop should be used to iterate through the rows, and a nested loop should be used to print the numbers in each row.

To display the pattern, a loop should be used to iterate through the rows, and a nested loop should be used to print the characters in each row.

Ans
```
import java.io.*;
public class FloydTriangle
{
  public static void main(String args[])
                          throws IOException
  {
    InputStreamReader IR=new
               InputStreamReader(System.in);
    BufferedReader br = new
                      BufferedReader(IR);
    System.out.println("1. To print the Floyd
                             triangle");
    System.out.println("2. To display the
                          ICSE pattern");
    System.out.println("Choose the correct
                             choice:");
    int ch = Integer.parseInt(br.readLine());
    switch(ch)
    {
      case 1:
        int p = 1;
        for(int i = 1; i <= 5; i++)
        {
           for(int j = 1; j <= i; j++)
           {
              System.out.print(p+"\t");
              p++;
           }
           System.out.println();
        }
        break;
      case 2:
        String s ="ICSE";
        for (int i=0; i<= s.length(); i++)
        {
           for (int j=0; j <=i; j++)
           {
              System.out.print(s.charAt[j]
                                  +" ");
           }
           System. out.println();
        }
        break;
        default:
           System.out. println("Your choice
                             is wrong");
    }
  }
}
```

6. Write two separate programs to generate the following patterns using iteration (loop) statements: ***ICSE 2015***

(i)	(ii)
*	5 4 3 2 1
* #	5 4 3 2
* # *	5 4 3
* # * #	5 4
* # * # *	5

Ans (i)
```
class Piramid1
{
  public static void main(String[] ar)
  {
    for(int i=1;i<=5;i++)
    {
      for(int j=1;j<=i;j++)
      {
        if(j%2==0)
          System.out.print("#");
        else
          System.out.print("*");
      }
      System.out.println(" ");
    }
  }
}
```

(ii)
```
class Piramid2
{
  public static void main(String[] ar)
  {
    for(int i=1;i<=5;i++)
    {
      for(int j=5;j>=i;j--)
      {
        System.out.print(j+" ");
      }
      System.out.println(" ");
    }
  }
}
```

7. Using the switch statement, write a menu driven program to: ***ICSE 2015***

(i) To find and display all the **factors** of a number input by the user (including 1 and excluding number itself).

Example:

Sample Input : n = 15

Sample Output : 1, 3, 5

(ii) To find and display the **factorial** of a number input by the user (the factorial of a non-negative integer n), denoted by n!, is the product of all integers less than or equal to n.

Example:

Sample Input : n = 5

Sample Output : $5! = 1\times 2\times 3\times 4\times 5 = 120.$

For an incorrect choice, an appropriate error message should be displayed.

Ans
```
import java.io.*;
class Main
{
  public static void main(String[] ar) throws IOException
  {
    int ch;
    do
    {
      System.out.println("\n 1  Factor\n 2 Factorial \n 3 Exit");
      InputStreamReader IR=new InputStreamReader(System.in);
      BufferedReader br=new BufferedReader(IR);
      ch=Integer.parseInt(br.readLine());
      switch(ch)
      {
        case 1:
           System.out.println("Enter number for factor");
              int n=Integer.parseInt(br.readLine());
           factor(n);
           break;
        case 2:
           System.out.println("Enter number for factorial");
           int x=Integer.parseInt(br.readLine());
           factorial(x);
           break;
        default:
           System.out.println("Wrong choice");
      }
    }while(ch!=3);
  }
  static void factor(int num)
  {
    System.out.print("Factor="+(1));
    for(int i=2;i<num;i++)
    {
      if(num%i==0)
        System.out.print(","+i);
    }
  }
  static void factorial(int num)
  {
    long fact=1;
    if(num<=0)
    {
      System.out.println("Please input value greater than 0");
      return;
    }
    else
    {
      for(int i=num;i>=1;i--)
        fact=fact*i;
      System.out.println(num+"!="+fact);
    }
  }
}
```

8. Using the switch statement, write a menu driven program to calculate the maturity amount of a BankDeposit.

The user is given the following options

(i) Term Deposit (ii) Recurring Deposit

For option (i) accept principal (P), rate of interest (r) and time period in years (n). Calculate and output the maturity amount (A) receivable using the formula

$$A = P\left[1 + \frac{r}{100}\right]^n$$

For option (ii) accept Monthly Installment (P), rate of interest (r) and time period in months (n). Calculate and output the maturity amount (A) receivable using the formula

$$A = P\times n + P\times \frac{n(n+1)}{2} \times \frac{r}{100} \times \frac{1}{12}$$

For an incorrect option, an appropriate error message should be displayed. ***ICSE 2014***

Ans

```
import java.io.*;
class BankDeposit
{
  public static void main(String[] args) throws IOException
  {
    InputStreamReader IR = new InputStreamReader(System.in);
    BufferedReader br = new BufferedReader(IR);
    System.out.println("User Menu:");
    System.out.println("1: Term Deposit");
    System.out.println("2: Recurring Deposit");
    System.out.println("Enter the choice (1 or 2):");
    int ch = Integer.parseInt(br.readLine());
    switch(ch)
    {
      case 1:    System.out.println("Enter principal:");
                 float P = Float.parseFloat(br.readLine());
                 System.out.println("Enter rate of Interest:");
                 float r = Float.parseFloat(br.readLine());
                 System.out.println("Enter time period in years:");
                 float n = Float.parseFloat(br.readLine());
                 double a = 1 + (r/100);
                 double A = P * Math.pow(a,n);
                 System.out.println("Maturity Amount:" +A);
                 break;
      case 2:    System.out.println("Enter Monthly Installment:");
                 P = Float.parseFloat(br.readLine());
                 System.out.println("Enter Rate of Interest:");
                 r = Float.parseFloat(br.readLine());
                 System.out.println("Enter time period in months:");
                 n = Float.parseFloat(br.readLine());
                 double as = (r/100)*(1/12);
                 double b = ((n*(n+1))/2)*as;
                 double Ab = (P*n)+(P*b);
                 System.out.println("Maturity Amount:"+Ab);
                 break;
        default:
                 System.out.println("Wrong choice");
      }
    }
}
```

Common Mistake One could be made using the switch statement to calculate the maturity amount of a Bank Deposit is not including a default case. If the user enters an invalid option and there is no default case to handle it, the program will simply exit without providing any feedback to the user.

9. The International Standard Book Number (ISBN) is a unique numeric book identifier which is printed on every book. The ISBN is based upon a 10-digit code. The ISBN is legal if

$$1\times digit_1 + 2\times digit_2 + 3\times digit_3 + 4\times digit_4 + 5\times digit_5 + 6\times digit_6 + 7 \times digit_7 + 8\times digit_8 + 9\times digit_9 + 10\times digit_{10}$$ is divisible by 11.

e.g. For an ISBN 1401601499

Sum = $1 \times 1 + 2 \times 4 + 3 \times 0 + 4 \times 1 + 5 \times 6 + 6 \times 0 + 7 \times 1 + 8 \times 4 + 9 \times 9 + 10 \times 9$

= 253 which is divisible by 11.

Write a program to

(i) Input the ISBN code as a 10-digit integer.

(ii) If the ISBN is not a 10-digit integer, output the message, "Illegal ISBN" and terminate the program.

(iii) If the number is 10-digit, extract the digits of the number and compute the sum as explained above. If the sum is divisible by 11, output the message, "Legal ISBN". If the sum is not divisible by 11, output the message, "Illegal ISBN". ***ICSE 2013***

Ans
```
import java.io.*;
class ISBN
{
  public static void main(String[] args) throws IOException
  {
    InputStreamReader IR = new InputStreamReader(System.in);
    BufferedReader input = new BufferedReader(IR);
    System.out.println("Enter a 10 digit code:");
    String s = input.readLine();
    int len = s.length();
    if(len != 10)
    {
      System.out.println("Illegal ISBN code");
    }
    else
    {
      String ch;
      int dig = 0, Sum = 0, k = 1;
      for(int i=0; i<len; i++)
      {
        ch = Character.toString(s.charAt(i));
        if(ch.equalsIgnoreCase("X"))
        {
          dig = 10;
        }
        else
        {
          dig=Integer.parseInt(ch);
          Sum=Sum+dig*k;
          k+ +;
        }
      }
      System.out.println("Output:Sum=" +Sum);
      if(Sum%11==0)
      {
        System.out.println("Valid ISBN Code");
      }
      else
      {
        System.out.println("Invalid ISBN Code");
      }
    }
  }
}
```

10. Using the switch statement, write a menu driven program

(i) To check and display whether a number, input by the user is a composite number or not (A number is said to be a composite, if it has one or more than one factor excluding 1 and the number itself).

e.g. 4, 6, 8, 9, ...

(ii) To find the smallest digit of an integer that is input

Sample input : 6524

Sample output : Smallest digit is 2

For an incorrect choice, an appropriate error message should be displayed. ***ICSE 2013***

Ans

```
import java.io.*;
class Digit
{
  public static void main(String[] args) throws IOException
  {
    InputStreamReader read = new InputStreamReader(System.in);
    BufferedReader in = new BufferedReader(read);
    System.out.println("Enter a digit:");
    String s = in.readLine();
    int x = Integer.parseInt(s);
    System.out.println("Enter your choice\n1 for composite number and
    2 for smallest digit");
    int ch=Integer.parseInt(in.readLine());
    switch(ch)
    {
        case 1:
          boolean comp = false;
          for(int i=2; i<x; i++)
          {
            if(x%i==0)
            {
              comp = true;
            }
          }
          if(comp)
          {
            System.out.println(x+" is a composite number");
          }
          else
          {
            System.out.println(x+" is not composite number");
          }
          break;
        case 2:
          int i,j=9,p,r,k=x;
          while(k!=0)
          {
            r=k%10;
            k=k/10;
            if(r<=j)
            {
              j=r;
            }
          }
          System.out.println("The smallest digit is : "+j);
          break;
        default:
          System.out.println("Invalid choice");
    }
  }
}
```

11. Given below is a hypothetical table showing rates of Income Tax for male citizens below the age of 65 years

Taxable Income (TI) **in Rs.**	**Income Tax in Rs.**
Does not exceed Rs. 1,60,000	Nil
Is greater than Rs. 1,60,000 and less than or equal to Rs. 5,00,000	(TI—1,60,000) × 10%
Is greater than Rs. 5,00,000 and less than or equal to Rs. 8,00,000	[(TI—5,00,000) × 20%] + 34,000
Is greater than Rs. 8,00,000	[(TI—8,00,000) × 30%] + 94,000

Write a program to input the age, gender (male or female) and Taxable Income of a person. If the age is more than 65 years or the gender is female, display "wrong category". If the age is less than or equal to 65 years and the gender is male, compute and display the Income Tax payable as per the table given above. ***ICSE 2012***

Ans
```
import java.io.*;
class IncomeTax
{
  public static void main(String[] args) throws IOException
  {
    InputStreamReader IR=new InputStreamReader(System.in);
    BufferedReader rd=new BufferedReader(IR);
    System.out.println("Enter age:");
    int age=Integer.parseInt(rd.readLine());
    System.out.println("Enter gender:");
    String gender=rd.readLine();
    System.out.println("Enter taxable income");
    int income=Integer.parseInt(rd.readLine());
    if(age>65||gender.equals("female"))
    {
      System.out.println("wrong category");
    }
    else
    {
      double tax= 0.0;
      if(income<=160000)
      {
        tax=0;
      }
      else if(income>160000 && income<=500000)
      {
        tax=(income-160000)*10/100;
      }
      else if(income>500000 && income<=800000)
      {
        tax=(income-500000)*20/100+34000;
      }
      else
      {
        tax=(income-800000)*30/100+94000;
      }
      System.out.println("Income tax is =" +tax);
    }
  }
}
```

12. Using the switch statement, write a menu driven program to ***ICSE 2012***

(i) Generate and display the first 10 terms of the Fibonacci series

0, 1, 1, 2, 3, 5, ...

The first two Fibonacci numbers are 0 and 1, and each subsequent number is the sum of the previous two.

(ii) Find the sum of the digits of an integer that is input.

Sample Input : 15390

Sample Output : Sum of the digits = 18

For an incorrect choice, an appropriate error message should be displayed.

> **KEY idea**
>
> For finding the sum of digits, the program takes an integer input and calculates the sum of its digits. If an incorrect choice is made, an error message is displayed.

Ans
```
import java.io.*;
class Menu
{
  public static void main(String[] args) throws IOException
```

```
    {
      InputStreamReader IR = new InputStreamReader(System.in);
      BufferedReader br = new BufferedReader(IR);
      System.out.println("Enter 1 for fibonacci series");
      System.out.println("Enter 2 for sum of the digit");
      System.out.println("Enter choice");
      int ch = Integer.parseInt(br.readLine());
      switch(ch)
      {
        case 1:
          int i = 0, j = 1, s = 0;
          System.out.println(i);
          System.out.println(j);
          for(int t = 1; t<= 8; t++)
          {
             s = i+j;
             System.out.println(s);
             i = j;
             j = s;
          }
          break;
        case 2:
          int r, sum=0;
          System.out.println("Enter any integer");
          int n = Integer.parseInt(br.readLine());
          while(n != 0)
          {
             r = n % 10;
             sum = sum + r;
             n = n/10;
          }
          System.out.println("Sum =" +sum);
          break;
        default:
          System.out.println("Incorrect choice");
      }
    }
  }
```

13. Write a program to input a number and print whether the number is a special number or not. (A number is said to be a special number, if the sum of the factorial of the digits of the number is same as the original number).
e.g. 145 is a special number, because 1! + 4! + 5! = 1 + 24 + 120 = 145
(where ! stands for factorial of the number and the factorial value of a number is the product of all integers from 1 to that number, e.g. 5! = 5×4×3×2×1= 120). **ICSE 2011**

Ans

```
import java.io.*;
class Special
{
  public static void main(String[] args) throws IOException
  {
    InputStreamReader IR=new InputStreamReader(System.in);
    BufferedReader br=new BufferedReader(IR);
    int n, f, sum=0, num;
    System.out.println("Enter any number:");
    n=Integer.parseInt(br.readLine());
    num=n;
    while(n!=0)
    {
      int R=n%10;
      f=1;
      for(int k=1; k<=R; k++)
      {
```

```
            f=f*k;
          }
          sum=sum+f;
          n=n/10;
        }
      if(num==sum)
      {
        System.out.println("It is special no.");
      }
      else
      {
        System.out.println("It is not special number");
      }
    }
}
```

14. Write a menu driven program to perform the following (Use switch-case statement)

(i) To print the series 0, 3, 8, 15, 24, ... n terms (value of 'n' is to be an input by the user).

(ii) To find the sum of the series given below

S = 1/2 + 3/4 + 5/6 + 7/8 .... 19/20 ***ICSE 2011***

Ans

```
import java.io.*;
class Series
{
  public static void main(String args[]) throws IOException
  {
    int ch, n;
    System.out.println("User Menu:");
    System.out.println("1:To print series");
    System.out.println("2:To find the sum of the series");
    InputStreamReader IR=new InputStreamReader(System.in);
    BufferedReader br=new BufferedReader(IR);
    ch=Integer.parseInt(br.readLine());
    switch(ch)
    {
      case 1:
        System.out.println("Enter the value of n");
        n =Integer.parseInt(br.readLine());
        for(int k=1; k<=n; k++)
        {
          System.out.println((k*k-1));
        }
        break;
      case 2:
        double sum=0;
        double k=2;
        for(int p=1; p<=19; p=p+2)
        {
          sum=sum+p/k;
          k=k+2;
        }
        System.out.println(sum);
        break;
      default:
        System.out.println("Invalid choice");
    }
  }
}
```

Common Mistake In this question, a common mistake could be forgetting to include break statements after each case in the switch-case statement, causing the program to execute multiple cases instead of just one.

15. Write a menu driven program to accept a number and check and display whether it is a prime number or not OR an automorphic number or not. (Use switch-case statement)

(i) **Prime number** A number is said to be a prime number if it is divisible only by 1 and itself and not by any other number. e.g. 3, 5, 7, 11, 13, etc.

(ii) **Automorphic number** An automorphic number is the number which is contained in the last digit(s) of its square. e.g. 25 is an automorphic number as its square is 625 and 25 is present as the last two digits.

ICSE 2010

Ans
```
import java.io.*;
class Solution
{
  public static void main(String args[]) throws IOException
  {
    InputStreamReader IR=new InputStreamReader(System.in);
    BufferedReader br=new BufferedReader(IR);
    int n, ch;
    System.out.println("Enter the number");
    n=Integer.parseInt(br.readLine());
    System.out.println("Enter your choice 1 for prime and
                                             2 for Automorphic");
    ch=Integer.parseInt(br.readLine());
    switch(ch)
    {
      case 1:
        int i;
        boolean flag=true;
        for(i=2; i<n; i++)
        {
          int res=n%i;
          if(res==0)
          {
            flag=false;
            break;
          }
        }
        if(flag)
        {
          System.out.println(n+" is a Prime Number");
        }
        else
        {
          System.out.println(n+" is not a Prime Number");
        }
        break;
      case 2:
        int num=n%100;
        int sq=(int)Math.sqrt(num);
        String number=Integer.toString(num);
        String square=Integer.toString(sq*sq);
        if(square.equals(number))
        {
          System.out.println(n+" is an automorphic number");
        }
        else
```

```
            {
              System.out.println(n+" is not an automorphic number");
            }
            break;
          default:
            System.out.println("wrong choice");
        }
      }
    }
```

Concept Enhancer To check if a number is prime, the program should iterate from 2 to the square root of the number and check if the number is divisible by any of these values. If the number is divisible by any value in this range, it is not prime. Otherwise, it is prime. To check if a number is an automorphic number, the program should square the number and check if the last digits of the square match the original number. If the last digit's match, the number is automorphic; otherwise, it is not.

16. An electronics shop has announced the following seasonal discounts on the purchase of certain items.

Purchase Amount in Rs.	Discount on Laptop	Discount on Desktop PC
0–25000	0.0%	5.0%
25001—57000	5.0%	7.5%
57001—100000	7.5%	10.0%
More than 100000	10.0%	15.0%

Write a program based on the above criteria, to input name, address, amount of purchase and the type of purchase (L for Laptop and D for Desktop) by a customer. Compute and print the net amount to be paid by a customer along with his name and address. ***ICSE 2009***

(**Hint** discount = (discount rate/100) * amount of purchase

Net amount = amount of purchase – discount)

Ans
```
import java.io.*;
class Purchase
{
  public static void main(String[] args) throws IOException
  {
    InputStreamReader IR = new InputStreamReader(System.in);
    BufferedReader br = new BufferedReader(IR);
    System.out.println("Enter Name:");
    String name = br.readLine();
    System.out.println("Enter Address:");
    String add = br.readLine();
    System.out.println("Enter the type of Purchase:");
    String type = br.readLine();
    System.out.println("Enter Amount of Purchase:");
    int amount = Integer.parseInt(br.readLine());
    double discountRate = 0.0;
    if(type.equals("L"))
    {
      if(amount <= 25000)
      {
        discountRate = 0;
      }
      else if(amount >= 25001 && amount <= 57000)
      {
        discountRate = 5.0;
      }
```

```
            else if(amount >= 57000 && amount <= 100000)
            {
                discountRate = 7.5;
            }
            else if(amount > 100000)
            {
                discountRate = 10.0;
            }
        }
        else if(type.equals("D"))
        {
            if(amount <= 25000)
            {
                discountRate = 5.0;
            }
            else if(amount >= 25001 && amount <= 57000)
            {
                discountRate = 7.5;
            }
            else if(amount >= 57001 && amount <= 100000)
            {
                discountRate = 10.0;
            }
            else if(amount > 100000)
            {
                discountRate=15.0;
            }
        }
        double discount=(discountRate/100) * amount;
        double netAmount=amount - discount;
        System.out.println("Customer Name=" +name);
        System.out.println("Customer Address=" +add);
        System.out.println("Purchase Type=" +type);
        System.out.println("Net amount to be paid=" +netAmount);
    }
}
```

17. Write a menu driven program to accept a number from the user and check whether it is a 'BUZZ' number or to accept any two numbers and print the 'GCD'of them

(i) A BUZZ number is the number which either ends with 7 or divisible by 7.

(ii) GCD (Greatest Common Divisor) of two integers is calculated by continued division method. Divide the larger number by the smaller, the remainder then divides the previous divisor. The process is repeated till the remainder is zero. The divisor then results the GCD. ***ICSE 2009***

Ans

```
import java.io.*;
class Number
{
    public static void main(String[] args) throws IOException
    {
        InputStreamReader IR=new InputStreamReader(System.in);
        BufferedReader br=new BufferedReader(IR);
        System.out.println("Press 1 for BUZZ number and 2 for GCD");
        int ch=Integer.parseInt(br.readLine());
        switch(ch)
        {
        case 1:
            int n;
            System.out.println("Enter the Number");
            n=Integer.parseInt(br.readLine());
            if(n%7==0 || n%10==7)
            {
                System.out.println("BUZZ Number");
            }
            else
```

```
          {
            System.out.println("Not BUZZ");
          }
          break;
        case 2:
          int a, b, gcd, l, s;
          System.out.println("Value of first number:");
          a=Integer.parseInt(br.readLine());
          System.out.println("Value of second number:");
          b=Integer.parseInt(br.readLine());
          if(a==b)
          {
            gcd=a;
          }
          else
          {
            if(a > b)
            {
               l=a;
               s=b;
            }
            else
            {
               l=b;
               s=a;
            }
            while(l%s!=0)
            {
               s=l%s;
               l=s;
            }
            gcd = s;
          }
          System.out.println("Value of GCD " +gcd);
        }
      }
    }
```

18. Write a program to generate a triangle or an inverted triangle till n terms based upon the user's choice of triangle to be displayed.

Example 1

Input Type 1 for a triangle and
Type 2 for an inverted triangle

1

Enter the number of terms - 5

Output

1
2 2
3 3 3
4 4 4 4
5 5 5 5 5

Example 2

Input Type 1 for a triangle and
Type 2 for an inverted triangle.

2

Enter the number of terms - 6

Output

6 6 6 6 6 6
5 5 5 5 5
4 4 4 4
3 3 3
2 2
1

ICSE 2009

Ans

```
import java.io.*;
class Triangle
{
  public static void main(String[ ] args) throws IOException
  {
    InputStreamReader IR=new InputStreamReader(System.in);
    BufferedReader br=new BufferedReader(IR);
    int ch, num, i, j;
    System.out.println("Enter 1 for a triangle and 2 for an
    inverted triangle");
    ch=Integer.parseInt(br.readLine());
    System.out.println("Enter the number of terms");
```

```
        num=Integer.parseInt(br.readLine());
        switch(ch)
        {
          case 1:
          for(i=1; i<=num; i++)
          {
            for(j=1; j<=i; j++)
            {
              System.out.print(i);
            }
            System.out.println();
          }
          break;
          case 2:
            for(i=num; i>=1; i--)
            {
              for(j=1; j<=i; j++)
              {
                System.out.print(i);
              }
              System.out.println();
            }
          break;
        }
      }
    }
```

19. Write a menu driven class to accept a number from the user and check whether it is a Palindrome or a Perfect number.

(i) Palindrome number (a number is a Palindrome which when read in reverse order in same as read in the right order). e.g. 11, 101, 151, etc.

(ii) Perfect number (a number is called Perfect if it is equal to the sum of its factors other than the number itself). e.g. $6 = 1 + 2 + 3$ ***ICSE 2008***

KEY idea

To check if the given number is a palindrome, the program should reverse the number and compare it with the original number. To check if the given number is a perfect number, the program should calculate the sum of all the factors of the number except the number itself and compare it with the original number.

Ans

```
import java.io.*;
class Number
{
  public static void main(String args[]) throws IOException
  {
    InputStreamReader IR=new InputStreamReader(System.in);
    BufferedReader br=new BufferedReader(IR);
    System.out.println("Enter 1 for palindrome and 2 for perfect number");
    int ch=Integer.parseInt(br.readLine());
    switch(ch)
    {
      case 1:
        System.out.println("Enter any number");
        int original = Integer.parseInt(br.readLine());
        int a=original,rev=0,rem;
        while(a>0)
        {
          rem=a%10;
          rev=rev*10+rem;
          a=a/10;
        }
        if(original==rev)
        {
          System.out.println("Number is palindrome");
```

```
            }
            else
            {
               System.out.println("Number is not palindrome");
            }
            break;
         case 2:
            int n, s=0;
            System.out.println("Enter a number");
            n=Integer.parseInt(br.readLine());
            for(int x=1; x<=n-1; x++)
            {
               if(n%x==0)
                  s=s+x;
            }
            if(s==n)
            {
               System.out.println("It is Perfect no");
               break;
            }
            else
            {
               System.out.println("It is not Perfect no");
               break;
            }
         default:
            System.out.println("Wrong choice");
            break;
      }
   }
}
```

20. Using a switch statement, write a menu driven program to convert a given temperature from Fahrenheit to Celsius and *vice-versa*. For an incorrect choice an appropriate error message should be displayed. ***ICSE 2007***

(**Hint** $C = \frac{5}{9} \times (F - 32)$ and $F = (1.8 \times C) + 32$)

Ans

```
import java.io.*;
class Menu
{
  public static void main(String args[]) throws IOException
  {
     InputStreamReader IR = new InputStreamReader(System.in);
     BufferedReader br = new BufferedReader(IR);
     int choice;
     double F, C;
     System.out.println("Press 1 for Fahrenheit to Celsius,
     2 for Celsius to Fahrenheit, 3 for Exit");
     choice = Integer.parseInt(br.readLine());
     switch(choice)
     {
        case 1:
           System.out.println("Enter the value of Fahrenheit");
           F=Double.parseDouble(br.readLine());
           C=(5*(F-32))/9;
           System.out.println("Temperature in Celsius=" +C);
           break;
        case 2:
           System.out.println("Enter the value of Celsius");
           C=Double.parseDouble(br.readLine());
           F=(1.8*C)+32;
           System.out.println("Temperature in Fahrenheit=" +F);
           break;
        case 3:
           System.exit(0);
```

```
            default:
                System.out.println("Wrong choice!");
        }
    }
}
```

21. Write a program to calculate and print the sum of odd numbers and the sum of even numbers for the first n natural numbers. The integer n is to be entered by the user. ***ICSE 2006***

Ans

```
import java.io.*;
class Sum
{
  public static void main(String args[]) throws IOException
  {
    InputStreamReader IR = new InputStreamReader(System.in);
    BufferedReader br = new BufferedReader(IR);
    int n, i, odd_sum = 0, even_sum = 0;
    System.out.println("Enter the value of n");
    n=Integer.parseInt(br.readLine());
    for(i=1; i<=n; i++)
    {
      if(i%2==0)
      {
        even_sum=even_sum + i;
      }
      else
      {
        odd_sum=odd_sum + i;
      }
    }
    System.out.println("Sum of all odd number " +odd_sum);
    System.out.println("Sum of all even number " +even_sum);
  }
}
```

Output Enter the value of n 10
Sum of all odd number 25
Sum of all even number 30

22. A cloth showroom has announced the following festival discounts on the purchase of items based on the total cost of the items purchased

Total Cost	**Discount** (in Percentage)
Less than ₹ 2000	5%
Rs. 2001 to ₹ 5000	25%
Rs. 5001 to ₹ 10000	35%
Above ₹ 10000	50%

Write a program to input the total cost and to compute and display the amount to be paid by the customer after availing the discount. ***ICSE 2006***

Ans

```
import java.io.*;
class Amount
{
  public static void main(String[] args) throws IOException
  {
    InputStreamReader IR = new InputStreamReader(System.in);
    BufferedReader br = new BufferedReader(IR);
    int tcost;
    double dis = 0.0, price;
    System.out.println("Enter the total cost");
    tcost = Integer.parseInt(br.readLine());
    if(tcost < 2000)
    {
      dis = 0.05*tcost;
    }
```

```
        else if(tcost >= 2001 && tcost <= 5000)
        {
          dis = 0.25*tcost;
        }
        else if(tcost >= 5001 && tcost <= 10000)
        {
          dis = 0.35*tcost;
        }
        else
        {
          dis=0.50*tcost;
        }
        price = tcost-dis;
        System.out.println("Total bill=" +price);
    }
}
```

Output Enter the total cost 4500
Total bill=3375.0

23. Write a program to input any given string to calculate the total number of characters and vowels present in the string and also reverse the string

e.g. INPUT : Enter string : SNOWY

OUTPUT : Total number of characters : 5

Number of vowels : 1

Reverse string : YWONS *ICSE 2005*

Ans

```
import java.io.*;
class Negative
{
  public static void main(String args[]) throws IOException
  {
    InputStreamReader IR=new InputStreamReader(System.in);
    BufferedReader br=new BufferedReader(IR);
    System.out.print("Enter a string : ");
    String s=br.readLine();
    int noVowels=0;
    String rev=" ";
    for(int i=0; i<s.length(); i++)
    {
      char C=s.toUpperCase().charAt(i);
      switch(C)
      {
        case 'A':
        case 'E':
        case 'I':
        case 'O':
        case 'U':
           noVowels++;
           break;
      }
      C = s.charAt(s.length()-1-i);
      rev = rev+C;
    }
    System.out.println("Total number of characters : "+s.length());
    System.out.println("Number of vowels : " +noVowels);
    System.out.println("Reverse string : " +rev);
  }
}
```

Output Enter a string : SNOWY
Total number of characters: 5
Number of vowels : 1
Reverse string : YWONS

24. Write a program to print the sum of negative numbers, sum of positive even numbers and sum of positive odd numbers from a list of numbers *(N)* entered by the user. The list terminates when the user enters zero. ***ICSE 2005***

Ans
```
import java.io.*;
class negative
{
  public static void main(String args[]) throws IOException
  {
    int n, sneg=0, seven=0, sodd=0;
    InputStreamReader IR=new InputStreamReader(System.in);
    BufferedReader br=new BufferedReader(IR);
    System.out.println("Enter list of numbers and 0 to terminate the list");
    do
    {
      n=Integer.parseInt(br.readLine());
      if(n<0)
      {
        sneg=sneg+n;
      }
      else
      {
        if(n%2==0)
        {
          seven=seven+n;
        }
        else
        {
          sodd=sodd+n;
        }
      }while(n!=0);
    }
    System.out.println("Sum of negative number=" +sneg);
    System.out.println("Sum of positive even number=" +seven);
    System.out.println("Sum of positive odd number=" +sodd);
  }
}
```

25. Write a class with name employee and Basic as its data member, to find the gross pay of an employee for the following allowances and deduction. Use meaningful variables.

Dearness Allowance = 25% of Basic Pay ***ICSE 2005***

House Rent Allowance = 15% of Basic Pay

Provident Fund = 8.33% of Basic Pay

Net Pay = Basic Pay + Dearness Allowance + House Rent Allowance

Gross Pay = Net Pay – Provident Fund

Ans
```
class employee
{
  private int Basic;
  void salary(int Basic, String name)  //Enter basic salary and name
  {
    double DA, HR, PF, NP, GP;
    DA=(25.0/100) * Basic;
    HR=(15.0/100) * Basic;
    PF=(8.33/100) * Basic;
    NP=Basic + DA + HR;
    GP=NP - PF;
    System.out.println("Gross Pay" +GP);
  }
}
```

CHAPTER TEST

1 Mark Questions

1. Which of the following a class defines that implement the data structure and operations of the data respectively?
(a) Attributes, Objects (b) Objects, Attributes (c) Attributes, Methods (d) None of these

2. Which of the following represent the state of an object?
(a) Properties (b) Name (c) Colour (d) None of these

3. What do you mean by nameless objects?
(a) An object created by using the new keyword.
(b) An object of a superclass created in the subclass.
(c) An object without having any name but having a reference.
(d) An object that has no reference.

2 Marks Questions

4. Choose from the following as primitive or non- primitive data types.
char, arrays, int, classes

5. Predict the return data type of 'r' and 'n' from the snippet

```
int p; float m;
r = p + m;
n=m/3* (Math.pow (4, 3));
System.out.println(r);
System.out.println(n);
```

15 Marks Questions

6. Define a class 'Student' described as below

Data members/instance variables: name, age, m1,m2,m3 (marks in 3 subjects), maximum, average

Member methods

(i) To accept the details of a student.
(ii) To compute the average and the maximum out of three marks.
(iii) To display the name, age, marks in three subjects, maximum and average.

Write a main method to create an object of a class and call the above member methods.

7. Define a class called Fruit Juice with the following description

Instance variables/data members	
int product_code	stores the product code number
String flavour	stores the flavour of the juice. (orange, apple, etc.)
String pack_type	stores the type of packaging (tetra-pack, bottle, etc.)
int pack_size	stores package size (200ml, 400ml, etc.)
int product price	stores the price of the product
Member Methods	
void input()	to input and store the product code, flavour, pack type, pack size and product price
void discount()	to reduce the product price by 10
void display()	to display the product code, flavour, pack type, pack size and product price

Write the main method to create an object of the class and call the above member methods.

03

User-Defined Methods

TREND ANALYSIS 3 YEARS

Average No. of Questions Across all Sets

	Types of Questions	2023	2019	2018
User-Defined Methods	1 Mark	4	–	–
	2 Marks	–	1	3
	15 Marks	1	–	2

Method

A Java method (function) is a collection of statements that are grouped together to perform a coherent task or any particular operation.

```
public static void main(String[] args)
{ .........
  .........
}
```

It is main method in Java, which is always called by the JVM at starting.

Declaration of a Method

To declare a method in Java, required components are

(i) **Modifier** public, private, protected, etc.

(ii) **Return type** int, float, void (if method does not return a value), etc.

(iii) **Method name** depends on user.

(iv) **Parameter list in parenthesis** proceeded by their data type.

(v) **Method body** The method code enclosed by curly braces.

(vi) **Method Signature** Every method has method signature. It is a part of the method declaration. It includes the method name and parameter list.

e.g. Access modifier | Return type | Method name | Parameters

```
public void add(int a, int b)
{
   //method body
}
```

Method Prototype

It is the first line of the method definition that tells the program about the type of the value returned by the method and number and type of arguments.

With the help of prototype, a compiler can compare each use of the method with the prototype to determine whether the function is invoked properly.

Types of Method (Function)

In Java, we have two different types of methods. These are as follows:

Instance Method

It is **non-static method** which is defined in a class and only accessible through the object of the class.

Syntax `<<objectname>>.<<methodname>>;`

Instance methods are classified into two ways:

(i) **Accessor Methods** (pure method) Used to read instance variable. e.g. 'get' method.

(ii) **Mutator Methods** (impure method) Used to not only read but also modify the data. e.g. 'set' method.

Class Method

Class method **(static method)** is a method that can be called and executed without creating an object. In general, static methods are used to create instance methods.

Syntax `class.classMethod(parameter lists);`

Need of Method

A function is a block of code that performs a particular task. Sometimes, we need to write a particular block of code for more than once in our program. This may lead to bugs and irritation for the programmer. To prevent programs from these problems, functions are needed.

Modular Programming

It is the process of subdividing a computer program into separate subprograms or methods. These subprograms or methods are called **modules**. These modules have their own functions within the class.

Calling/Invoking an Object's Method

We can use an object reference to invoke an object's method. We append the method's simple name to the object reference, with an intervening dot operator(.).

Syntax `objectReference.methodName();`

Note Object creation has already discussed in Chapter 2.

Instance Function

Instance functions are the group of codes that performs a particular task. There are two types of instance functions in Java

(i) **Pure functions** define a relationship between input and output. A pure function does not depend on any state beyond its local scope. It does not modify arguments, since it is used only for input/output. Operations like square root, sine and cosine are pure functions.

(ii) **Impure functions** are those functions, which modify their behaviour based on external state. It is also called **modifier function** that can cause a change of state in the object.
e.g. `printf(), random()`

Pure and impure are mainly used to access or set the value for the private member of the class in the main method.

Use of static Data Member with static Function

static Keyword

It becomes important when we want to define a class member that will be used independently at class level. When a class member is declared 'static', it can be accessed without creating any object of its class.

Note When function name comes without static keyword, that means this function will be non-static.

Java static Data Member

Data members or fields of a Java class declared static are called **class members**. There exists exactly only one copy of static field or class member, no matter how many objects of the class are finally created.

Java static Method (Function)

It is used to implement class behaviours that are not affected by the state of any instance. Java static methods have many restrictions over themselves:

- They can only call **static** method within from them.
- Java **static** methods can only access **static** data members.
- Java **static** methods cannot refer **this** and **super**.

e.g.
```
class StaticMethod
{
   int instVar=10;
   static int staticVar=20;
   public static void staticmethod()
   {
      System.out.println(instVar);
         // Here, an error will occur as it
            // is a non static variable.
      System.out.println(staticVar);
      StaticMethod sm=new StaticMethod();
      System.out.println(sm.instVar);
   }
}
public class StaticMethodDemo
{
   public static void main(String[] args)
   {
      StaticMethod.staticmethod();
   }
}
```

Ways of Invoke/Calling Functions

In Java, we can call functions through two ways. These are, call by value and call by reference. The main objective of passing arguments to functions is message passing.

Call by Value

Call by value or **pass by value** in Java means passing a copy of the value, which is to be passed. Primitive types are passed through call by value.

e.g.
```
int a=34;
public void math(int num)
math(a);

   a       num      memory
 | 34 |   | 34 |
```

Call by Reference

Call by reference or **pass by reference** in Java means the passing reference itself. Reference types are passed through call by reference.

e.g.
```
Student S1 = new Student();
Student S2 = new Student();
      S2.copy(S1);          Call by reference
void copy(Student S)
{
   –
   –  } body of the copy function
   –
   –
}
```

Actual Parameter and Formal Parameter

In relation to function calling, parameters are two types

(i) Actual parameter (ii) Formal parameter

Actual parameters are situated in caller method and **formal parameters** are written in called funciton.

e.g.
```
class Addition                    Formal Parameter
{
    int sum ( int a, int b )
    {
      return a + b;
    }
    public static void main ()
    {
      Addition ad = new Addition ();
      int x = 10, y = 20;      Actual Parameter
      int z = sum ( x, y );
      System.out.print('Output' + z);
    }
}
```

Returning from a Function

It does not only terminate the function's execution but also passes the control back to the calling function.

Return Statement

On executing the return statement, it immediately transfers the control back to the calling function. There is no restriction on the number of return statements that may be present in a function.

Returning Values

The functions which are not declared as void or declared as any data type, return a value. A function can return only a single value.

```
                        Function definition
return type Function( )
{
  :::::::::
  return(Variable/Datavalue);
}
void main( )
{                       Function calling
  :::::::::
  Variable = Function();
  :::::::::
}
```
Return value is passed to variable

Function Overloading (Polymorphism)

If two or more methods in a class have the same name but different parameters, it is known as **method overloading.** Method overloading can be done by changing number of arguments or by changing the data type of arguments. There are two ways of method overloading

By Changing Data Type of Arguments

e.g.
```
class Calculate
{
    void sum(int a, int b)        //method 1
    {
      System.out.println("sum is " +(a+b));
    }
    void sum(double a, float b)   //method 2
    {
      System.out.println("sum is " +(a+b));
    }
    public static void main(String[] args)
    {
      Calculate cal=new Calculate();
      cal.sum(8,5);    //method 1 is called
      cal.sum(4.6, 3.8F);
                       //method 2 is called
    }
}
```

Output sum is 13
sum is 8.399999952316284

By Changing Number of Arguments

e.g.

```
class Area
{
    void find(int l, int b)        //method 1
    {
        System.out.println("Area is " +(l * b));
    }
    void find(int l, int b, int h) //method 2
    {
        System.out.println("Area is " +(l*b*h));
    }
    public static void main(String[] args)
    {
        Area ar = new Area();
        ar.find(8, 5);
            //method 1 is called
        ar.find(4, 6, 2);
            //method 2 is called
    }
}
```

Output Area is 40
Area is 48

PYQs Previous Years Questions

1 Mark Questions

1. The number of values that a method can return is *ICSE 2023*

   (a) 1 (b) 2 (c) 3 (d) 4

Ans (a) 1

2. Write a method prototype name check() which takes an integer argument and returns a char *ICSE 2023*

   (a) char check () (b) void check (int x)
   (c) check (int x) (d) char check (int x)

Ans (d) char check (int x)

3. Method which is a part of a class rather than an instance of the class is termed as *ICSE 2023*

   (a) static method (b) non-static method
   (c) wrapper class (d) string method

Ans (a) static method

4. A method which does not modify the value of variables is termed as *ICSE 2023*

   (a) impure method (b) pure method
   (c) primitive method (d) user defined method

Ans (b) pure method

5. A method needs to be called with help of an object. *ICSE 2022 (Sem I)*

   (a) void (b) class (c) non-static (d) static

Ans (c) non-static

6. Parameters used in the method call statement are *ICSE 2022 (Sem I)*

   (a) actual parameters (b) informal parameters
   (c) formal parameters (d) void parameters

Ans (a) actual parameters

7. The keyword which indicates that the method returns no value. *ICSE 2022 (Sem I)*

   (a) public (b) static (c) void (d) abstract

Ans (c) void

8. Invoking a method by passing the objects of a class is termed as *ICSE SQP 2022 (Sem I)*

   (a) call by value (b) call by reference
   (c) call by method

Ans (b) call by reference

2 Marks Questions

1. Write the prototype of a function search which takes two arguments a string and a character and returns an integer value. *ICSE SQP 2020*

Ans `int search(string str, char ch);`

2. State a difference between call by value and call by reference. *ICSE 2019*

Or Differentiate between call by value or pass by value and call by reference or pass by reference. *ICSE 2012*

Ans

Call by Value	Call by Reference
It works with primitive data type.	It works with non-primitive data type.
The original value of variable remains unchanged.	The original value of variable changes.
Operation is performed on duplicate value of variables.	Operation is performed on original values of variables.

3. Write the prototype of a function check which takes an integer as an argument and returns a character. **ICSE 2018**

Ans `public char check(int x)`

4. What are the two ways of invoking functions? **ICSE 2018, 11**

Ans In Java, two ways to invoke a function are

(i) Call by value

(ii) Call by reference

If the function is static, it can be invoked by using the class name. If the function is non-static, it can be invoked by using object.

5. Differentiate between actual parameter and formal parameter. **ICSE 2018, SQP 2017, 16, 08, 07**

Ans Difference between actual parameter and formal parameter are as follows

Actual Parameter	Formal Parameter
It is used when method is called.	It appears in the definition of a method.
e.g. `int a=5;` `int b=4;` `sum(a,b); //actual`	e.g. `int a=5;` `int b=4;` `public sum(int c,int d); //formal`

6. Write a function prototype of the following
A function PosChar which takes a string argument and a character argument and returns an integer value. **ICSE 2016**

Ans `int PosChar (String s, char c)`

7. What are the values of a and b after the following function is executed, if the values passed are 30 and 50? **ICSE 2015**

```
void paws(int a, int b)
{
    a = a + b;
    b = a - b;
    a = a - b;
    System.out.println(a+“,”+b);
}
```

Ans **Output** 50, 30

8. Give the output of the following method **ICSE 2014**

```
public static void main(String[] args)
{
  int a=5;
  a++;
  System.out.println(a);
  a-=(a--)-(-a);
  System.out.println(a);
}
```

Ans **Output**

6

–5

9. What is the role of keyword void in declaring functions? **ICSE 2014, 07**

Ans The keyword void indicates that the function would not return any value.

10. Give the prototype of a function search which receives a sentence sentnc and a word wrd and returns 1 or 0. **ICSE 2011**

Ans `int search(String sentnc, String wrd)`

11. Write two advantages of using functions in a program. **ICSE 2010**

Ans There are two advantages of using functions in a program:

(i) Functions make code reusable.

(ii) Functions improve modularity and facilitate easy debugging.

12. Give the prototype of a function check which receives a character ch and an integer n and returns true or false. **ICSE 2010**

Ans The prototype of a function check
`boolean(char ch, int n)`

13. Differentiate between static and non-static data members. **ICSE 2010**

Ans Difference between static and non-static data members

Static	Non-static
These variable are preceded by static keyword.	These variable should not be preceded by static keyword.
Memory for static variable is created only one in the program at the time of loading of class.	Memory for non-static variable is created at the time of create an object of class.

14. Write the function prototype for the function ‘sum’ that takes an integer variable(x) as its argument and returns a value of float data type. **ICSE 2009**

Ans The function prototype which returns a value of float data type is
`public float sum(int x)`

15. Difference between pure and impure functions. *ICSE 2009*

Ans Difference between pure and impure functions are as follows

Pure Function	Impure Function
Pure function does not change the state of the object.	Impure function changes the state of the object by modifying instance variables.
Example of pure function is get function.	Example of impure function is set function.

16. When there are multiple definitions with the same function name, what make them different from each other? *ICSE 2009*

Ans The function prototype makes multiple definitions with the same function name and make different to each other by differentiate their (number and types) parameters. This helps the compiler to recognise, which function is to be executed.

17. If a function contains several return statements, how many of them will be executed? *ICSE 2007*

Ans In any call of function, only one return statement can be executed at a time.

3/4 Marks Questions

1. Consider the following code and answer the questions that follow *ICSE 2009*

```
class academic
{
   int x, y;
   void access()
   {
      int a, b;
      academic student = new academic();
      System.out.println("object created");
   }
}
```

(i) What is the object name of class academic?
(ii) Name the instance variable used in the program.
(iii) Write the local variable used in the program.
(iv) Give the type of function used and its name.

Ans The output of the given code will be
(i) Object name → student
(ii) Instance variable used in the program → x and y
(iii) Local variable used in the program → a and b
(iv) Type of function → instance (impure type)
Name of function → access( )

2. Explain function overloading with an example. *ICSE 2006*

Ans Function overloading is the process of defining functions/methods with the same function names but with different numbers and types of parameters. i.e. function name is the same but function signature (numbers and types of parameters) is different.
e.g.

```
class Display
{
    public void disp(char c)
    {
      System.out.println(c);
    }
    public void disp(char c, int num)
    {
      System.out.println(c+ "" + num);
    }
}
class Sample
{
    public static void main(string args [])
    {
      Display ob = new Display();
      ob.disp('a');
      ob.disp('a', 10);
    }
}
```

Output
a
a   10

3. (i) What is call by value?
(ii) How are the following passed
(a) Primitive Types?
(b) Reference Types? *ICSE 2005*

Ans (i) Call by value is that when a copy of the variable is passed to the function as an argument. Any change to the copy in the function will not change the original variables' value. It is used to primitive data type passing only, in Java.
(ii) (a) Primitive types, are passed through call by value.
(b) Reference types, are passed through call by reference.

6 Marks Questions

1. The following program segment checks whether number is an Abundant number or not. A number is said to be an Abundant number when the sum of its factors (excluding the number itself) is greater than the number. *ICSE 2022 (Sem I)*
Example:
Factors of number 12 are 1, 2, 3, 4, 6

Sum of factors is 1 +2 + 3+ 4 +6 = 16

Fill in the blanks with appropriate Java statements.

```
void abundant(int n)
{
  int s=0;
  for((i) ________; (ii) _______;i++)
  {
    if((iii) ________ )
    s=s+i;
  }
  if((iv)________ )
    System.out.println(" Abundant Number");
  else
    System.out.println("Not Abundant
                                    Number");
}
```

(i) (a) int i=1 (b) int i=0
(c) int i=2 (d) Int i=1

(ii) (a) i<=n (b) i<n
(c) i>n (d) i>=n

(iii) (a) n%i= =0 (b) n%i= =1
(c) n%2= =0 (d) n/2= =0

(iv) (a) s<n (b) s>n
(c) s= =n (d) s=n

Ans (i) (a) int i=1

(ii) (b) i < n

(iii) (a) n%i = = 0

(iv) (b) s > n

2. A school is giving away merit certificates for the students who have scored 90 percentage and above in class 10.

The following program is based on the specification given below. ***ICSE 2022 (Sem I)***

Class name	Student
Member variables	
String name	To enter name of a student
double per	To enter percentage obtained by the student
String cer	To store the message
Member methods	
void input( )	To accept the detail
void merit( )	To check the percentage and award the merit
void display( )	To display the detail
void main ( )	To create an object of the class and invoke the methods

Fill in the blanks with appropriate Java statements.

```
import java. (i)__________.*;
class Student
{
  String name;
  double per;
  String cer;
  void input()
  {
    Scanner obj= new Scanner(System.in);
    System.out.println(" Enter name,
                                  Percentage");
    name = obj.next();
    per = (ii) ________
  }
  void merit()
  {
    if ((iii)___________ )
    {
      cer="AWARDED";
    }
    else
      cer=(iv)__________
  }
  void (v) __________
  {
    System.out.println(name);
    System.out.println(per);
    System.out.println( cer);
  }
  void main()
  {
    Student s = new (vi) __________
    s.input();
    s.merit();
    s.display();
  }
}
```

(i) (a) utility (b) Util
(c) util (d) UTILITY

(ii) (a) obj.nextDouble( ); (b) nextDouble( );
(c) obj.nextFloat( ); (d) nextFloat()

(iii) (a) per>=90 (b) per<=90
(c) per>90 (d) per==90

(iv) (a) NOT AWARDED; (b) "NOT AWARDED";
(c) "AWARDED"; (d) "NOT AWARDED"

(v) (a) display( ) (b) Display( )
(c) Print( ) (d) DISPLAY( )

(vi) (a) Student( ); (b) STUDENT( )
(c) student( ) (d) Student( )

Ans (i) (c) util (ii) (a) obj.nextDouble( );

(iii) (a) per>=90 (iv) (b) "NOT AWARDED";

(v) (a) display( ) (vi) (a) Student( );

3. Given below is a class with following specifications **ICSE 2022 (Sem I)**

class name	Number
void Display(int n)	To extract and print each digit of given number from last digit of the first digit on separate lines: Example: n=674 **Output** 4 7 6
void Display( )	To print numbers from 0.5 to 5.0 with updation of 0.5.

Fill in the blanks of the given program with appropriate statements.

```
class (i) _________
{
   void Display(int n)
   {
      while((ii) _________ )
      {
         int rem= (iii) _________
         System.out.println(rem);
         n=(iv)_________
      }
   }
   void Display( )
   {
      for((v)_____ ; x<= (vi) _____; x+=0.5)
      System.out.println(x);
   }
}
```

(i) (a) Number (b) number (c) NUMBER (d) NUM

(ii) (a) n<0 (b) n>0 (c) n==0 (d) n=0

(iii) (a) n%100; (b) n/10; (c) n%10; (d) n/100

(iv) (a) n%10; (b) n/10; (c) n/100; (d) n%100

(v) (a) double x=0.5 (b) Double x=0.5 (c) double x=0.0 (d) Double x=0.0

(vi) (a) x>=5.0 (b) x<=5.0 (c) x==5.0 (d) x=5.0

Ans (i) (a) Number

(ii) (b) n > 0

(iii) (c) n%10;

(iv) (b) n/10;

(v) (a) double x=0.5

(vi) (b) x<=5.0

15 Marks Questions

1. Define a class to overload the function print as follows **ICSE 2023**

void print ()	To print the following format 1 1 1 1 2 2 2 2 3 3 3 3 4 4 4 4 5 5 5 5
void print (int n)	To check whether the number is a lead number. A lead number is the one whose sum of even digits are equal to sum of odd digits. e.g. 3669 odd digits sum = 3 + 9 = 12 even digits sum = 6 + 6 = 12 3669 is a lead number.

KEY idea

The class should be defined with a name "Example", have two methods named "print". The first method "print" should have a void return type and take no arguments. The second "print" method should take an integer "n" as an argument and also have a void return type.

Ans

```
public class Example
{
    public void print()
    {
        for (int i = 1; i <= 5; i++)
        {
            for (int j = 1; j <= 4; j++)
            {
                System.out.print(i + " ");
            }
            System.out.println();
        }
    }
    public void print(int n)
    {
        int oddSum = 0;
        int evenSum = 0;
        while(n!=0)
        {
            int digit = n % 10;
            if (digit % 2 == 0)
            {
                evenSum += digit;
            }
            else
            {
                oddSum += digit;
            }
            n /= 10;
        }
        if (oddSum == evenSum)
        {
            System.out.println(n + " is a lead
                                            number");
        }
```

```
        else
        {
            System.out.println(n + " is not a
                                    lead number");
        }
    }
    public static void main (String[] args)
    {
        Example ex = new Example ();
        ex.print();
        ex.print(123456);
        // prints "123456 is not a lead number"
        ex.print(3669);
        // prints "3669 is a lead number"
    }
}
```

2. Define a class with the following specifications

Class name	**employee**
Member variables	
eno	employee number
ename	name of the employee
age	age of the employee
basic	basic salary (Declare the variables using appropriate data types)
Member methods	
void accept ()	accept the details using scanner class
void calculate ()	to calculate the net salary as per the given specifications net = basic + hra + da − pf hra =18.5% of basic da =17.45% of basic pf = 8.10% of basic if the age of the employee is above 50 he/she gets an additional allowance of ₹ 5000
void print ()	to print the details as per the following format eno ename age basic net
void main ()	to create an object of the class and invoke the methods

ICSE SQP 2023

Ans

```
import java.util.Scanner;
class Employee
{
    int eno;
    String ename;
    int age;
    double basic;
    double net;
    public void accept ()
    {
        Scanner in = new Scanner (System.in);
        System.out.print("Employee number: ");
        eno = Integer.parseInt(in.nextLine());
        System.out.print("Employee name: ");
        ename = in.nextLine();
        System.out.print("Age: ");
        age = Integer.parseInt(in.nextLine());
        System.out.print("Basic salary: ");
        basic = Double.parseDouble
                            (in.nextLine());
    }
    public void calculate ()
    {
        double hra = 0.185 * basic;
        double da = 0.1745 * basic;
        double pf = 0.0810 * basic;
        net = basic + hra + da - pf;
        if (age > 50)
        {
            net += 5000;
        }
    }
    public void print ()
    {
        System.out.println("eno\tename\tage
                            \tbasic\tnet");
        System.out.println("\n" + eno + "
                \t" + ename + "\t" + age + "
                  \t" + basic + "\t" + net);
    }
    public static void main (String[] args)
    {
        Employee obj = new Employee ();
        obj.accept();
        obj.calculate();
        obj.print();
    }
}
```

3. Define a class to overload the method print as follows

ICSE SQP 2023

void print ()	to print the format 1 2 3 4 5 6 7 8 9 10
boolean print (int n)	to check whether the number is a Dudeney number, a number is dudeney if the cube of the sum of the digits is equal to the number itself. e.g. $512=(5+1+2)^3=(8)^3=512$
void print (int a, char ch)	if ch = s or S print the square of the number else if ch = c or C print the cube of the number.

Ans

```
import java.util.Scanner;
class Overload
{
    public void print ()
    {
        int k = 1;
        for (int i = 1; i <= 4; i++)
        {
            for (int j = 1; j <= i; j++)
                System.out.print(k++ + " ");
            System.out.println();
        }
    }
    public boolean print (int n)
    {
        int sum = 0;
        for (int i = n; i != 0; i /= 10)
        sum += i % 10;
        int cube = (int) Math.pow (sum, 3);
        if (n == cube)
            return true;
        return false;
    }
    public void print(int a, char ch)
    {
        if (ch == 'S' || ch == 's')
            System.out.println("Square ="+(a*a));
        else if (ch == 'C' || ch == 'c')
            System.out.println("Cube ="+(a*a*a));
    }
    public static void main (String [] args)
    {
        Scanner in = new Scanner (System.in);
        System.out.print("Enter a number: ");
        int n = Integer.parseInt(in.nextLine());
        System.out.print("Enter character 'c' or 's' ");
        char c = in.next().charAt(0);
        Overload obj = new Overload ();
        obj.print();
        boolean r=obj.print(n);
        System.out.println(r);
        obj.print(n,c);
    }
}
```

Common Mistake One common mistake for this question could be missing the method signature or parameters for the print() method. Without specifying the method signature or parameters, the method overloading won't be implemented correctly.

4. Anshul transport company charges for the parcels of its customers as per the following specifications given below ***ICSE SQP 2020***

Class name	**Atransport**
Member variables	
String name	to store the name of the customer
int w	to store the weight of the parcel in Kg
int charge	to store the charge of the parcel
Member functions	
void accept ()	to accept the name of the customer, weight of the parcel from the user (using Scanner class)

void calculate()	To calculate the charge as per the weight of the parcel as per the following criteria **Weight in Kg** — **Charge per Kg** Upto 10 Kgs — Rs. 25 per Kg Next 20 Kgs — Rs. 20 per Kg Above 30 Kgs — Rs. 10 per Kg A surcharge of 5 % is charged on the bill.
void print ()	to print the name of the customer, weight of the parcel, total bill inclusive of surcharge in a tabular form in the following format: Name Weight Bill amount ....

Define a class with the above-mentioned specifications, create the main method, create an object and invoke the member methods.

Ans

```
import java.util.Scanner;
public class Atransport
{
    private String name;
    private int w;
    private int charge;
    public void accept()
    {
      Scanner in = new Scanner(System.in);
      System.out.print("Enter Customer Name:");
      name = in.nextLine();
      System.out.print("Enter Parcel Weight:");
      w = in.nextInt();
    }
    public void calculate()
    {
      if (w <= 10)
         charge = w * 25;
      else if (w <= 30)
         charge = 250 + ((w - 10) * 20);
      else
         charge = 250 + 400 + ((w - 30)*10);
         charge += charge * 5 / 100;
    }
    public void print()
    {
      System.out.println("Name\tWeight\tBill amount");
      System.out.println("----\t------\t-----------");
      System.out.println(name + "\t" + w + "\t" + charge);
    }
    public static void main(String args[])
    {
      Atransport obj = new Atransport();
      obj.accept();
      obj.calculate();
      obj.print();
    }
}
```

5. Design a class to overload a function Sum () as follows

(i) int Sum (int A, int B) - with two integer arguments (A and B) calculate and return sum of all the even numbers in the range of A and B.

Sample input: A = 4 and B = 16

Sample output: sum = 4 + 6 + 8 + 10 + 12 + 14 + 16

(ii) double Sum (double N) - with one double arguments (N) calculate and return the product of the following series:

sum = $1.0 \times 1.2 \times 1.4 \times \ldots\ldots\ldots \times N$

(iii) int Sum (int N) - with one integer argument (N) calculate and return sum of only odd digits of the number N.

Sample input : N = 43961

Sample output : sum = 3 + 9 + 1 = 13

Write the main method to create an object and invoke the above methods. ***ICSE SQP 2020***

Ans

```
public class SumOverload
{
    public int Sum(int A, int B)
    {
        int sum = 0;
        for (int i = A; i <= B; i++)
        {
            if (i % 2 == 0)
            sum += i;
        }
        return sum;
    }
    public double Sum(double N)
    {
        double p = 1.0;
        for (double i = 1.0; i <= N; i += 0.2)
            p *= i;
        return p;
    }
    public int Sum(int N)
    {
        int sum = 0;
        while (N != 0)
        {
            int d = N % 10;
            if (d % 2 != 0)
                sum += d;
            N /= 10;
        }
        return sum;
    }
    public static void main(String args[])
    {
        SumOverload obj = new SumOverload();
        int evenSum = obj.Sum(4, 16);
        System.out.println("Even sum from 4 to 16 = " + evenSum);
        double seriesProduct = obj.Sum(2.0);
        System.out.println("Series Product =" + seriesProduct);
        int oddDigitSum = obj.Sum(43961);
        System.out.println("Odd Digits Sum =" + oddDigitSum);
    }
}
```

6. Design a class **RailwayTicket** with following description ***ICSE 2018***

Instance variables/data members	
String name	To store the name of the customer
String coach	To store the type of coach customer wants to travel
long mobno	To store customer's mobile number
int amt	To store basic amount of ticket
int totalamt	To store the amount to be paid after updating the original amount

Member methods	
void accept ()	To take input for name, coach, mobile number and amount.
void update()	To update the amount as per the coach selected (extra amount to be added in the amount as follows)

Type of Coaches	Amount
First_AC	700
Second_AC	500
Third_AC	250
Sleeper	None

void display()	To display all details of a customer such as name, coach, total amount and mobile number.

Write a main method to create an object of the class and call the above member methods.

Ans

```
import java.io.* ;
class RailwayTicket
{
    String name, coach;
    double mobno;
    int amt, totalamt;
    void accept () throws IOException
    {
      BufferedReader br = new BufferedReader
        (new InputStreamReader (System.in));
      System.out.println("Enter the name of the customer");
      name = br.readLine();
      System.out.println("Enter the type of coach customer wants to travel");
      coach = br.readLine();
      System.out.println("Enter the customer's mobile number");
      mobno = Double. parseDouble (br.readLine());
      System.out.println("Enter the basic amount of ticket");
      amt = Integer.parseInt(br.readLine ());
    }
    void update ()
    {
      String Type;
      switch (Type)
      {
         case "First_AC":
              totalamt = amt + 700 ;
              break;
         case "Second_AC":
              totalamt = amt + 500;
              break;
         case "Third_AC":
              totalamt = amt + 250;
              break;
         case "Sleeper":
              totalamt=amt;
              break;
      }
    }
    void display ()
    {
      System.out.println ("Name:" +name);
      System.out.println ("Coach type:" + coach);
      System.out.println ("Mobile number:" + mobno);
```

```
        System.out.println ("Total amount:" + totalamt);
    }
    public static void main (string args[]) throws IOException
    {
        RailwayTicket RT=new RailwayTicket ();
        RT. accept ();
        RT. update ();
        RT. display ();
    }
}
```

7. Design a class to overload a function volume() as follows **ICSE 2018**

(i) double volume (double R) – with radius (R) as an argument, returns the volume of sphere using the formula.

$$V = 4/3 \times 22/7 \times R^3$$

(ii) double volume (double H, double R) – with height(H) and Radius(R) as the arguments, returns the volume of a cylinder using the formula.

$$V = 22/7 \times R^2 \times H$$

(iii) double volume (double L, double B, double H) – with length(L), breadth(B) and Height(H) as the arguments, returns the volume of a cuboid using the formula.

$$V = L \times B \times H$$

Ans

```
class OverloadFunction
{
    double volume (double R)
    {
        double V;
        V=(4/3)*(22/7)*R*R*R;
        return V;
    }
    double volume (double H,double R)
    {
        double V= (22/7)*R*R*H;
        return V;
    }
    double volume (double L, double B, double H)
    {
        double V=L*B*H;
        return V;
    }
    public static void main (String[]args)
    {
        OverloadFunction ofn=new OverloadFunction();
        System.out.println("Sphere volume="+ofn.volume(5));
        System.out.println("Cylinder volume="+ofn.volume(5, 4));
        System.out.println("Cuboid volume="+ofn.volume(3, 4, 5));
    }
}
```

8. Define a class ElectricBill with the following specifications **ICSE 2017**

class	**ElectricBill**
Instance variables / data members	
String n	to store the name of the customer
int units	to store the number of units consumed
double bill	to store the amount to be paid

Member methods	
void accept()	to accept the name of the customer and number of units consumed
void calculate()	to calculate the bill as per the following tariff Number of units — Rate per unit First 100 units — Rs.2.00 Next 200 units — Rs.3.00 Above 300 units — Rs.5.00 A surcharge of 2.5% charged if the number of units consumed is above 300 units.
void print ()	To print the details as follows Name of the customer: .... Number of units consumed: .... Bill amount: ....

Write a main method to create an object of the class and call the above member methods.

Ans

```
import java.io.*;
class ElectricBill
{
    String n;
    int units;
    double bill;
    void accept() throws IOException
    {
      InputStreamReader IR=new InputStreamReader(System.in);
      BufferedReader br=new BufferedReader(IR);
      System.out.println("Enter the name of customer");
      n=br.readLine();
      System.out.println("Enter the number of units consumed");
      units=Integer.parseInt(br.readLine());
    }
    void calculate()
    {
      if(units<=100)
         bill=units*2;
      else if(units>100 && units<=300)
         bill=units*3;
      else
         bill=units*5+(units*2.5)/100;
    }
    void print()
    {
      System.out.println("Name of the customer: "+n);
      System.out.println("Number of units consumed: "+units);
      System.out.println("Bill amount: "+bill);
    }
    public static void main(String args[]) throws IOException
    {
      ElectricBill EB=new ElectricBill();
      EB.accept();
      EB.calculate();
      EB.print();
    }
}
```

9. Design a class to overload a function SumSeries() as follows **ICSE 2016**

(a) void SumSeries(int n, double x) – with one integer argument and one double argument to find and display the sum of the series given below:

$$s = \frac{x}{1} - \frac{x}{2} + \frac{x}{3} - \frac{x}{4} + \frac{x}{5} \ldots \ldots \ldots \text{ to n terms}$$

(b) void SumSeries() – To find and display the sum of the following series

$$s = 1 + (1\times 2) + (1\times 2\times 3) + \ldots \ldots \ldots + (1\times 2\times 3\times 4 \ldots \ldots \ldots \ldots \ldots \times 20)$$

Ans

```
import java.io.*;
public class SumofSeries
{
    void SumSeries(int n, double x)
    {
      double s=0.0;
      for(int i=1;i<=n;i+ +)
         if(i%2= =0)
               s=s-(x/i);
         else
            s=s+(x/i);
      System.out.println("Sum of series:"+s);
    }
    void SumSeries()
    {
      int s=0,f=1;
      for(int i=1;i<=20; i + +)
      {
         for (int j=1;j < =i; j+ +)
               f=f*j;
         s=s+f;
      }
      System.out.println("Sum of series:"+s);
    }
    public static void main(String args[]) throws IOException
    {
      SumofSeries ss1 = new SumofSeries();
      ss1.SumSeries();
      InputStreamReader IR=new InputStreamReader(System.in);
      BufferedReader br = new BufferedReader(IR);
      System.out.println("Enter the value of n and x");
      int n=Integer.parseInt(br.readLine());
      double x=Double.parseDouble (br.readLine());
      SumofSeries ss2=new SumofSeries();
      ss2.SumSeries(n, x);
    }
}
```

10. Define a class **ParkingLot** with the following description **ICSE 2015**

Instance variables/data members	
int vno	To store the vehicle number
int hours	To store the number of hours, the vehicle is parked in the parking lot
double bill	To store the bill amount
Member methods	
void input()	To input and store the vno and hours.
void calculate()	To compute the parking charge at the rate of ₹3 for the first hour or part thereof and ₹ 1.50 for each additional hour or part thereof.
void display()	To display the detail.

Write a main method to create an object of the class and call the above methods.

Ans

```
import java.io.*;
class ParkingLot
{
    int vno;
    int hours;
    double bill;
    void input() throws IOException
    {
      InputStreamReaderIR=new InputstreamReader(system.in);
      BufferedReader br=new BufferedReader(IR)
      System.out.println("Enter Vehicle Number :");
      vno=Integer.parseInt(br.readLine());
      System.out.println("Enter total hours  :");
      hours=Integer.parseInt(br.readLine());
    }
    void calculate()
    {
      if(hours>1)
         bill=3+1.5*(hours-1);
      else
         bill=3;
    }
    void display()
    {
      System.out.println("Vehicle Number :"+vno);
      System.out.println("Total hours :"+hours);
      System.out.println("Total charges :"+bill);
    }
    public static void main(String args[] throws IOException
    {
      ParkingLot p1=new ParkingLot();
      p1.input();
      p1.calculate();
      p1.display();
    }
}
```

11. Design a class to overload a function Joystring() as follows: ***ICSE 2015***

(a) void Joystring (String s, char ch1, char ch2) with one string argument and two character arguments that replaces the character argument ch1 with the character argument ch2 in the given String s and prints the new string.

Example:

Input value of s = "TECHNALAGY"

ch1 = 'A'

ch2 = 'O'

Output: "TECHNOLOGY"

(b) void Joystring (String s) with one string argument that prints the position of the first space and the last space of the given String s.

Example:

Input value of = "Cloud computing means Internet based computing"

Output: First index : 5

Last index : 36

(c) void Joystring (String s1, String s2) with two string arguments that combine the two strings with a space between them and prints the resultant string.

Example:

Input value of s1 = "COMMON WEALTH"

Input value of s2 = "GAMES"

Output : COMMON WEALTH GAMES

(use library functions)

Ans

```
import java.io.*;
class JoyString
{
    static void Joystring(String s,char ch1,char ch2)
    {
      System.out.println(s.replace(ch1,ch2));
    }
    static void Joystring(String s)
    {
      System.out.println("First index:"+s.indexOf(32));
      System.out.println("Last index:"+s.lastIndexOf(32));
    }
    static void Joystring(String s1,String s2)
    {
      System.out.println(s1.concat(" ").concat(s2));
    }
    public static void main(String[] args) throws IOException
    {
      InputStreamReader IR=new InputStreamReader(System.in);
      BufferedReader br=new BufferedReader(IR);
      System.out.println("Enter String");
      String s=br.readLine();
      System.out.println("Enter character which you want to replace");
      char ch1=br.readLine().charAt(0);
      System.out.println("Enter character from which you want to replace");
      char ch2=br.readLine().charAt(0);
      Joystring(s,ch1,ch2);
      System.out.println("Enter string");
      String s1=br.readLine();
      Joystring(s1);
      System.out.println("Enter two strings");
      String s3=br.readLine();
      String s4=br.readLine();
      Joystring(s3,s4);
    }
}
```

12. A special two-digit number is such that when the sum of its digits is added to the product of its digits, the result is equal to the original two-digit number.

e.g. consider the number 59

Sum of digits = 5 + 9 = 14; Product of its digits = 5 × 9 = 45

Sum of the sum of digits and product of digits = 14 + 45 = 59

Write a program to accept a two-digit number. Add the sum of its digits to the product of its digits. If the value is equal to the number input, output the message "Special 2-digit number" otherwise, output the message "Not a special 2-digit number". ***ICSE 2014***

Ans

```
import java.io.*;
class Special
```

```
{
    int num, sum=0, pro=1, fs=0;
    void accept() throws IOException
    {
        InputStreamReader IR=new InputStreamReader(System.in);
        BufferedReader br=new BufferedReader(IR);
        System.out.println("Enter any two digit number:");
        num=Integer.parseInt(br.readLine());
    }
    void compute()
    {
        int digit, n=num;
        while(num!=0)
        {
            digit=num % 10;
            sum=sum + digit;
            pro=pro * digit;
            num=num/10;
        }
        fs=sum + pro;
        if(fs==n)
        {
            System.out.println("Special 2-digit number");
        }
        else
        {
            System.out.println("Not a special 2-digit number");
        }
    }
    public static void main(String[] args) throws IOException
    {
        Special sp = new Special();
        sp.accept();
        sp.compute();
    }
}
```

13. Design a class to overload a function area( ) as follows *ICSE 2014*

(i) double area (double a, double b, double c) with three double arguments, returns the area of a scalene triangle using the formula

$$\text{Area} = \sqrt{s(s-a)(s-b)(s-c)}$$

where $s = (a + b + c) / 2$

(ii) double area (int a, int b, int height) with three integer arguments, returns the area of a trapezium using the formula

area = 1/2 * height (a + b)

(iii) double area (double diagonal1, double diagonal2) with two double arguments, returns the area of a rhombus using the formula

area = 1/2 * (diagonal1 * diagonal2)

Ans

```
class Overloadfunction
{
    double area(double a, double b, double c)
    {
        double s, r;
        s=(a + b + c)/2;
        r=s*(s - a)*(s - b)*(s - c);
        double ar=Math.sqrt(r);
        return ar;
    }
    double area(int a, int b, int height)
```

```
        {
            double ar=(height * (a + b))/2;
            return ar;
        }
        double area(double diagonal1, double diagonal2)
        {
            double ar=(diagonal1 * diagonal2)/2;
            return ar;
        }
        public static void main(String[] args)
        {
            Overloadfunction ofn=new Overloadfunction();
            ofn.area(2.5, 3.2, 1.2);
            ofn.area(10, 20, 5);
            ofn.area(20, 30);
        }
}
```

14. Design a class to overload a function series() as follows *ICSE 2013*

(i) double series (double n) with one double argument and returns the sum of the series.

$$\text{sum} = \frac{1}{1} + \frac{1}{2} + \frac{1}{3} + \ldots + \frac{1}{n}$$

(ii) double series (double a, double n) with two double arguments and returns the sum of the series.

$$\text{sum} = \frac{1}{a^2} + \frac{4}{a^5} + \frac{7}{a^8} + \frac{10}{a^{11}} + \ldots + n \text{ terms}$$

Ans

```
import java.io.*;
class seriesofsum
{
    public static double series(double n)
    {
        double sum = 0.0;
        int terms = (int) (Math.round(n));
        for(int i = 1; i <= terms; i++)
        {
            double term = 1.00/(double) i;
            sum += term;
        }
        return sum;
    }
    public static double series(double a, double n)
    {
        double sum = 0.0;
        int terms = (int) (Math.round(n));
        double nr = 1.0, dr = 2.0;
        for(int i = 1; i <= terms; i++)
        {
            double term = nr/(Math.pow(a, dr));
            sum += term;
            nr += 3.0;
            dr += 3.0;
        }
        return sum;
    }
    public static void main(String[] args) throws IOException
    {
        InputStreamReader IR = new InputStreamReader(System.in);
        BufferedReader br = new BufferedReader(IR);
```

```
            System.out.println("Enter a and n : ");
            double a = Double.parseDouble(br.readLine());
            double n = Double.parseDouble(br.readLine());
            seriesofsum ss = new seriesofsum();
            double sum1 = ss.series(n);
            System.out.println("sum1 : " + sum1);
            double sum2 = ss.series(a, n);
            System.out.println("sum2 : " + sum2);
        }
    }
```

Output
Enter a and n :
1.1
5
sum1 : 2.283333333333333
sum2 : 13.503928535489445

Common Mistake One common mistake for designing a Java class to overload the function series() is forgetting to properly implement the function for the second overloaded version. In this case, the first overloaded version is straightforward and calculates the sum of a series based on a single input value. However, the second overloaded version has a more complex formula that involves both input values a and n. Therefore, it is important to ensure that the function is implemented correctly with the appropriate formula to calculate the sum of the series up to n terms.

---

15. Design a class to overload a function polygon() as follows

(i) void polygon(int n, char ch)
with one integer argument and one character type argument that draws a filled square of side n using the character stored in ch.

(ii) void polygon(int x, int y)
two integer arguments that draws filled rectangle of length x and breadth y, using the symbol '@'.

(iii) void polygon()
with no argument that draws a filled triangle shown below. ***ICSE 2012***

```
*
* *
* * *
```

Ans

```
class Poly
{
    public static void polygon(int n, char ch)
    {
        System.out.println("Overloaded method 1");
        for(int i = 1; i <= n; i++)
        {
            printChar(ch, n);
            System.out.println();
        }
    }
    public static void polygon(int n, int y)
    {
        System.out.println("Overloaded method 2");
        for(int i = 1; i <= n; i++)
        {
            printChar('@', y);
            System.out.println();
        }
```

```
    }
    public static void polygon()
    {
       System.out.println("Overloaded method 3");
       for(int i = 1; i <= 3; i++)
       {
          printChar('*', i);
          System.out.println();
       }
    }
    public static void printChar(char ch, int n)
    {
       for(int i=1; i <= n; i++)
          System.out.print(ch);
    }
    public static void main(String[] args) throws IOException
    {
       Poly ss=new Poly();
       ss.polygon(2, '0');
       ss.polygon(2, 5);
       ss.polygon();
    }
}
```

Output

Overloaded method 1
OO
Overloaded method 2
@@@@@
@@@@@
Overloaded method 3
*
* *
* * *

16. Define a class called mobike with the following description *ICSE 2011*

Instance variables/data members	
`int bno`	to store the bike's number
`int phno`	to store the phone number of the customer
`String name`	to store the name of the customer
`int days`	to store the number of days the bike is taken on rent
`int charge`	to calculate and store the rental charge
Member methods	
`void input()`	to input and store the details of the customer
`void compute()`	to compute the rental charge The rent for a mobike is charged on the following basis First five days Rs. 500 per day. Next five days Rs. 400 per day. Rest of the days Rs. 200 per day.
`void display()`	to display the details in the following format Bike No. Phone No. Name No. of days Charge ....

Ans

```
import java.io.*;
class mobike
{
    int bno, phno, days, charge;
```

```
    String name;
    public void input() throws IOException
    {
       InputStreamReader IR=new InputStreamReader(System.in);
       BufferedReader br=new BufferedReader(IR);
       System.out.println("Enter bike number, phone, days and name:");
       bno=Integer.parseInt(br.readLine());
       phno=Integer.parseInt(br.readLine());
       days=Integer.parseInt(br.readLine());
       name=br.readLine();
    }
    public void compute()
    {
       charge=0;
       int n500, n400, n200;
       n500=(days>5)?5:days;
       n400=(days>10)?5:((days>5)?(days-5):0);
       n200=(days>10)?(days-10):0;
       charge=(n500*500)+(n400*400)+(n200*200);
    }
    public void display()
    {
       System.out.println("Bike No. Phone No. Name No. of Days Charge");
       printInt(bno, 8 + 1);
       printInt(phno, 9 + 1);
       System.out.print(name+"\t");
       printInt(days, 11 + 1);
       printInt(charge, 6);
       System.out.println();
    }
    public static void printInt(int n, int width)
    {
       String s=" " + n;
       int spaces=width-s.length();
       System.out.print(n);
       while(spaces > 0)
       {
          System.out.print(" ");
          spaces--;
       }
    }
    public static void main(String[] args) throws IOException
    {
       mobike m1=new mobike();
       mobike m2=new mobike();
       mobike m3=new mobike();
       m1.input();
       m1.compute();
       m1.display();
       m2.input();
       m2.compute();
       m2.display();
       m3.input();
       m3.compute();
       m3.display();
    }
}
```

Output

Enter bike number, phone, days and name : 1234 22226 4 John

Bike No.	Phone No.	Name	No. of Days	Charge
1234	2222	John	4	2000

Enter bike number, phone, days and name : 2001 22228 9 John

Bike No.	Phone No.	Name	No. of Days	Charge
2001	22228	John	9	4100

Enter bike number, phone, days and name : 3400 22232 10 John

Bike No.	Phone No.	Name	No. of Days	Charge
3400	22232	John	10	5300

17. Design a class to overload a function compare( ) as follows *ICSE 2011*

(i) void compare(int, int) to compare two integer values and print the greater of the two integers.

(ii) void compare(char, char) to compare the numeric value of two characters and print the character with higher numeric value.

(iii) void compare(String, String) to compare the length of the two strings and print the longer of the two.

Ans

```
import java.io.*;
class CompareString
{
    public void compare(int a, int b)
    {
      if(a>b)
         System.out.println(a);
      else
         System.out.println(b);
    }
    public void compare(char ch1, char ch2)
    {
      if(ch1>ch2)
         System.out.println(ch1);
      else
         System.out.println(ch2);
    }
    public void compare(String s1, String s2)
    {
      if(s1.length()>s2.length())
      {
         System.out.println(s1);
      }
      else
      {
         System.out.println(s2);
      }
    }
    public static void main(String[] args)
    {
      CompareString cs = new CompareString();
      cs.compare(3, 4);
      cs.compare(5, 4);
      cs.compare('A', 'a');
      cs.compare('b', 'B');
      cs.compare("Hello", "Everyone");
      cs.compare("Good Night", "Everyone");
    }
}
```

Output
4
5
a
b
Everyone
Good Night

Concept Enhancer The concept of overloading a function in Java allows us to define methods with the same name but with different input parameters. The method selected to execute is determined by the number, type, and order of arguments passed to it.

18. Design a class to overload a function num_calc() as follows *ICSE 2009*

(i) void num_calc(int num, char ch) with one integer argument and one character argument, computes the square of integer argument if choice ch is 's' otherwise finds its cube.

(ii) void num_calc(int a, int b, char ch) with two integer arguments and one character argument. It computes the product of integer arguments if ch is 'p' else adds the integers.

(iii) void num_calc(String s1, String s2) with two string arguments, which prints whether the strings are equal or not.

Ans

```
class Overloading
{
    public void num_calc(int num, char ch)
    {
      if(ch=='s')
      {
         double square=Math.pow(num, 2);
         System.out.println("Square is "+square);
      }
      else
      {
         double cube=Math.pow(num, 3);
         System.out.println("Cube is "+cube);
      }
    }
    public void num_calc(int a, int b, char ch)
    {
      if(ch=='p')
      {
         int product=a*b;
         System.out.println("Product is "+product);
      }
      else
      {
         int sum=a + b;
         System.out.println("Sum is "+sum);
      }
    }
    public void num_calc(String s1, String s2)
    {
      if(s1.equals(s2))
      {
         System.out.println("Strings are same");
      }
      else
      {
         System.out.println("Strings are not same");
      }
    }
}
```

```
class Match
{
    public static void main(String[] args)
    {
        System.out.println("Strings are matching");
        Overloading m = new Overloading();
        m.num_calc(10, 's');
        m.num_calc(10, 2, 'p');
        m.num_calc("Hello", "Hello");
    }
}
```

Output

Strings are matching
Square is 100.0
Product is 20
Strings are same

19. Write a program to calculate and print the sum of each of the following series

(i) Sum (S) = 2 – 4 + 6 – 8 + ... –20

(ii) Sum (S) = $\frac{x}{2} + \frac{x}{5} + \frac{x}{8} + \frac{x}{11} = \ldots + \frac{x}{20}$ (Value of x to be input by the user). *ICSE 2008*

Ans

```
import java.io.*;
class Series
{
    public static void doseries1()
    {
        int s=0;
        for(int i=2; i<=20; i+=1)
        {
            if(i%4==0)
            {
                s=s-i;
            }
            else if(i%2==0)
            {
                s=s+i;
            }
        }
        System.out.println("Sum 1:" +s);
    }
    public static void doseries2(double x)
    {
        double s=0.0, term, nr;
        int dr;
        nr=x;
        for(dr=2; dr<=20; dr+=3)
        {
            term=nr/(double)dr;
            s+=term;
        }
        System.out.println("Sum 2:" +s);
    }
    public static void main(String[] args) throws IOException
    {
        //user input of x
        InputStreamReader IR=new InputStreamReader(System.in);
        BufferedReader br=new BufferedReader(IR);
        System.out.print("Enter x:");
        double x=Double.parseDouble(br.readLine());
        doseries1();
        doseries2(x);
    }
}
```

Output
Enter x : 1
Sum 1 : –10
Sum 2 : 1.096161191749427

20. Define a class employee having the following description *ICSE 2008*

Data members/Instance variables	
`int pan`	to store personal account number
`String name`	to store name
`double taxincome`	to store annual taxable income
`double tax`	to store tax that is calculated
Member functions	
`input()`	Store the pan number, name, taxable income
`calc()`	Calculate tax for an employee
`display()`	Output details of an employee

Write a program to compute the tax according to the given conditions and display the output as per given format.

Total Annual Taxable Income	Tax Rate
Upto Rs. 1,00,000	No tax
From 1,00,001 to 1,50,000	10% of the income exceeding Rs. 1,00,000
From 1,50,001 to 2,50,000	Rs. 5000 + 20% of the income exceeding Rs. 1,50,000
Above Rs. 2,50,000	Rs. 25000 + 30% of the income exceeding Rs. 2,50,000

Output

Pan Number	Name	Tax-income	Tax
–	–	–	–
–	–	–	–
–	–	–	–
–	–	–	–

Ans

```
import java.io.*;
class employee
{
    int pan;
    String name;
    double taxincome;
    double tax;
    public void input()
    {
      InputStreamReader IR=new InputStreamReader(System.in);
      BufferedReader br=new BufferedReader(IR);
      pan=Integer.parseInt(br.readLine());
      name=br.readLine();
      taxincome=Double.parseDouble(br.readLine());
    }
    public void calc()
    {
      if(taxincome <= 100000)
      {
         tax=0.0;
      }
      else if(taxincome >= 100001 && taxincome <= 150000)
      {
         tax=0.1*(taxincome - 100000);
      }
```

```
        else if(taxincome >= 150001 && taxincome <= 250000)
        {
            tax = 5000 + 0.2*(taxincome - 150000);
        }
        else
        {
            tax=25000 + 0.3*(taxincome - 250000);
        }
    }
    public void display ()
    {
        System.out.println("Pan number"+"\t"+"Name"+"\t"+"Tax-income"+"\t" + "Tax");
        System.out.println(pan + "\t"+"\t" + name + "\t" + taxincome + "\t"+ tax + "\t");
    }
    public static void main(string[] args)
    {
        employee e = new employee ();
        e.input ();
        e.calc();
        e.display();
    }
}
```

Output

20
Smith
456888

Pan number	Name	Tax-income	Tax
20	Smith	456888.0	87066.4

21. Write a class with the name volume using function overloading that computes the volume of a cube, a sphere and a cuboid.

Formula

Volume of a cube (vc) = s*s*s

Volume of a sphere (vs) = 4/3* pi* r* r*r (where pi = 3.14 or 22/7)

Volume of a cuboid (vcd) = l*b*h

ICSE 2008

Ans

```
import java.io.*;
class Volume
{
    public void vol(double s)
    {
        double vc = s*s*s,
        System.out.println("Volume:"+vc);
    }
    public void vol(double r, double pi)
    {
        double vs=4.0/3.0 * pi * Math.pow(r, 3);
        System.out.println("Volume : " +vs);
    }
    public void vol(double l, double b, double h)
    {
        double vcd = l * b * h;
        System.out.println("Volume : " +vcd);
    }
    public static void main(String[] args) throws IOException
    {
        InputStreamReader IR=new InputStreamReader(System.in);
        BufferedReader br=new BufferedReader(IR);
        Volume v=new Volume(); //Object of class volume
        double S, L, B, H, R;
        System.out.println("Enter S of Cube : ");
        S=Double.parseDouble(br.readLine());
        v.vol(S);
```

```
            System.out.println("Enter R of Sphere : ");
            R=Double.parseDouble(br.readLine());
            v.vol(R, 3.14);
            System.out.println("Enter L, B, H of Cuboid : ");
            L=Double.parseDouble(br.readLine());
            B=Double.parseDouble(br.readLine());
            H=Double.parseDouble(br.readLine());
            v.vol(L, B, H);
        }
    }
```

Output

Enter S of Cube :
4
Volume : 64.0
Enter R of Sphere :
2
Volume : 33.493333333333333
Enter L, B, H of Cuboid :
2
3
4
Volume : 24.0

22. Write a program to compute and display the sum of the following series *ICSE 2007*

$$\frac{1+2}{1\times 2}+\frac{1+2+3}{1\times 2\times 3}+\ldots+\frac{1+2+3+4\ldots n}{1\times 2\times 3\times 4\ldots n}$$

Ans

```
import java.io.*;
class Series
{
    public static int getsum(int num)
    {
        int f=0;
        for(int i=1; i<=num; i++)
        {
            f=f+i;
        return f;
    }
    public static int getmul(int num)
    {
        int f=1;
        for(int i=1; i<=num; i++)
        {
            f=f*i;
        }
        return f;
    }
    public static void main(String[] args) throws IOException
    {
        InputStreamReader IR=new InputStreamReader(System.in);
        BufferedReader br=new BufferedReader(IR);
        System.out.println("Enter the value of n");
        int n=Integer.parseInt(br.readLine());
        float sum=0;
        int i;
        float term1, term2;
        for(i=2; i<=n; i++)
        {
            term1=(float)getsum(i);
            term2=(float)getmul(i);
            sum+=term1/term2;
        }
        System.out.println("Sum=" +sum);
    }
}
```

Output : Enter the value of n

10

Sum=3.0774229

23. Define a class salary described as below

Data Members Name, Address, Phone, Subject, MonthlySalary, Incometax.

Member methods (i) To accept the details of a teacher including the monthly salary.

(ii) To display the details of the teacher.

(iii) To compute the annual Income Tax as 5% of the annual salary above Rs. 1,75,000/.

Write a main method to create object of a class and call the above member methods. ***ICSE 2007***

Ans

```
import java.io.*;
import java.lang.*;
class salary
{
    String Name, Address;
    long Phone;
    String Subject;
    int MonthlySalary;
    double IncomeTax;
    public void accept() throws Exception
    {
      InputStreamReader IR=new InputStreamReader(System.in);
      BufferedReader br=new BufferedReader(IR);
      System.out.println("Enter the name : ");
      this.Name=br.readLine();
      System.out.println("Enter the address : ");
      this.Address=br.readLine();
      System.out.println("Enter the phone : ");
      this.Phone=Integer.parseInt(br.readLine());
      System.out.println("Enter the subject : ");
      this.Subject=br.readLine();
      System.out.println("Enter the monthly salary : ");
      this.MonthlySalary=Integer.parseInt(br.readLine());
    }
    public void display()
    {
      System.out.println("DISPLAY");
      System.out.println("Name : " +this.Name);
      System.out.println("Address : " +this.Address);
      System.out.println("Phone : " +this.Phone);
      System.out.println("Subject : " +this.Subject);
      System.out.println("Monthly Income : " +this.MonthlySalary);
      System.out.println("Income Tax : " +this.IncomeTax);
    }
    public void compute()
    {
      int annualSalary=this.MonthlySalary * 12;
      double taxRate=(annualSalary > 175000) ? 5.0 : 0.0;
      double tax=(annualSalary - 175000) * taxRate/100;
      this.IncomeTax=tax;
    }
    //main method
```

```
    public static void main(String[] args)throws Exception
    {
      salary s=new salary();
      s.accept();
      s.compute();
      s.display();
    }
}
```

Output

Enter the name :
SMITH
Enter the address :
India
Enter the phone :
0965898979
Enter the subject :
Computer Application
Enter the monthly salary :
1000000
DISPLAY
Name : SMITH
Address : India
Phone : 0965898979
Subject : Computer Application
Monthly Income : 1000000
Income Tax : 591250.0

24. Write a program using a function called area() to compute the area of a *ICSE 2005*

(i) circle ($\pi * r^2$), where $\pi = 3.14$
(ii) square (side * side)
(iii) rectangle (length * breadth)

Display the menu to output the area as per user's choice.

Ans

```
import java.io.*;
class Area
{
    public static void main(String[] args)
    {
      char menuOption = ' ';
      double radius, side, length, breadth;
      do
      {
        menuOption = askMenuOption();
        switch(menuOption)
        {
          case 'R' :      //Rectangle
            length = askDouble("Enter the length : ");
            breadth = askDouble("Enter the breadth : ");
            area(length, breadth);
            break;
          case 'S' :      //Square
            side = askDouble("Enter the side : ");
            area(side, side);
            break;
          case 'C' :      //Circle
            radius = askDouble("Enter the radius : ");
```

```
                area(radius);  //overloaded function #2
                break;
            case 'X' :
                System.out.println("Exiting program. Thank you ! ");
                break;
            default:
                System.out.println("Incorrect option. Try again...");
        }
    }while(menuOption != 'X');
  }
  //Ask user to enter menu option.
  //If invalid option, ask to enter again.
  //Return the option selected.
  public static char askMenuOption() throws Exception
  {
    InputStreamReader IR=new InputStreamReader(System.in);
    BufferedReader br=new BufferedReader(IR);
    char option=' ';
    System.out.println("Enter R-Rectangle, S-Square, C-Circle,
    X-Exit : ");
    option=(char)br.read();
    return option;
  }
  public static double askDouble(String prompt)
  {
    InputStreamReader IR=new InputStreamReader(System.in);
    BufferedReader br=new BufferedReader(IR);
    System.out.println(prompt);
    double d=Double.parseDouble(br.readLine());
    return d;
  }
  public static void area(double length, double breadth)
  {
    System.out.println("Area : " +(length * breadth));
  }
  public static void area(double radius)
  {
    System.out.println("Area : " +(3.14 * Math.pow(radius, 2)));
  }
}
```

Output

Enter R-Rectangle, S-Square, C-Circle, X-Exit : T
Incorrect option. Try again...
Enter R-Rectangle, S-Square, C-Circle, X-Exit : R
Enter the length : 4
Enter the breadth : 5
Area : 20.0
Enter R-Rectangle, S-Square, C-Circle, X-Exit : S
Enter the radius: 2.0
Area : 4.0
Enter R-Rectangle, S-Square, C-Circle, X-Exit : C
Enter the radius 2.0
Area : 12.56
Enter R-Rectangle, S-Square, C-Circle, X-Exit : X
Exiting program. Thank you !

CHAPTER TEST

1 Mark Questions

1. What makes the two or more functions having the same name different?
(a) Number of arguments (b) Type of arguments (c) Return type (d) Both (a) and (b)

2. Which of the following is a correct prototype of a function check which receives a character ch and integer n and returns true or false.
(a) `pubic int check (char ch,int n);`
(b) `public boolean check (char ch, int n);`
(c) `public boolean check (char ch, integer n);`
(d) `public boolean check (char ch, int n);`

3. void math(int i, int j)
Type of argument passing in the above statement.
(a) Passing argument by integer (b) Passing argument by reference
(c) Passing argument by interchange y (d) None of these

2 Marks Questions

4. When will you define a method as static?

5. Define a function. What is meant by function prototype?

6. When a function returns the value, the entire function call can be assigned to a variable. Do you agree with the statement?

15 Marks Questions

7. Define a class Salary as under
Data Members
Name, Address, Phone, Subject-Specialisation, Monthly Salary, Income Tax
Member methods
(i) To accept the details of a teacher including the monthly salary
(ii) To display the details of the teacher
(iii) To compute the annual income tax as 5% of the annual salary above 1,75,000/-

8. Write a program to input a number. Use a function int Armstrong (int n) to accept the number. The function returns 1, if the number is Armstrong, otherwise zero (0).
Sample input: 153
Sample Output: 153 $\Rightarrow 1^3 + 5^3 + 3^3 = 153$
It is an Armstrong Number.

04

Constructors

TREND ANALYSIS 3 YEARS

Average No. of Questions Across all Sets

	Types of Questions	2023	2019	2018
Constructors	1 Mark	1	–	–
	2 Marks	–	–	1
	15 Marks	–	1	–

It has the same name as the name of the class to which it belongs. Constructor's syntax does not include a return type, since constructors never return a value. It may include parameters of various types. It is used to initialise the property of an object.

Characteristics of Constructor

The characteristics of constructor are as follows:

- They are invoked directly when an object is created.
- They cannot be inherited, through a derived class, can call the base class constructor.
- Constructor cannot be friend function.
- They cannot be used in union.
- They make implicit calls to the operators new and delete when memory allocation is required.

Uses of Constructor

The uses of constructor are as follows:

(i) Constructors are used to initialize the instances of classes.

(ii) You can use a constructor to create new objects often with parameters specifying the initial state about the object.

Types of Constructors

Constructors have different types and these are:

Default Constructor

It is the no argument constructor that is automatically created by compiler in the absence of explicit constructor.

e.g.
```
public class Smart
{
  public Smart()
  {
    System.out.println("Default
                                constructor");
  }
  public static void main(String[] args)
  {
    Smart sc=new Smart();
  }
}
```

Parameterised Constructor

These constructors are required to pass parameters on creation of objects.

e.g.
```
public class Smart
{
  private String name;
```

```
    public Smart(String str)
    {
      this.name=str;
      System.out.println("The parameterised
                              constructor" +str);
    }
    public static void main(String args[])
    {
      Smart sc=new Smart("Aaliya");
    }
  }
```

Constructor with Default Arguments

It is possible to define constructors with default arguments.

e.g. `complex(float real, float imag=0);`

The default argument imag is zero.

Constructor Overloading

Constructor overloading is the way of having more than one constructors, which do different-different tasks. In other words, constructor overloading in Java allows to have more than one constructor inside one class. The number of parameters can be same but it can have different data types.

e.g.

```
public class Smart
{
  public Smart()
  {
    //statement
  }
  public Smart(int i)
  {
    //statement
  }
  public Smart(String str)
  {
    //statement
  }
  public static void main(String args[])
  {
    Smart s=New Smart();
    Smart ss=New Smart(10);
    Smart st=New Smart("java");
  }
}
```

Using this( ) with a Constructor

The this( ) can be used to invoke another constructor in the same class. Also, this constructor can be used to implement local chaining of constructors in a class.

The this( ) call in a constructor invokes an other constructor with the corresponding parameter list within the same class. This approach, is better if you have many constructor in the class and want to reuse the constructor.

e.g.

```
class Student
{
  int id;
  String name;
  Student()
  {
    System.out.println("default
                          constructor");
  }
  Student(int id, String name)
  {
    this();
    this.id=id;
    this.name=name;
  }
  void display()
  {
    System.out.println(id + " " +name);
  }
  public static void main(String args[])
  {
    Student e1=new Student(111, "Karan");
    Student e2=new Student(222, "Arjun");
    e1.display();
    e2.display();
  }
}
```

Output

default constructor
default constructor
111 Karan
222 Arjun

Difference between Constructor and Method

Difference between constructor and method are as follows :

Constructor	Method
(i) It should not have any return type.	(i) It should have return type.
(ii) It will be called automatically whenever object is created.	(ii) It should be called explicitly either with object reference or class reference.
(iii) Constructor must be class name.	(iii) Method can be any user defined name.
(iv) The Java compiler provides a default constructor, if we do not have any constructor.	(iv) Method is not provided by compiler in any case.

PYQs Previous Years Questions

1 Mark Questions

1. The method which has same name as that of the class name. **ICSE 2023**

Ans Constructor

2. A method with the same name as of the class and with arguments and no return data type is termed as **ICSE SQP 2023**

   (a) parameterized constructor
   (b) default constructor
   (c) non-parameterized constructor
   (d) wrapper class method

Ans (a) parameterized constructor

3. The concept of having more than one constructor with different types of parameters. **ICSE 2022 (Sem I)**

   (a) Copy constructor
   (b) Method overloading
   (c) Constructor overloading
   (d) Overloaded methods

Ans (c) Constructor overloading

4. Java compiler automatically creates a default constructor, in case no constructor is present in the Java class . **ICSE 2022 (Sem I)**

   (a) True (b) False

Ans (a) True

5. The method with the same name as of the class and which does not have a return data type is called as **ICSE SQP 2022 (Sem I)**

   (a) constructor (b) function
   (c) method

Ans (a) constructor

6. The statement to stop the execution of a construct. **ICSE SQP 2022 (Sem I)**

   (a) System.exit(0) (b) break
   (c) STOP

Ans (b) break

2 Marks Questions

1. Explain the concept of constructor overloading with an example. **ICSE SQP 2020, 2017, SQP 2016, 2011**

Ans Constructor overloading is the concept to make constructor with same name of class and using different signature. A class can have more than one constructors.

Example of constructor overloading

```
class Age
{
    int age; //variable declaration
    public Age()              //Constructor 1
    {
      age = -1;
    }
    public Age(int age)       //Constructor 2
    {
      this.age = age;
    }
    public static void main(String[] args)
    {
      Age a1 = new Age();
                           //Calling constructor 1
      Age a2 = new Age(20);
                           //Calling constructor 2
    }
}
```

2. State two features of a constructor. **ICSE 2018, 10**

Or

Write two characteristics of a constructor.

Ans There are two features of a constructor

   (i) A constructor does not have any return type
   (ii) A constructor automatically called whenever object is created.

3. What is parameterised constructor? **ICSE 2016**

Ans Parameterised constructors are required to pass parameters on creation of objects. Unlike default constructor which does not have any parameters, it is however possible to have one or more parameters in a constructor.

Sample (int a, int b) is a parameterised constructor in which Sample is a class name and a, b are arguments.

4. Name the two types of constructor. **ICSE 2015**

Ans Two types of constructor are

   (i) Default constructor
   (ii) Parameterised constructor

5. What is constructor? When is it invoked? **ICSE 2014**

Ans Constructor in Java is a block of code, which is executed at the time of object creation. It has the same name as the name of the class to which it belongs. It never returns a value.

6. Differentiate between constructor and function. **ICSE 2017; ICSE SQP 2017**

Or

Give a difference between a constructor and a method. **ICSE 2013**

Or

State the difference between constructor and method. **ICSE 2005**

Ans Difference between constructor and method (function) are as follows

Constructor	Method (Function)
It has no return type.	It has a return type.
Constructor name should be same as the class name.	Method name can be any valid identifier.
Constructor is automatically called upon object creation.	Method are invoked explicitly.

7. Create a class with one integer instance variable. Initialize the variable using
(i) default constructor
(ii) parameterized constructor **ICSE 2012**

Ans (i)
```
class Books
{
  int que;
  public Books()   //default constructor
  {
    System.out.println("Computer
                          Application");
    que=0;
  }
  public static void main(String[] args)
  {
    Books bs=new Books();
    System.out.println("Question="
                             +bs.que);
  }
}
```
Output Computer Application
Question = 0

(ii)
```
class Books1
{
  int que1;
  public Books1(int que1)
                //parameterised constructor
  {
    this.que1 = que1;
  }
  public static void main(String[] args)
  {
    Books1 bs1 = new Books1(40);
    System.out.println("Questions
                          =" +bs1.que1);
  }
}
```
Output Questions = 40

8. Why do we need a constructor as a class member? **ICSE 2007**

Ans A constructor is like a method with no return type. We need a constructor as a class type to create objects and to initialise value for an instance variable.

9. What is a default constructor? **ICSE 2006**

Ans The default constructor automatically initializes all instance variables to zero. When we do not explicitly define a constructor for a class, then Java creates a default constructor for that class.

4 Marks Question

1. Enter any two variables through constructor parameters and write a program to swap and print the values. **ICSE 2005**

Ans
```
class point
{
    int x, y;     //instance variables
    public point(int a, int b)
                      // parameterised constructor
    {
      this.x = a;
      this.y = b;
    }
    public void swap()
    {
      int temp = x;
      x = y;
      y = temp;
    }
    public void display()
    {
      System.out.println("Point = ("+x+",
                                "+y+")");
    }
    public static void main(String[] args)
    {
      point p = new point(3, 4);
      p.display();  //value before swapping
      p.swap();
      p.display();
                  //value after swapping
    }
}
```
Output Point = (3, 4)
Point = (4, 3)

15 Marks Questions

1. Design a class name **ShowRoom** with the following description

Instance variables/Data members:	
String name	To store the name of the customer
long mobno	To store the mobile number of the customer
double cost	To store the cost of the items purchased
double dis	To store the discount amount
double amount	To store the amount to be paid after discount
Member methods:	
ShowRoom( )	default constructor to initialize data members
void input( )	To input customer name, mobile number, cost
void calculate( )	To calculate discount on the cost of purchased items, based on following criteria
void display( )	To display customer name, mobile number, amount to be paid after discount

Cost	Discount (in percentage)
Less than or equal to ₹ 10000	5%
More than ₹ 10000 and less than or equal to ₹ 20000	10%
More than ₹ 20000 and less than or equal to ₹ 35000	15%
More than ₹ 35000	20%

Write a main method to create an object of the class and call the above member methods.

ICSE 2019

Ans

```
import java.io.*;
public class ShowRoom
{
      String name;
      long mobno;
      double cost, dis, amount;
      ShowRoom()
      {
         name="";
         mobno=0.0;
         cost=0.0;
         dis=0.0;
         amount=0.0;
      }
      void input() throws IOException
      {
         InputStreamReader IR= new InputStreamReader(System.in);
         BufferedReader br=new BufferedReader(IR);
         System.out.println("Enter Customer Name:");
         name=br.readLine();
         System.out.println("Enter Customer Mobile no.:");
         mobno=Long.parseLong(br.readLine());
         System.out.println("Enter Cost:");
         cost=Double.parseDouble(br.readLine());
      }
      void calculate()
```

```
    {
        if(cost<=10000)
            dis=(5*cost)/100;
        else if(cost>10000 && cost<=20000)
            dis=(10*cost)/100;
        else if(cost>20000 && cost<=35000)
            dis=(15*cost)/100;
        else
            dis=(20*cost)/100;
        amount=cost-dis;
    }
    void display()
    {
        System.out.println("Customer name:"+name);
        System.out.println("Customer mobile no.:"+mobno);
        System.out.println("Amount after discount:"+amount);
    }
    public static void main(String args[]) throws IOException
    {
        ShowRoom SR=new ShowRoom();
        SR.input();
        SR.calculate();
        SR.display();
    }
}
```

2. Define a class taximeter having the following description **ICSE SQP 2017**

Data members/instance variables	
int taxino	to store taxi number
String name	to store passenger's name
int km	to store number of kilometers travelled
Member functions	
taximeter()	constructor to initialize taxino to 0, name to " " and b to 0.
input()	to store taxino, name, km
calculate()	to calculate bill for a customer according to given conditions

kilometers travelled (km)	Rate/km
≤ 1 km	Rs 25
$1 < km \le 6$	Rs 10
$6 < km \le 12$	Rs 15
$12 < km \le 18$	Rs 20
> 18 km	Rs 25

display()	To display the details in the following format Taxino Name Kilometres travelled Bill amount – – – –

Create an object in the main method and call all the above methods in it.

Ans

```
import java.util.*;
public class taximeter
{
    int taxino;
```

```
    String name;
    int km;
    int b;
    taximeter()
    {
      taxino=0;
      name="";
      km=0;
      b=0;
    }
    void input()
    {
      Scanner sc=new Scanner(System.in);
      System.out.println("Enter the Taxi number ");
         taxino=sc.nextInt();
      System.out.println("Enter the name ");
         name=sc.nextLine();
      System.out.println("Enter the distance travelled ");
         km=sc.nextInt();
    }
    void calculate()
    {
      if(km<=1)
         b=25;
      if(km>1 && km<=6)
         b=km*10;
      if(km>6 && km<=12)
         b=km*15;
      if(km>12 && km<=18)
         b=km*20;
      if(km>18)
         b=km*25;
    }
    void display()
    {
      System.out.println("Taxino  Name  Kilometres travelled  Bill amount ");
      System.out.println(taxino+"  "+name+"  "+km+"  "+b+"  ");
    }
    public static void main (String args[])
    {
      taximeter ob= new taximeter ();
      ob.input();
      ob.calculate();
      ob.display();
    }
}
```

Output:

Enter the Taxi number 632

Enter the name Amit

Enter the distance travelled 20

Taxino	Name	Kilometres travelled	Bill amount
632	Amit	20	500

Common Mistake Most student appeared confused in constructor and class name and done mistake on bill amount conditions which is given in the question.

3. Define a class named **movieMagic** with the following description

Instance variables/data members	
`int year`	to store the year of release of a movie
`String title`	to store the title of the movie
`float rating`	to store the popularity rating of the movie (minimum rating = 0.0 and maximum rating = 5.0)
Member methods	
`movieMagic()`	Default constructor to initialize numeric data members to 0 and String data member to " ".
`void accept()`	To input and store year, title and rating.
`void display()`	To display the title of a movie and a message based on the rating as per the table below.

Rating	Message to be Displayed
0.0 to 2.0	Flop
2.1 to 3.4	Semi-hit
3.5 to 4.5	Hit
4.6 to 5.0	Super Hit

Write a main method to create an object of the class and call the above member methods.

ICSE 2014

Ans

```
import java.io.*;
class movieMagic
{
    int year;
    String title;
    float rating;
    public movieMagic()                //constructor
    {
      year = 0;
      title = " ";
      rating = 0.0;
    }
    public void accept() throws IOException     //method 1
    {
      InputStreamReader IR=new InputStreamReader(System.in);
      BufferedReader br=new BufferedReader(IR);
      System.out.println("Enter title : ");
      title=br.readLine();
      System.out.println("Enter year : ");
      year=Integer.parseInt(br.readLine());
      System.out.println("Enter rating : ");
      rating = Float.parseFloat(br.readLine());
    }
    public void display()          //method 2
    {
      String message = " ";
      System.out.println("Title : " + title);
      if(rating >= 0.0F && rating <= 2.0F) message = "Flop";
      else if(rating >= 2.1F && rating <= 3.4F) message = "Semi-Hit";
      else if(rating >= 3.5F && rating <= 4.5F) message = "Hit";
      else if(rating >= 4.6F && rating <= 5.0F) message = "Super-Hit";
      System.out.println("Result : " + message);
    }
    public static void main(String[] args) throws IOException
```

```
    {
      movieMagic obj=new movieMagic();
      obj.accept();
      obj.display();
    }
}
```

Output
Enter title : Rockstar
Enter year : 2013
Enter rating : 2.5
Result : Semi-Hit

4. Define a class named **FruitJuice** with the following description

Instance variables/data members	
`int product_code`	stores the product code number
`String flavour`	stores the flavour of the juice (e.g. orange, apple, etc.)
`String pack_type`	stores the type of packaging (e.g. tetra-pack, PET bottle, etc.)
`int pack_size`	stores package size (e.g. 200 ml, 400 ml, etc.)
`int product_price`	stores the price of the product
Member methods	
`FruitJuice()`	Default constructor to initialize integer data members to 0 and String data members to " ".
`void input()`	To input and store the product code, flavour, pack type, pack size and product price.
`void discount()`	To reduce the product price by 10.
`void display()`	To display the product code, flavour, pack type, pack size and product price.

Write a main method to create an object of the class and call the above member methods.

ICSE 2013

Ans
```
import java.io.*;
class FruitJuice
{
    int product_code;
    String flavour;
    String pack_type;
    int pack_size, product_price;
    public FruitJuice()
    {
      product_code=0;
      flavour=" ";
      pack_type=" ";
      pack_size=0;
      product_price=0;
    }
    public void input() throws IOException
    {
      InputStreamReader IR=new InputStreamReader(System.in);
      BufferedReader br=new BufferedReader(IR);
      System.out.println("Enter Product code, Flavour, Pack Type, Pack Size and
                                                              Product Price");
      product_code=Integer.parseInt(br.readLine());
      flavour=br.readLine();
      pack_type=br.readLine();
      pack_size=Integer.parseInt(br.readLine());
      product_price=Integer.parseInt(br.readLine());
    }
    public void discount()
```

```
    {
        product_price=product_price-10;
    }
    public void display()
    {
        System.out.println("Product code : " + product_code);
        System.out.println("Flavour : " + flavour);
        System.out.println("Pack type : " + pack_type);
        System.out.println("Pack size : " + pack_size);
        System.out.println("Product Price : " + product_price);
    }
    public static void main(String[] args) throws IOException
    {
        FruitJuice f=new FruitJuice();
        f.input();
        f.display();
        System.out.println("After Discount");
        f.discount();
        f.display();
    }
}
```

Output

Enter Product code, Flavour, Pack Type, Pack
Size and Product Price
10
Mango flavour
Short pack type
200
20
Product code : 10
Flavour : Mango flavour
Pack type : Short pack type
Pack size : 200
Product price : 20
After Discount
Product code : 10
Flavour : Mango flavour
Pack type : Short pack type
Pack size : 200
Product price : 10

5. Define a class called Library with the following description **ICSE 2013**

Instance variables/data members	
`int acc_num`	stores the accession number of the book
`String title`	stores the title of the book
`String author`	stores the name of the author
Member methods	
`void input()`	To input and store the accession number, title and author.
`void compute()`	To accept the number of days late, calculate the display the fine charged at the rate of Rs. 2 per day.
`void display()`	To display the details in the following format
	Accession Number
	Title Author

Write a main method to create an object of the class and call the above member methods.

Ans
```
import java.io.*;
class Library
{
    int acc_num;
    String title, author;
    public Library()                    //Constructor
    {
      acc_num=0;
      title=" ";
      author=" ";
    }
    public void input() throws IOException //Input method
    {
      InputStreamReader IR=new InputStreamReader(System.in);
      BufferedReader br=new BufferedReader(IR);
      System.out.println("Enter the Accession Number :");
      acc_num=Integer.parseInt(br.readLine());
      System.out.println("Enter the title : ");
      title=br.readLine();
      System.out.println("Enter the Author : ");
      author=br.readLine();
    }
    public void compute(int nDays)
    {
      int fine=nDays * 2;
      System.out.println("Fine charged : " +fine);
    }
    public void display()
    {
      printInt(acc_num, 16 + 1);
      printStr(title, 30 + 1);
      printStr(author, 20);
      System.out.println();
    }
    //Static method to print the header once only
    public static void displayHeader()
    {
      printStr("Accession Number ", 16 + 1);
      printStr("Title", 30 + 1);
      printStr("Author", 20);
      System.out.println();
      printStr(" ", 16 + 1);
      printStr(" ", 30 + 1);
      printStr(" ", 20);
      System.out.println();
    }
    public static void printInt(int n, int width)
    {
      String s = " " + n;
      printStr(s, width); //Call the string method
    }
    public static void printStr(String s, int width)
    {
      System.out.print(s);
      for(int i=s.length() + 1; i <= width; i++)
         System.out.print(" ");
    }
    public static void main(String[] args) throws IOException
    {
      Library book1=new Library();
```

```
        Library book2=new Library();
        book1.input();
        book2.input();
        book1.compute(5);
        book2.compute(7);
        Library.displayHeader();
        book1.display();
        book2.display();
    }
}
```

Output

Enter the Accession Number : 101
Enter the title : Computer Application
Enter the Author : Alistair
Enter the Accession number : 110
Enter the title : Java
Enter the Author : Robert
Fine charged : 10
Fine charged : 14

Accession Number	Title	Author
101	Computer Application	Alistair
110	Java	Robert

6. Define a class Student described as below

Data members/instance variables

name, age, m1, m2, m3 (marks in 3 subjects), maximum, average

Member methods

(i) A parameterized constructor to initialize the data numbers.
(ii) To accept the details of a student.
(iii) To compute the average and the maximum out of three marks.
(iv) To display the name, age, marks in three subjects, maximum and average.

Write a main method to create an object of a class and call the above member methods.

ICSE 2010

Ans

```
import java.io.*;
class Student
{
    String name;
    int age;
    int m1, m2, m3;
    int maximum;
    double average;
    public Student()
    {
    }
    public Student(String n, int a, int marks1, int marks2,
                                int marks3, int max, double avg)
    {
      name = n;
      age = a;
      m1 = marks1;
      m2 = marks2;
      m3 = marks3;
      maximum = max;
      average = avg;
    }
    public void acceptDetails() throws IOException
```

```
    {
        InputStreamReader IR = new InputStreamReader(System.in);
        BufferedReader br = new BufferedReader(IR);
        System.out.println("Enter name : ");
        name = br.readLine();
        System.out.println("Enter age : ");
        age = Integer.parseInt(br.readLine());
        System.out.println("Enter marks1 : ");
        m1 = Integer.parseInt(br.readLine());
        System.out.println("Enter marks2 : ");
        m2 = Integer.parseInt(br.readLine());
        System.out.println("Enter marks3 : ");
        m3 = Integer.parseInt(br.readLine());
    }
    public void compute()
    {
        average = (m1 + m2 + m3)/3.0;
        maximum = Math.max(m1,(Math.max(m2, m3)));
    }
    public void display()
    {
        System.out.println("Name =" +name);
        System.out.println("Age =" +age);
        System.out.println("Marks1 =" +m1);
        System.out.println("Marks2 =" +m2);
        System.out.println("Marks3 =" +m3);
        System.out.println("Maximum =" +maximum);
        System.out.println("Average =" +average);
    }
    public static void main(String[] args) throws IOException
    {
        Student student = new Student();
        student.acceptDetails();
        student.compute();
        student.display();
    }
}
```

Output

Enter name : Smith
Enter age : 18
Enter marks1 : 80
Enter marks2 : 70
Enter marks3 : 60
Name = Smith
Age = 10
Marks1 = 80
Marks2 = 70
Marks3 = 60
Maximum = 80
Average = 70.0

CHAPTER TEST

1 Mark Questions

1. The statement to invoke the default constructor of a class "State" is
   (a) `State obj= new state;`
   (b) `State obj = State();`
   (c) `State obj= new State();`
   (d) `State obj= new State()`
2. Constructor that creates objects by passing value is called
   (a) Default constructor
   (b) Parameterized constructor
   (c) Copy constructor
   (d) Non-parameterized constructor
3. The argument of a copy constructor is always passed by
   (a) Reference
   (b) Value
   (c) Both (a) and (b)
   (d) None of these

2 Marks Questions

4. Why return type is not allowed for constructors?
5. What is no arguments constructor?
6. Difference between constructor and function with respect to their return types.

15 Marks Questions

7. Create a class Rectangle with data members length, breadth and height. Use a parameterized constructor to initialize the object. With the help of function surfacearea() and volume(), calculate and display the surface area and volume of the rectangle.
8. Write a program in Java with the following specification

Class name	Hcf Lcm
Data members	int a,b
Member functions	
Hcflcm(int x, int y)	Constructor to initialize a and b.
void calculate()	To find and print Hcf and Lcm of both the numbers.

05

Library Classes

TREND ANALYSIS 3 YEARS

Library Classes

Average No. of Questions Across all Sets

Types of Questions	2023	2019	2018
1 Mark	2	–	1
2 Marks	1	3	1
15 Marks	–	–	–

There are some pre-defined classes available with Java system, which provide an effective support to the programmers in developing their program logic. These classes are known as library classes. They are also called as standard Java classes or built-in Java classes. These library classes are contained in packages.

Packages

The package contains a set of classes in order to ensure that class names are unique. Package is a group of classes, which can be imported to a program so that the user may exercise the implicit facility available in it. Some of the examples of packages are: java.lang, java.applet, java.awt, java.io, java.util, java.net, etc. java.lang package is imported by default in Java program.

There are several advantages of using java package, some of them are as follows

- Easy search
- Avoid naming conflicts
- Reuse classes
- Implement data encapsulation
- Provide controlled access
- Uniquely compare classes

All we need to do is put related classes into packages. After that, we can simply write an import class from existing packages and use it in our program. A package is a container of a group of related classes, where some of the classes are accessible.

We can reuse existing classes from the packages as many time as we need it in our program.

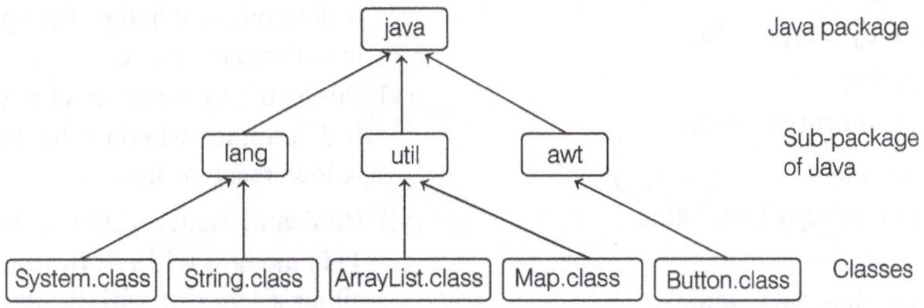

Import Statements

These statements in Java, allow to refer those classes, which are declared in other packages to be accessed without referring to the full package name.

Syntax `import package_name.classname;`

e.g. the package java.util contains many useful classes, such as ArrayList, then instead of referring to java.util.ArrayList wherever the ArrayList class is being used, you can just refer it by ArrayList.

Such as:

```
import java.util.ArrayList;
...............
...............
ArrayList ArrayList1=new ArrayList();
```

Wrapper Class

A variable of primitive data type is by default called by value. To achieve call by reference, we use the wrapper class. Wrapper class is used to convert any primitive data type into object. A wrapper class also contains a number of other different methods, which may be used in the processing of the corresponding data type. Package or library that contains wrapper classes is Java.lang.

Following table shows data type with its wrapper class:

Data Type	Wrapper Class
byte	Byte
short	Short
int	Integer
long	Long
float	Float
double	Double
char	Character
boolean	Boolean

Methods of Java Wrapper Class

parse...( ) Methods of Wrapper Class

It is used to convert a string into different numeric types. There are different types of parse methods in Java. These are:

(i) `Byte.parseByte(String s)`
Convert a string into a byte type value.

(ii) `Short.parseShort(String s)`
Convert a string into a short type value.

(iii) `Integer.parseInt(String s)`
Convert a string into an integer type value.

(iv) `Long.parseLong(String s)`
Convert a string into a long type value.

(v) `Float.parseFloat(String s)`
Convert a string into a float type value.

(vi) `Double.parseDouble(String s)`
Convert a string into a double type value.

e.g.
```
class A
{
    public static void main(string[]
                                args)
    {
        int i=Integer.parseInt("10");
        double d=Double.parseDouble
                              ("10.5");
        boolean b=Boolean.parseBoolean
                              ("true");
        System.out.println(i);
        System.out.println(d);
        System.out.println(b);
    }
}
```

Output

10
10.5
true

Methods of Character Wrapper Class

The character wrapper class has many useful methods. It includes:

(i) Boolean isLetter (char ch)
This method is used to determine whether the specified char value (ch) is a letter or not. This method will return true if it is letter, otherwise return false.

(ii) Boolean isDigit (char ch)
This method is used to determine whether the specified char value (ch) is a digit or not.

(iii) Boolean isWhitespace (char ch)
It determines whether the specified char value (ch) is white space. A whitespace includes space, tab, or new line.

(iv) Boolean isUppercase (char ch)
It determines whether the specified char value (ch) is uppercase or not.

(v) Boolean isLowercase (char ch)
It determines whether the specified char value (ch) is lowercase or not.

(vi) Boolean isLetterorDigit (char ch)
This method will return true if char value (ch) is either a letter or a digit, otherwise return false.

(vii) Char toLowercase (char ch)

This method will return the lowercase of the specified char value (ch).

(viii) Char toUppercase (char ch)

This method will return the uppercase of the specified char value (ch).

e.g.
```
public class test
{
   public static void main(string []
                                args)
   {
      system.out. println(character
                  .toUppercase ('a'));
   }
}
```

Output

A

Autoboxing and Unboxing in Wrapper Classes

Autoboxing

Automatic conversion of primitive data types to the object of their corresponding wrapper classes is known as autoboxing.

e.g., Conversion of int to Integer, long to Long, double to Double etc.

Unboxing

It is just the reverse process of autoboxing. Automatically converting an object of a wrapper class to its corresponding primitive type is known as unboxing.

e.g., Conversion of Integer to Int, Long to long, Double to double etc.

PYQs Previous Years Questions

1 Mark Questions

1. Predict the output of the following code snippet **ICSE 2023**

```
String P="20", Q="22";
int a = Integer.parseInt(P);
int b = Integer.valueOf(Q);
System.out.println(a+""+b);
```

(a) 20 (b) 20 22 (c) 2220 (d) 22

Ans (b) 20 22

2. When an object of a Wrapper class is converted to its corresponding primitive data type, it is called as **ICSE 2023**

(a) boxing (b) explicit type conversion
(c) unboxing (d) implicit type conversion

Ans (c) unboxing

3. The output of Double.parseDouble("71.25")+0.75 is **ICSE SQP 2023**

(a) 72 (b) 72.0 (c) 71.0 (d) 71.75

Ans (b) 72.0

4. The method to check if a character is an alphabet or not is **ICSE SQP 2023**

(a) isLetter(char) (b) isAlpha(char)
(c) isUppercase(char) (d) isLowercase(char)

Ans (a) isLetter(char)

5. Return data type of isLetter(char) is ______________ . **ICSE 2022 (Sem II)**

(a) Boolean (b) boolean
(c) bool (d) char

Ans (b) boolean

6. Method that converts a character to uppercase is ______________ . **ICSE 2022 (Sem II)**

(a) toUpper( )
(b) ToUpperCase( )
(c) toUppercase( )
(d) toUpperCase(char)

Ans (d) toUpperCase(char)

7. Corresponding wrapper class of float data type is ______________. **ICSE 2022 (Sem II)**

(a) FLOAT (b) float
(c) Float (d) Floating

Ans (c) Float

8. ______________ class is used to convert a primitive data type to its corresponding object. **ICSE 2022 (Sem II)**

(a) String (b) Wrapper
(c) System (d) Math

Ans (b) Wrapper

9. Give the output of the following code: *ICSE 2022 (Sem II)*

```
String A ="56.0",B="94.0";
double C=Double.parseDouble(A);
double D= Double.parseDouble(B);
System.out.println((C+D));
```

(a) 100 (b) 150.0 (c) 100.0 (d) 150

Ans (b) 150.0

10. Wrapper classes are available in ...... package. *ICSE SQP 2022 (Sem II)*

(a) java. io (b) java.util
(c) java.lang (d) java.awt

Ans (c) java.lang

11. Corresponding wrapper class of int data type is .... *ICSE SQP 2022 (Sem II)*

(a) integer (b) INTEGER
(c) Int (d) Integer

Ans (d) Integer

12. State the value of y after the following is executed. *ICSE SQP 2022 (Sem II)*

```
char x = '7' ;
y = Character.isLetter(x);
```

(a) false (b) 7 (c) true (d) '7'

Ans (a) false

13. Give the output of the following code. *ICSE SQP 2022 (Sem II)*

```
String A = "26.0", B = "74.0";
double C = Double.parseDouble(A);
double D = Double.parseDouble(B);
System.out.println((C+D));
```

(a) 26 (b) 74 (c) 100.0 (d) 2674

Ans (c) 100.0

14. When primitive data type is converted to its corresponding object of its class, it is called as .... *ICSE SQP 2022 (Sem II)*

(a) boxing (b) explicit type conversion
(c) unboxing (d) implicit type conversion

Ans (a) boxing

15. Name the package that contains wrapper classes. *ICSE 2018*

Ans java.lang

2 Marks Questions

1. Give the output of the following Character class methods *ICSE 2023*

(a) Character.toUpperCase('a')
(b) Character.isLetterOrDigit ('#')

Ans (a) A (b) False

2. Define boxing with an example. *ICSE SQP 2023*

Ans It is used to convert the primitive data type into corresponding objects.

e.g. Conversion of int to Integer.

```
Integer obj = new Integer ("2526");
```

3. Differentiate between boxing and unboxing. *ICSE SQP 2020*

Ans

Boxing	Unboxing
Boxing is used to store value types in the Garbage-collected Heap.	Unboxing an Interface type of a value type that implements the interface.
Convert the value type to reference type.	Convert to reference type to value type.
Implicit Conversion	Explicit Conversion

4. Give the output of the following code *ICSE 2019*

```
String P = ''20'', Q = ''19'';
int a = Integer.parseInt(P);
int b = Integer.valueOf(Q);
System.out.println(a + " " + b);
```

Ans **Output** 2019

5. State the data type and value of res after the following is executed *ICSE 2019*

```
char ch = '9';
res = Character.isDigit(ch);
```

Ans The data type of res is boolean and value of res after executing the code will be true.

Common Mistake Many students were not clear about the difference between the data type and wrapper classes. Some students write the data type and result is uppercase [Boolean/true].

6. What is meant by a package? Name any two Java application programming interface packages. *ICSE 2014*

Or

What is package? Give an example. *ICSE 2019, 06*

Ans A package is a namespace that organises a set of related types (classes, interfaces, enumerations and annotations) providing access protection. It allows classes in the same package to access each other's package access members.

Two Java application programming interface packages are:

(i) java.lang (ii) java.io

7. Write a difference between the functions isUpperCase( ) and toUpperCase(). *ICSE 2018; SQP 2017*

Ans Difference between isUpperCase ( ) and toUpperCase ( ) are as follows :

isUpperCase()	toUpperCase()
Checks whether a given character is an uppercase letter or not.	Converts the character to its upper case form and all the digits and special characters will remain as it is.
It returns a Boolean data type.	Returns char or String type.

8. Name any two library packages. ***ICSE 2016***

Ans Two library packages are

(i) java.lang (ii) java.applet

9. Name the wrapper classes of char type and boolean type. ***ICSE 2015***

Ans

Primitive Type	Wrapper Classes
char	Character
boolean	Boolean

10. State the data type and value of y after the following code is executed ***ICSE 2015***

```
char x = '7';
y = character.isletter(x);
```

Ans data type of y = boolean

value of y = false

11. Name any two wrapper classes. ***ICSE 2013***

Ans Wrapper classes are

(i) Integer

(ii) Boolean

12. What are library classes? Give an example. ***ICSE 2011***

Ans Predefined classes of Java, which get included in an application program themself are called library classes. They are also known as standard Java classes or built-in Java classes. These classes also have built-in member variables, constructors and methods like ordinary classes developed by programmer. These library classes are contained in packages.

e.g. java.io, java.lang, etc.

13. Name of following

(i) A package that is invoked by default.

(ii) A keyword, to use the classes defined in package. ***ICSE 2007***

Ans (i) java.lang package is invoked by default.

(ii) import keyword is used to define the package.

14. What is a wrapper class? Give an example. ***ICSE 2006***

Ans Wrapper class is used to convert any primitive data type into object. A wrapper class also contains a number of methods, which may be used in the processing of the corresponding data type. e.g. the wrapper class for int data type is Integer.

CHAPTER TEST

1 Mark Questions

1. The automatic conversion of a primitive data type to its corresponding wrapper object is called
(a) Boxing (b) Autoboxing
(c) Preboxing (d) ReverseBoxing

2. float f=3.14;
Here f is of type
(a) Object (b) Primitive
(c) Wrapper (d) None of these

3. .... and .... are the numeric wrapper classes in Java.
(a) String and Integer (b) STRING and INTEGER
(c) Byte and Short (d) Int and Boolean

4. .... is the wrapper class for the char data type.
(a) Char (b) CHAR
(c) CHARACTER (d) Character

2 Marks Questions

5. What is the significance of '*' while importing a package?
6. Define a wrapper class.
7. Write the purpose of the following functions
(i) Float.parseFloat() (ii) Double.toString()

15 Marks Question

8. Define a class Email with a function checkemail() that inputs an email id and checks whether its last character is in lowercase or not. If it is in lowercase it converts the entire emailid to uppercase and adds the domain name "@gmail.com" to the email id. Finally, it prints the converted email id.

06

Encapsulation

TREND ANALYSIS 3 YEARS

Average No. of Questions Across all Sets

	Types of Questions	2023	2019	2018
Encapsulation	1 Mark	–	–	–
	2 Marks	–	–	1
	15 Marks	–	–	–

Encapsulation in Java is a mechanism of wrapping the data (variables) and code acting on the data (methods) together as a single unit. In encapsulation, the variables of a class will be hidden from other classes, and can be accessed only through the methods of their current class. Therefore it also implements data hiding. Encapsulation is ineffective in absence of access specifiers.

Access Specifier

Java allows use of access specifiers for encapsulation and limiting access of class members outside the class.

Access specifier defines, who can use a method or variables. It is a feature of a class. These are the keywords, which are put down before the declaration of variables or methods. Access specifiers are also known as **access modifiers**.

Java provides four types of access specifier:

(i) public
(ii) protected
(iii) private
(iv) default (friendly)

Public

The public access specifier is the most open access level. Classes, methods and fields declared as public can be accessed from any class in Java program, whether these classes are in the same package or in another package.

e.g.

```
public class Book  //public class
{
   public int x,y;
                //public instance variables
}
```

Protected

The protected access specifier cannot be applied to class and interfaces. Methods, fields can be declared protected, however methods and fields in a interface cannot be declared protected. It can be accessed only by the subclass in other package or any class within the same package.

e.g.

```
class Book
{
   protected boolean colour()
      //protected method
   {
      //implementation details
   }
}
```

Private

The private access specifier achieves the lowest level of accessibility. The private methods and fields can be accessed only within the same class to which the methods and fields belong. The private methods and fields are not visible within the subclasses and are not inherited by subclasses. Using the private modifier, we can encapsulate an object itself and hide data from the outside world.

e.g.
```
class Book
{
   private double x, y;
         //private instance variables
}
```

Difference between Public and Private Access Modifier

Public	Private
A public access specifier is the most open access level.	A private access specifier is the lowest level of accessibility.
It allows variables and methods visible to all classes.	Private methods and variables are not visible within the subclasses.
Public access specifier uses public keyword.	Private access specifier uses private keyword.

Default (friendly)

Default access specifier means, we do not explicitly declare an access modifier for a class, field, method, etc. In terms of Java, this specifier is also known as **package-private**.

e.g.
```
class Book
{
   int i; //default instance variable
}
```

Difference between Default and Protected Access Modifier

Default	Protected
It is not necessary to put this modifier.	It is used, if members of the class are declared to be protected.
Without any class control, default modifier is available to any other class in the same package.	It can be accessed by only the subclasses in other package.
Default is not secure because anybody can access it.	Protected is much better than default in order to security purpose.

Access Specifier for Classes

When a class is declared as public, it is accessible to other classes defined in the same package as well as those defined in other package. A class cannot be declared as private.

Access Specifier for Methods

Access specifier for methods work in a similar way that of variables. Methods can use all four levels of access specifiers.

Access Specifier for Constructors

A constructor can have the same access specifiers used for variables and methods. When a constructor is declared "private", only the class itself can create a instance of it.

Visibility of Access Specifiers

Access Location \ Acess Modifier	Default	Private	Protected	Public
Same Class	Yes	Yes	Yes	Yes
Same Package	Yes	No	Yes	Yes
Outside Package	No	No	No	Yes
Subclass	Yes	No	Yes	Yes

Scope of Variables

Scope of variables refers to the lifetime and accessibility of a variable. It is useful because it provides the facility to access the variable or method of other class. e.g. If a variable is declared outside the class, then it will be accessible by all of the class methods. If it is declared in a method, then it can be used by that method only.

Thus, a Java variable can have one of the three scope:

(i) Instance variables

(ii) Class variables/Static variables

(iii) Local variables

Instance Variables

Instance variables are declared in a class, but outside a method. They are also called **member** or **field variables**. Instance variable is created each time with a different value, whenever a new object is created. Initial value of instance variable is zero for numbers, false for booleans, or null for object references. Instance variable should generally be declared as private.

e.g.
```
class Address
{
   private String phone;
                     // Instance variable
   public void setphone(String phone)
   {
      this.phone = phone;
   }
}
class Main_class
{
   public static void main(String[] args)
   { // access the Address class
      Address a=new Address();
      a.setphone("001");
   }
}
```

Class/Static Variables

Static variables or **class variables** are declared with the static keyword in a class, but outside a method. They are stored in static memory. Only one copy of this variable is allocated in the memory and each objects share it.

The initial value will depend on the data type of this variable, i.e. zero for integral type, false for boolean or null for object reference. It is created when the program starts and destroyed when the program stops.

e.g.
```
class MyAddress
{
   static int count=0;
            //class variable
   public void increment()
   {
      count + +;
   }
   public static void main(String args[])
   {
      MyAddress ma=new MyAddress();
      MyAddress ma1=new MyAddress();
      ma.increment();
      ma1.increment();
      System.out.println("ma : count
                          is="+ma.count);
      System.out.println("ma1: count
                          is="+ma1.count);
   }
}
```

Output

ma : count is = 2
ma1: count is = 2

Note Static variables (or class variables) are common to all the instance (or object) of the same class.

Local Variables

Local variables are declared in a method, constructor or block. Local variables are not visible outside the method, constructor or block. Access modifiers (private, protected, public, default) cannot be used with local variables.

e.g.
```
public class Calc
{
   public void Age()
   {
      int age = 0;        //local variable
      age = age + 7;
      System.out.println("Age is:"+age);
   }
   public static void main(String args[])
   {
      Calc m = new Calc();
      m.Age();
   }
}
```

Output Age is: 7

Argument Variables

These are the variables that are defined in the header of constructor or a method. The scope of these variables is the method or constructor in which they are defined. Once the method finishes execution, these variables are destroyed.

e.g.
```
public class myprogram
{
   public static void main(string[] args)
   {
      double r;
      r = ToolBox.min (1.0, 4.0);
            //argument variable
   }
}
public class ToolBox
{
   public static double min(double a,
                            double b)
   {
      double m= 0;
      if (a<b)
      {
         m = a ;
      }
      else
      {
         m = b;
      }
         return (m);
      }
   {
```

PYQs Previous Years Questions

1 Mark Questions

1. The access modifier that gives least accessibility is **ICSE 2022 (Sem II)**

   (a) private (b) public
   (c) protected (d) package

Ans (a) private

2. The access modifier that gives most accessibility is **ICSE SQP 2022 (Sem II)**

   (a) private (b) public
   (c) protected (d) package

Ans (b) public

2 Marks Questions

1. Define encapsulation. **ICSE SQP 2020, 16**

Ans Refer to text on page 117.

2. Mention the types of access specifiers. **ICSE SQP 2020**

Or Name any two types of access specifier. **ICSE 2017, 08**

Ans Java provides four types of access specifier

   (i) default (ii) public
   (iii) private (iv) protected

3. How are private members of a class different from public members? **ICSE 2018, 12**

Or Differentiate between public and private modifiers for members of a class.

Ans Refer to text on page 118.

4. The access specifier that gives the most accessibility is .... and the least accessibility is .... **ICSE 2015**

Ans The access specifier that gives the most accessibility is public and the least accessibility is private.

5. Consider the following class

```
public class MyClass
{
   public static int x = 3, y = 4;
   public int a = 2, b = 3;
}
```

   (i) Name the variables for which each object of the class will have its own distinct copy.
   (ii) Name the variables that are common to all object of the class. **ICSE 2014**

Ans (i) 'a' and 'b'
   (ii) 'x' and 'y'

6. Differentiate between private and protected visibility modifiers. **ICSE 2010**

Ans Differences between private and protected visibility modifiers

Private Visibility Modifier	Protected Visibility Modifier
It can be accessed by the same class to which the methods and fields belong.	It can be accessed by the subclass.
Private method and fields are not visible within the subclass.	Protected methods and fields are visible within subclass.

7. What is meant by private visibility of a method? **ICSE 2006**

Ans Private visibility of a method means that methods is accessible only in same class and cannot be accessed by subclass or in other class.

Additional Questions

1. Access specifiers are used for
   (a) removing objects
   (b) deallocating objects
   (c) renaming objects
   (d) restricting accessibility of class members

Ans (d) restricting accessibility of class members

2. The variable that is accessible to all parts of the program is called
   (a) local variable (b) global variable
   (c) static variable (d) final variable

Ans (b) global variable

3. Can a private member of a public class can be accessed by
   (i) same class?
   (ii) other class in the same package?

Ans (i) Yes, private member of a public class can be accessed by same class.
   (ii) No, other classes are unable to access private member of a public class.

4. Give reasons
   (i) In what circumstances is a class derived publicly?
   (ii) In what circumstances is a class derived privately?

Ans (i) In Java, a base class can be derived by a sub class by using only public mode of inheritance. When a class is derived publicly, the public and protected members of the base class are accessible to the derived class. Private members of the base class are not inherited by derived class.
   (ii) Java does not support private and protected modes of inheritance. Classes are always derived publicly in Java.

CHAPTER TEST

1 Mark Questions

1. The non- static data members of a class are also called
   (a) Non-instance variables (b) Instance variables
   (c) Constant variables (d) Final variables
2. A data member of a class that carries a single shared value for all the objects of the class is called
   (a) Class variable (b) Instance variable
   (c) Static variable (d) Both (a) and (c)
3. The variables declared in the function signature are named as
   (a) parameter variables (b) argument variables
   (c) global variables (d) return variables
4. Arti tells that the variable she had declared without any access specifier will be accessible to the entire package. Is she True?
   (a) Yes (b) No

2 Marks Questions

5. Describe the methods of accessing the data members and member functions of a class in the following cases
   (i) in the member function of the same class.
   (ii) in the member function of another class.
6. What are the types of visibility modes used in Java?
7. What will happen if data members are declared private?

15 Marks Questions

8. What is meant by a static data member? Show its application with the help of an example.
9. Write a program by using a class with the following specifications

Class name	Factorial
Data members	private int n
Member functions	
void input()	to input a number
void fact()	to find and print the factorial of the number

Use a main function to create an object and call member methods of the class.

07

Arrays

TREND ANALYSIS 3 YEARS

Average No. of Questions Across all Sets

	Types of Questions	2023	2019	2018
Arrays	1 Mark	–	–	–
	2 Marks	1	1	1
	15 Marks	3	1	1

An array is a type of composite data type and collection of the same type of variables that are referred by a common name. An array is a fixed number of elements of the same type, which are stored in memory sequentially. Therefore, an integer array holds integers, a character array holds characters and so on.

An array containing 5 integer values of type int called abc could be represented as:

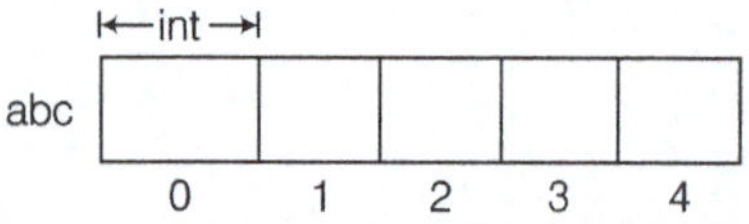

Where, each blank box represents an element of the array. These elements are numbered from 0 to 4, being 0 the first element and 4 the last element.

Subscripts Elements of array will be referred as array_name[n], where *n* is the number of element in the array. A pair of square brackets, i.e. [ ] is called subscript or index. The subscript or index designate element and their position in the array's ordering.

Uses of Array

We use array for the following purposes:

(i) To group storage locations.
(ii) To declare elements in a brief manner using subscripts.
(iii) To store elements in continuous locations.

Types of Array

There are two types of array

(i) Single Dimensional Array
(ii) Double Dimensional Array

Single Dimensional Array

When the elements are specified by a single subscript, the array is called single dimensional array or single subscripted array.

To create an array use the following syntax

```
array_name = new type[size];
```

e.g.
```
age = new int[20];
```

where, new is a keyword that allocates memory for an array.

Declaration of Single Dimensional Array

To declare an array, first we give the type of array such as int, double, float, boolean, etc. and then the name of the array.

Syntax `Type array_name[];`
or `Type[] array_name;`
or `Type []array_name;`
e.g. `int roll_No[];`
or `int[] roll_No;`
or `int []roll_No;`

Initialization of Single Dimensional Array

Individual components of an array are referenced by array name and its subscripts which represents their position in the array. By default, positions are always begun with 0.

Syntax `Array_name[subscript] = value;`

e.g.
```
age[0] = 21;
age[1] = 22;
age[2] = 23;
:
:
age[19] = 100;
```

Note We can declare, create and initialize the array together by
```
type array_name[] = {value0, value1,
                     ..., valuen};
```
e.g. `int age[] = {21, 22, 23, 24, 25};`

Length of Single Dimensional Array

Java allows storage in an array according to the variable length. It can be accessed using the following format
```
int age[]={21, 22, 23, 24, 25};
int size = age.length;
```

Accessing Array Elements of Single Dimensional Array

In order to process the stored data in an array, we refer each individual element by specifying the array name and identifying the element desired by a subscript.

Syntax `array_name[subscript];`

Double Dimensional Array

Double dimensional array is a structure created in memory to contain the data values by using rows and columns. It is also referred as a double subscripted array because of using two types of subscripts, one for row number and other for column number represent array.

To create an array use the following syntax
```
type[][] array_name = new type[size][size];
```
e.g. `int[][] arr = new int[10][20];`

Declaration of Double Dimensional Array

To declare double dimensional array, first we give the type of array such as int, double, float, Boolean etc. and then the name of the array.

Syntax
```
Type array_name[][];
or Type[][] array_name;
or Type [][]array_name;
or Type[] array_name[];
```
e.g. `int a[][];` or `int[][] a;` or `int [][]a;` or `int[] a[];`

Initialization of Double Dimensional Array

Individual components of an array are referenced by array name and its subscripts which represents their position in the array. By default, positions are always begun with [0][0] index.

Syntax
```
int a[0][0] = 2;
int a[0][1] = 4;
int a[0][2] = 6;
......
......
int a[1][2] = 12;
```

Length of Double Dimensional Array

Length of double dimensional array is number of rows present in it. The row index runs from 0 to length −1.
```
int a[][] = new int [2][3];
int size = a.length;
```

Accessing Array Elements of Double Dimensional Array

To access elements of a double dimensional array we use array name followed by row index value and column index value of the element that to be accessed. In case of the double dimensional array the compiler assigns separate index values for rows and columns.

Syntax `array_name[][];`

Accepting Data in Array from User

In an array, the data is input by InputStreamReader and BufferedReader and the data output is performed by System.out.println() function.

There are two ways to input the elements in the array
(i) Without using loop (ii) Using loop

Basic Operations on Arrays

Arrays provide the following basic operations, which can be performed on them. They are

Searching

It is the process to determine whether the given item is present in the array or not. There are two ways to search an item:

(i) **Linear Search** In linear search method, given array is scanned from lower bound to upper bound and each element is compared with the element to be searched. This is one of the simplest way of searching a particular element in array.

Linear search can be applied even if the array is not sorted. The main disadvantage of this search is that it requires more comparisons with respect to binary search.

Code Segment for Linear Search

(Loop variable: c; Size of array: n; Element to be search: search)

```
for(c = 0; c < n; c++)
{
    if(array[c] == search)
    {
        System.out.println(search+ "is
         present at location"+ (c + 1) +".");
        break;
    }
}
if(c==n)
    System.out.println(search+ " is not
                             present in array");
```

(ii) **Binary Search** Binary search is one of the best and fast ways of searching the element in array. It provides the search result in least possible time with compare to linear search. Binary search can be applicable only if an array is in sorted order.

Under this search, initially the comparison is made with the middle element of the concerned array and if not found there, the searching is then done to the first or the second half according to the condition (less than/greater than).

The process is again repeated to the further sub-division of the first or the second half till the desired element is matched.

Binary search is based on Divide and Conquer principle. This is one of the efficient ways of searching for voluminous data.

Following conditions to be followed in binary *search*:

(a) Array should be in sorted order

(b) If array[mid] = data; pos = mid

(c) If array[mid] < data; lb = mid+1

(d) If array[mid] > data; ub = mid – 1

(e) If lb > ub element not in array

where,

lb = lower bound, ub = upper bound

mid = mid value of an array,

data = element to be search and

pos = storing index.

Code Segment of Binary Search

```
pos=-1;
while(lb <= ub)
{
    mid =(lb+ub)/2;
    if(array[mid] = = data)
    {
        pos = mid;
        break;
    }
    else if(data > array[mid])
        lb = mid + 1;
    else if(data < array[mid])
        ub = mid - 1;
}
if(pos = = -1)
    System.out.println("\n number does
                                not exist");
else
    System.out.println("\n index is"
                                   +pos);
```

Difference between Linear Search and Binary Search

Linear Search	Binary Search
It takes place in both sorted and unsorted list or array.	It takes place in only sorted list or array either in ascending or descending order.
It searches an element in a sequential manner.	An array is divided into two halves and then the element is searched.

Sorting

Sorting is a process of arranging data in ascending or descending order. There are two ways to sort the data

(i) **Bubble Sort** This type of sorting is based on exchange sort technique, as it is related to exchange mechanism. In this technique, consecutive array elements are compared and if not in order it exchanges them up to end of the array. This process will be repeated till all the elements are arranged in desired order. If an array is having N elements, we can obtain N-1 comparisons in each pass.

Code Segment for Bubble Sort

```
for(int k = 0 ; k < n; k++)
{
    for(int KK = 0; KK < n - k; KK++)
    {
        if(M[KK] > M[KK+1]
            // for descending order
        {
            temp = M[KK];
            M[kk] = M[KK+1];
            M[KK + 1] = temp;
        }
    }
}
```

(ii) **Selection Sort** It is an in-place comparison sorting algorithm. In this algorithm, the array is divided into two parts, first is sorted part, and another one is the unsorted part. Initially, the sorted part of the array is empty, and unsorted part is the given array. Sorted part is placed at the left, while the unsorted part is placed at the right.

In selection sort, the first smallest element is selected from the unsorted array and placed at the first position. After that second smallest element is selected and placed in the second position. The process continues until the array is entirely sorted.

Code segment for selection sort

```
for (int i=0; i<arr.length - 1; i++)
{
    int index = i;
    for (int j=i+1; j<arr.length; j++)
    {
        if (arr[j] < arr[index])
        {
            index = j;
              //searching for lowest index
        }
    }
    int smallerNumber = arr[index];
    arr[index] = arr[i];
    arr[i] = smallerNumber;
}
```

Memory Required to Store the Elements

In one dimensional array, number of bytes required to store the element in the memory = size of the type of data * size of the array.

e.g. `char A[4]` will require $2 \times 4 = 8$ bytes of storing place because char data type requires 2 bytes and A[4] contains 4 elements.

PYQs Previous Years Questions

1 Mark Questions

1. The array int x[10] occupies *ICSE SQP 2023*

(a) 10 bytes (b) 40 bytes
(c) 20 bytes (d) 80 bytes

Ans (b) 40 bytes

2. The element in x[4] of the array {3, 5, 7, 12, 16, 18, 20, 35, 42, 89} is *ICSE SQP 2023*

(a) 16 (b) 12
(c) 7 (d) 18

Ans (a) 16

3. A single dimensional array contains N elements. What will be the last subscript? *ICSE 2022 (Sem II)*

(a) N (b) N – 1
(c) N – 2 (d) N+1

Ans (b) N – 1

4. Identify the correct array declaration statement. *ICSE SQP 2022 (Sem II)*

(a) int a [10];
(b) int a [ ]= new int [10];
(c) int arr [i] = 10;
(d) int a [10] = new int [ ];

Ans (b) int a [ ]= new int [10];

5. Name the search or sort algorithm that

At each stage, compares the sought key value with the key value of the middle element of the array. *ICSE 2012*

Ans Binary search

2 Marks Questions

1. Consider the given array and answer the questions given below *ICSE 2023*

`int x[ ] = {4,7,9,66,72,0,16};`

(i) What is the length of the array?
(ii) What is the value in x[4]?

Ans (i) Length-wise, the size is 7.
Memory-wise, the size is 28 bytes.
(ii) 72

2. Consider the following array and answer the questions given below *ICSE SQP 2023*

`int x[ ] = {23,45,67,12,45,89,24,12,9,7};`

(i) What is the size of the array ?
(ii) What is the position of 89 ?

Ans (i) Length-wise, the size is 10.
Memory-wise, the size is 40 bytes.
(ii) x[5]

3. What is the difference between the linear search and the binary search technique? *ICSE 2019*

Or

Write one difference between linear search and binary search. *ICSE SQP 2020; 2011*

Or

Differentiate between binary search and linear search. *ICSE SQP 2020; 2007*

Ans Difference between linear search and binary search:

Linear Search	Binary Search
(i) This process can be carried on unsorted array.	(i) This is applied only on sorted arrays.
(ii) Linear search, searches an element in a sequential manner.	(ii) In binary search, an array is divided into two halves and then the element is searched.

4. State the number of bytes and bits occupied by a character array of 10 elements. *ICSE SQP 2020*

Ans As size of char is 2 bytes, a character array of 10 elements occupies 2 × 10 = 20 bytes.

1 byte = 8 bits so 20 bytes convert to 8 × 20 = 160 bits.

5. Differentiate between searching and sorting. *ICSE 2018*

Ans Differences between searching and sorting are as follows

Searching	Sorting
(i) It is the process to determine whether the given item is present in the array or not.	(i) It is a process of arranging data in ascending or descending order.
(ii) It includes linear search and binary search.	(ii) It includes bubble sort, quick sort, insertion sort etc.

6. Write statements to show how finding the length of a character array char[ ] differs from finding the length of a String object str. *ICSE 2013*

Ans Array char[ ] provides the set of characters so with array, we use length property to return the length of array.

But with String object str, we use length( ) function to return the length of a string (i.e. number of characters present in str).

7. What is an array? Write a statement to declare an integer array of 10 elements. *ICSE 2012*

Ans Array is a collection of the same data type variables, which are referenced by a common name. An array is an object.

Declaration of integer array

```
int[] arr = new int[10];
```

8. State the total size in bytes, of the arrays a[4] of char data type and p[4] of float data type. *ICSE 2011*

Ans One char value takes 2 bytes so

size of char a[4] is 4 × 2 = 8 bytes

One float value takes 4 bytes so

size of float p[4] is 4 × 4 = 16 bytes

9. Write one difference between length and length( ) functions. *ICSE 2010*

Ans Length parameter is used with array to get the number of elements of array and length( ) method is used with String to get the length of String. Both return an integer value.

10. If array[]={1,9,8,5,2}; *ICSE 2008*

(i) What is array.length?

(ii) What is array[2]?

Ans (i) array.length determines the length of array, so array.length = 5

(ii) array[2] = 8

11. Find and correct the errors in the following program segment *ICSE 2006*

```
int n[] = (2, 4, 6, 8, 10);
for(int i = 0; i <= 5; i++)
  System.out.println("n ["+i+"]=" + n[i]);
```

Ans int n[]=(2, 4, 6, 8, 10); → error 1 ('{' and '}' bracket should be used)

int n[]={2, 4, 6, 8, 10}; → correct

for(i=0; i<=5; i++) → error 2 (array out of bound)

for(i=0; i<5; i++) → correct (range should be from 0-4)

10 Marks Questions

1. Define a class to perform binary search on a list of integers given below, to search for an element input by the user, if it is found display the element along with its position, otherwise display the message "Search element not found".

2, 5, 7, 10, 15, 20, 29, 30, 46, 50 *ICSE 2022 (Sem II)*

Ans

```
import java.util.*;
public class Search
{
   public static void main(String[] args)
   {
      int intarray[]=new int[10];
      Scanner sc=new Scanner(System.in);
      int beg=0,mid=-1,end=9,se=0,i,
                                     found=-1;
      System.out.println("Enter 10
            integers in ascending order ");
```

```
        for (i=0;i<=9;i++)
        intarray[i]=sc.nextInt();
        System.out.println("Enter search element ");
        se=sc.nextInt();
        while (beg<=end)
        {
          mid=(beg+end)/2;
          if (intarray[mid]==se)
          {
            found=1;
            break;
          }
          else if(se>intarray[mid])
            beg=mid+1;
          else
            end=mid-1;
        }
        if (found==1)
        System.out.println("Found at :"+(mid+1));
        else
          System.out.println("Search element not found!!!");
      }
    }
```

2. Define a class to declare a character array of size ten, accept the characters into the array and display the characters with highest and lowest ASCII (American Standard Code for Information Interchange) value.

EXAMPLE:

INPUT:

'R','z','q','A','N','p','m','U','Q','F',

OUTPUT:

Character with highest ASCII value =z

Character with lowest ASCII value = A **ICSE 2022 (Sem II)**

Ans

```
import java.util.*;
public class HighLowAscii
{
  public static void main(String [] args)
  {
    char charArray[] = new char[10];
    Scanner sc=new Scanner(System.in);
    char hc='A',lc='z',c;
    int i;
    System.out.println("Enter 10 characters :");
    for(i=0;i<10;i++)
    charArray[i]=sc.nextLine().charAt(0);
    for(i=0;i<10;i++)
    {
      c=charArray[i];
      System.out.println(c);
      if (c>hc)
        hc=c;
```

```
            if (c<lc)
                lc=c;
        }
        System.out.println("Character with highest ASCII value :"+hc);
        System.out.println("Character with lowest ASCII value :"+lc);
    }
}
```

3. Define a class to declare an array of size twenty of double data type, accept the elements into the array and perform the following:

- Calculate and print the product of all the elements.
- Print the square of each element of the array. ***ICSE 2022 (Sem II)***

Ans

```
import java.util.*;
public class SquareProduct
{
    public static void main(String [] args)
    {
        double numbers[]=new double[20];
        Scanner sc=new Scanner(System.in);
        double prod=1.0,sq=0.0;
        int i;
        System.out.println("Enter 20 numbers :");
        for(i=0;i<20;i++)
        numbers[i]=sc.nextDouble();
        for(i=0;i<20;i++)
        {
            prod*=numbers[i];
            System.out.println("Product of all the elements =" + prod);
        }
        System.out.println("Square of :"+ numbers[i] + "="
                                          + numbers[i]*numbers[i]);
    }
}
```

4. Define a class to declare an integer array of size n and accept the elements into the array. Search for an element input by the user using linear search technique, display the element if it is found, otherwise display the message "NO SUCH ELEMENT. ***ICSE SQP 2022 (Sem II)***

Ans

```
import java.util.Scanner;
public class LinearSearch
{
    private int[] arr;
    private int n;
    public LinearSearch(int size)
    {
        n = size;
        arr = new int[n];
    }
    public void accept()
    {
        Scanner input = new Scanner(System.in);
        System.out.println("Enter " + n + " elements:");
        for (int i = 0; i < n; i++)
        {
            arr[i] = input.nextInt();
        }
```

```
    }
    public void search(int x)
    {
        boolean found = false;
        for (int i = 0; i < n; i++)
        {
            if (arr[i] == x)
            {
                System.out.println(x + " found at index " + i);
                found = true;
                break;
            }
        }
        if (!found)
        {
            System.out.println("NO SUCH ELEMENT");
        }
    }
    public static void main(String[] args)
    {
        Scanner input = new Scanner(System.in);
        System.out.print("Enter the size of the array: ");
        int size = input.nextInt();
        LinearSearch obj = new LinearSearch(size);
        obj.accept();
        System.out.print("Enter the element to search: ");
        int element = input.nextInt();
        obj.search(element);
    }
}
```

Output

Enter the size of the array: 5
Enter 5 elements:
45
67
43
89
78
Enter the element to search: 67
67 found at index 1

5. Define a class to declare a character array of size ten, accept the character into the array and perform the following:
   - Count the number of uppercase letters in the array and print.
   - Count the number of vowels in the array and print. ***ICSE SQP 2022 (Sem II)***

Ans

```
import java.util.Scanner;
public class CharArray
{
    public static void main(String[] args)
    {
        char[] arr = new char[10];        // declare character array of size 10
        Scanner sc = new Scanner(System.in);
        System.out.println("Enter 10 characters: ");
        String input = sc.nextLine();   // fill the array with the user input
        for (int i = 0; i < 10; i++)
        {
            if (i < input.length())
            {
                arr[i] = input.charAt(i);
```

```
            }
            else
            {
                arr[i] = ' '; // fill with spaces if input length < 10
            }
        }
        int upperCount = 0;
        int vowelCount = 0;
            // iterate through the array and count uppercase letters and vowels
        for (char c : arr)
        {
            if (Character.isUpperCase(c))
            {
                upperCount++;
            }
            if (isVowel(c))
            {
                vowelCount++;
            }
        }     // print the counts
        System.out.println("Number of uppercase letters: " + upperCount);
        System.out.println("Number of vowels: " + vowelCount);

    } // method to check if a character is a vowel
    public static boolean isVowel(char c)
    {
        char ch = Character.toLowerCase(c);
        return ch == 'a' || ch == 'e' || ch == 'i' || ch == 'o' || ch == 'u';
    }
}
```

Output

Enter 10 characters: SuPriYaPat

Number of uppercase letters: 4

Number of vowels: 4

6. Define a class to declare an array of size 20 of double datatype, accept the elements into the array and perform the following:
   - Calculate and print the sum of all the elements.
   - Calculate and print the highest value of the array. ***ICSE SQP 2022 (Sem II)***

Ans

```
import java.util.Scanner;
public class DoubleArray
{
    public static void main(String[] args)
    {
        Scanner scanner = new Scanner(System.in);
        double[] arr = new double[20];  // Accepting elements into the array
        System.out.println("Enter 20 double values:");
        for (int i = 0; i < arr.length; i++)
        {
            arr[i] = scanner.nextDouble();
        } // Calculating the sum of all elements
        double sum = 0;
        for (int i = 0; i < arr.length; i++)
        {
            sum += arr[i];
        }
        System.out.println("Sum of all elements: " + sum);
            // Calculating the highest value of the array
        double max = arr[0];
```

```
        for (int i = 1; i < arr.length; i++)
        {
            if (arr[i] > max)
            {
                max = arr[i];
            }
        }
        System.out.println("Highest value in the array: " + max);
    }
}
```

Output

Enter 20 double values:
2.3
1.2
3.5
7.8
5.6
9.0
0.5
2.2
4.1
1.0
3.2
2.1
8.7
6.5
4.3
7.6
0.9
5.4
1.8
3.6
Sum of all elements: 72.5
Highest value in the array: 9.0

Concept Enhancer In Java, an array is a collection of similar data types that are stored in contiguous memory locations. To calculate the sum of all the elements in an array, we can use a loop to iterate through each element and add them together. To find the highest value, we can use a loop to compare each element with the current highest value and update it if a higher value is found. It is important to note that arrays in Java are zero-indexed, meaning the first element is at index 0 and the last element is at index size-1.

15 Marks Questions

1. Define a class to accept values in integer array of size 10. Find sum of one digit number and sum of two digit numbers entered. Display them separately. *ICSE 2023*

   Example: Input:

   a [] = {2, 12, 4, 9, 18, 25, 3, 32, 20, 1}

   Output:

   Sum of one digit numbers

   2+4+9+3+1=19

   Sum of two digit numbers

   12+18+25+32+20=107

Ans
```
import java.util.Scanner;
public class Example
{
   public static void main (String[] args)
   {
      Scanner sc = new Scanner (System.in);
      int [] arr = new int[10];    // Taking input array from user
      System.out.println("Enter 10 integer values:");
      for (int i = 0; i < 10; i++)
      {
         arr[i] = sc.nextInt();

      }
      // Calculating sum of one-digit and two-digit numbers in the array
      int oneDigitSum = 0;
      int twoDigitSum = 0;
      for (int i = 0; i < 10; i++)
      {
         if (arr[i] >= 0 && arr[i] <= 9)
         {
            oneDigitSum += arr[i];
         } else if (arr[i] >= 10 && arr[i] <= 99)
         {
            twoDigitSum += arr[i];
         }
      }
      // Printing sum of one-digit and two-digit numbers in the array
      System.out.println("Sum of one-digit numbers in the array: " + oneDigitSum);
      System.out.println("Sum of two-digit numbers in the array: " + twoDigitSum);
   }
}
```

Output

Enter 10 integer values:
23
4
6
5
33
76
5
89
66
54
Sum of one-digit numbers in the array: 20
Sum of two-digit numbers in the array: 341

2. Define a class to accept values into an array of double data type of size 20. Accept a double value from user and search in the array using linear search method. If value is found display message "Found" with its position where it is present in the array. Otherwise display message "not found".
ICSE 2023

Ans
```
import java.util.Scanner;
public class Example
{
   public static void main (String[] args)
   {
      Scanner sc = new Scanner (System.in);
      double[] arr = new double[20];     // Taking input array from user
      System.out.println("Enter 20 double values:");
      for (int i = 0; i < 20; i++)
```

```
        {
            arr[i] = sc.nextDouble();
        }     // Taking input value from user
        System.out.println("Enter a double value to search:");

        double val = sc.nextDouble();      // Performing linear search
        boolean found = false;
        for (int i = 0; i < 20; i++)
        {
            if (arr[i] == val)
            {
                found = true;
                System.out.println(val + " found at index " + i);
                    break;
            }
        }
        if (!found)
        {
            System.out.println(val + " not found in the array");
        }
    }
}
```

Output

Enter 20 double values:
20.7
23.5
12.3
34.7
67.5
43.0
56.9
75.4
89.6
55.0
39.7
80.9
33.0
29.8
66.0
48.7
86.9
112.0
705.9
323.7
Enter a double value to search:
29.8
29.8 found at index 13

3. Define a class to accept 10 characters from a user. Using bubble sort technique arrange them in ascending order. Display the sorted array and original array. ***ICSE 2023***

KEY idea

To define a class in Java to accept user input and sort it using the bubble sort technique, you will need to declare a character array, initialize it with user input using the Scanner class, implement the bubble sort algorithm to sort the array, and then display the sorted array and original array using loops.

Ans
```
import java.util.Arrays;
import java.util.Scanner;
public class Main
{
   public static void main(String[] args)
   {

      Scanner sc = new Scanner(System.in);
      char[] arr = new char[10];
      System.out.println("Enter 10 characters:");
      for (int i = 0; i < arr.length; i++)
      {
         arr[i] = sc.next().charAt(0);
      }
      System.out.println("Original array:");
      System.out.println(Arrays.toString(arr));
      char temp;
      for (int i = 0; i < arr.length; i++)
      {
         for (int j = 1; j < (arr.length - i); j++)
         {
            if (arr[j - 1] > arr[j])
            {
               temp = arr[j - 1];
               arr[j - 1] = arr[j];
               arr[j] = temp;
            }
         }
      }
      System.out.println("Sorted array:");
      System.out.println(Arrays.toString(arr));
   }
}
```

Output

Enter 10 characters:
e
f
h
c
u
j
d
n
w
s
Original array:
[e, f, h, c, u, j, d, n, w, s]
Sorted array:
[c, d, e, f, h, j, n, s, u, w]

4. Define a class to accept 10 integers and arrange them in descending order using bubble sort. Print the original array and the sorted array. ***ICSE SQP 2023***

Ans
```
import java.util.Scanner;
class Bubble
{
   public static void main (String[] args)
   {
      Scanner in = new Scanner(System.in);
```

```
        int a[] = new int[10];
        System.out.println("Enter 10 integers:");
        for (int i = 0; i < a.length; i++)
        {
          a[i] = Integer.parseInt(in.nextLine());
        }
        System.out.println("Original array:");
        for (int i = 0; i < a.length; i++)
        System.out.print(a[i] + " ");
        System.out.println();
        for (int i = 0; i < a.length; i++)
        {

          for (int j = 0; j < a.length - 1 - i; j++)
          {
            if (a[j] < a[j + 1])
            {
              int temp = a[j];
              a[j] = a[j + 1];
              a[j + 1] = temp;
            }
          }
        }
        System.out.println();
        System.out.println("Sorted array:");
        for (int i = 0; i < a.length; i++)
        System.out.print(a[i] + " ");
        System.out.println();
    }
}
```

Output

Enter 10 integers:
1
2
3
5
4
6
7
9
8
0
Original array:
1 2 3 5 4 6 7 9 8 0
Sorted array:
9 8 7 6 5 4 3 2 1 0

5. Define a class to accept values into a double array of size 20 and print the range of the array, range is the difference between the largest and the smallest elements of the array. ***ICSE SQP 2023***

Ans

```
import java.util.Scanner;
class Range
{
    public static void main (String[] args)
    {
        Scanner in = new Scanner(System.in);
        double a [] = new double [20];
        double large = 0.0;
```

```
        double small = 0.0;
        System.out.println("Enter 20 numbers:");
        for (int i = 0; i < a.length; i++)
        {
            a[i] = Double.parseDouble(in.nextLine());
            if (i == 0)
            {
                large = a[i];
                small = a[i];
            }
            else
            {
                if (large < a[i])
                    large = a[i];
                if (small > a[i])
                    small = a[i];
            }
        }
        double range = large - small;
        System.out.println("Range = " + range);
    }
}
```

Output

Enter 20 numbers:1
2
3
4
5
6
7
8
9
10
11
12
13
14
15
16
17
18
19
20
Range = 19.0

6. Define a class to accept the names of 10 students in an array and check for the existence of the given name in the array using linear search, if found print the position of the name, if not found print the appropriate message. Also print the names which begins with the word "SRI".

ICSE SQP 2023

KEY idea

To define a class in Java that accepts 10 names of students in an array and performs linear search to check the existence of a given name in the array. If the name is found, the position of the name is printed. If not found, an appropriate message is displayed. The class should also print the names that begin with the word "SRI".

Ans
```
import java.util.Scanner;
class Search
{
   public static void main(String[] args)
   {
      Scanner in = new Scanner(System.in);
      String a[] = new String[10];
      int count = 0;
      int pos = 0;
      System.out.println("Enter 10 names:");
      for (int i = 0; i < a.length; i++)
      a[i] = in.nextLine();
      System.out.print("Enter name to be searched: ");
      String key = in.nextLine();
      boolean found = false;
      for (int i=0; i < a.length; i++)
      {
         if (key.equalsIgnoreCase(a[i]) && !found)
         {
            found = true;
            pos = i;
         }
         if (a[i].startsWith("SRI"))
         count++;
      }
      if (found)
         System.out.println("Found at position: " + (pos + 1));
      else
         System.out.println("Not found!");
         System.out.println("No. of names beginning with SRI = " + count);
   }
}
```

Output

Enter 10 names:
suman
bhavana
sapna
adishree
farah
gautam
harsha
rakesh
shivani
supriya
Enter name to be searched: supriya
Found at position: 10
No. of names beginning with SRI = 0

7. Write a program to input name and percentage of 35 students of class X in two separate one dimensional arrays. Arrange students details according to their percentage in the descending order using selection sort method. Display name and percentage of first ten toppers of the class.
ICSE SQP 2020

Ans
```
import java.util.Scanner;
public class StudentPercentage
{
   public static void main(String args[])
   {
      Scanner in = new Scanner(System.in);
```

```
        String names[] = new String[35];
        double percentage[] = new double[35];
        for (int i = 0; i < names.length; i++)
        {
          System.out.print("Enter name of student " + (i + 1) + ": ");
          names[i] = in.nextLine();
          System.out.print("Enter percentage of student " + (i + 1) + ": ");
          percentage[i] = in.nextDouble();
          in.nextLine();
        }
        for (int i = 0; i < percentage.length - 1; i++)
        {
          int maxIdx = i;
          for (int j = i + 1; j < percentage.length; j++)
          {
             if (percentage[j] > percentage[maxIdx])
             maxIdx = j;
          }
          double t = percentage[i];
          percentage[i] = percentage[maxIdx];
          percentage[maxIdx] = t;
          String name = names[i];
          names[i] = names[maxIdx];
          names[maxIdx] = name;
        }
        //Display first ten toppers
        System.out.println("Name\tPercentage");
        for (int  i = 0; i < 10; i++)
        {
          System.out.println(names[i] + '\t' + percentage[i]);
        }
     }
  }
```

Output

Enter name of student 1: Supriya
Enter percentage of student 1: 78.0
Enter name of student 2: Amit
Enter percentage of student 2: 89.7
Enter name of student 3: Priya
Enter percentage of student 1: 88.0
Enter name of student 4: Smiti
Enter percentage of student 2: 79.8
......
......
Name Percentage
Amit 89.7
Priya 88.0
Smiti 79.8
Supriya 78.0

8. Write a program to input and store integer elements in a double dimensional array of size 4 × 4 and find the sum of all the elements. ***ICSE SQP 2020***

```
7 3 4 5
5 4 6 1
6 9 4 2
3 2 7 5
```

Sum of all the elements: 73

Ans
```
import java.util.Scanner;
public class arraySum
{
   public static void main(String args[])
   {
      Scanner in = new Scanner(System.in);
      int arr[][] = new int[4][4];
      long sum = 0;
      System.out.println("Enter the elements of 4x4 array:");
      for (int i = 0; i < 4; i++)
      {
         for (int j = 0; j < 4; j++)
         {
            arr[i][j] = in.nextInt();
         }
      }
      for (int i = 0; i < 4; i++)
      {
         for (int j = 0; j < 4; j++)
         {
            sum += arr[i][j];

         }
      }
      System.out.println("Sum of all the elements: " + sum);
   }
}
```

Output

Enter the elements of 4 × 4 array:

7 3 4 5
5 4 6 1
6 9 4 2
3 2 7 5

Sum of all the elements: 73

9. Write a program to input 15 integer elements in an array and sort them in ascending order using the bubble sort technique. ***ICSE 2019***

Ans
```
import java.util.Scanner;
class BubbleSortAsc
{
   public static void main(String[] args)
   {
      int num=15, i, j, temp;
      Scanner input = new Scanner(System.in);
      int array[] = new int[num];
      System.out.println("Enter " + num + " integers: ");
      for (i = 0; i <num; i++)
      {
         array[i] = input.nextInt();
         for (i = 0; i < ( num - 1 ); i++)
         {
            for (j = 0; j <num - i - 1; j++)
            {
               if (array[j] > array[j+1])
               {
                  temp = array[j];
                  array[j] = array[j+1];
```

```
                    array[j+1] = temp;
                }
            }
        }
        System.out.println("Sorted list of integers:");
        for (i = 0; i <num; i++)
        System.out. println(array[i]);
    }
  }
}
```

10. Write a program to accept name and total marks of N number of students in two single subscript array name[ ] and totalmarks[ ]. ***ICSE 2018***

Calculate and print:

(i) The average of the total marks obtained by N number of students.
[average = (sum of total marks of all the students)/N]

(ii) Deviation of each student's total marks with the average.
[deviation = total marks of a student – average]

Ans

```
import java.io.*;
class Students
{
  public static void main (String[] args) throws IOException
  {
    int N;
    int totmarks[] = new int [N];
    String names[] = new String [N];
    BufferedReader br = new BufferedReader (new InputStreamReader(System.in));
    for (int i =0 ; i< N ; i ++)
    {
      System.out.println ("Enter the name of students");
      names[i] = br. readLine();
      System.out.println ("Enter his total marks");
      totmarks[i] = Integer.parseInt (br.readLines());
    }
    double avg,dev;
    int sum;
    for(int i=0; i < N ; i ++)
    {
      sum = sum + marks [i];
    }
    avg = sum/N;
    for(int i = 0 ; i < N ; i ++)
    {
      dev = totmarks - avg ;
    }
    System.out.println ("Average of total marks by N students = "+ avg);
    System.out.println ("Deviation of each student's total marks with Average"
                                                                    + dev);
  }
}
```

11. Write a program to input integer elements into an array of size 20 and perform the following operations ***ICSE 2017***

(i) Display largest number from the array.

(ii) Display smallest number from the array.

(iii) Display sum of all the elements of the array.

Ans

```
import java.io.*;
class ArrayOperation
{
   public static void main(String args[]) throws IOException
   {
      int arr[] = new int[20];
      InputStreamReader IR=new InputStreamReader(System.in);
      BufferedReader br=new BufferedReader(IR);
      System.out.println("Enter the array elements");
      for(int i=0;i<20;i++)
         arr[i]=Integer.parseInt(br.readLine());
      int MIN=arr[0],MAX=arr[0],SUM=0;
      for(int i=0;i<20;i++)
      {
         if(MIN>arr[i])
            MIN=arr[i];
         else if(MAX<arr[i])
            MAX=arr[i];
         SUM=SUM+arr[i];
      }
      System.out.println("Largest number from array = "+MAX);
      System.out.println("Smallest number from array = "+MIN);
      System.out.println("Sum of all the elements of the array = "+SUM);
   }
}
```

12. Write a program to store 10 names in an array. Arrange these in alphabetical order by sorting. Print the sorted list. Take single word names, all in capital letters, e.g. SAMSON, AJAY, LUCY, etc.

ICSE SQP 2017

Ans

```
import java.util.Arrays;
public class NameSorter
{
   public static void main(String[] args)
   {
      String[] names = {"SAMSON", "AJAY", "LUCY", "DAVID", "JOHN", "MARY", "PETER",
                                                         "TOM", "XAVIER", "ZOE"};
      Arrays.sort(names);
      for (String name : names)
      {
         System.out.println(name);
      }
   }
}
```

Output

AJAY
DAVID
JOHN
LUCY
MARY
PETER
SAMSON
TOM
XAVIER
ZOE

13. Write a program to create an array to store 10 integers and print the largest integer and the smallest integer in that array.

ICSE SQP 2017

KEY idea

To create an array to store 10 integers and print the largest integer and the smallest integer in that array, you need to declare an integer array of size 10, initialize it with values and then iterate through the array to find the largest and smallest values.

Ans

```
import java.util.*;
public class Main
{
   public static void main(String[] args)
   {
      // Create an array of 10 integers
      int[] arr = {4, 8, 1, 9, 3, 7, 2, 6, 10, 5};
      // Find the largest and smallest integers in the array
      int smallest = arr[0];
      int largest = arr[0];
      for (int i = 1; i < arr.length; i++)
      {
         if (arr[i] < smallest)
         {
            smallest = arr[i];
         }
         if (arr[i] > largest)
         {
            largest = arr[i];
         }
      }
      // Print the largest and smallest integers
      System.out.println("The smallest integer is " + smallest);
      System.out.println("The largest integer is " + largest);
   }
}
```

Output

The smallest integer is 1
The largest integer is 10

Concept Enhancer To better understand this concept, it's helpful to learn about sorting algorithms and how they can be used to find the largest and smallest values in an array efficiently. Additionally, understanding the concept of time complexity can help you optimize your code for performance.

14. Write a program to input and store roll numbers, names and marks in 3 subjects of n number of students in five single dimensional array and display the remark based on average marks as given below: (The maximum marks in the subject are 100) ***ICSE 2015***

$$\text{Average marks} = \frac{\text{Total marks}}{3}$$

Average marks	Remark
85-100	EXCELLENT
75-84	DISTINCTION
60-74	FIRST CLASS
40-59	PASS
Less than 40	POOR

Ans
```
import java.io.*;
class StudentRemarks
{
   public static void main(String[] args) throws IOException
   {
      InputStreamReader IR=new InputStreamReader(System.in);
      BufferedReader br=new BufferedReader(IR);
      System.out.println("Enter the total number of Students");
      int n=Integer.parseInt(br.readLine());
      int rollNo[]=new int[n];
      String name[]=new String[n];
      int marks1[]=new int[n];
      int marks2[]=new int[n];
      int marks3[]=new int[n];
      for(int i=0;i<n;i++)
      {
         rollNo[i]=Integer.parseInt(br.readLine());
         name[i]=br.readLine();
         marks1[i]=Integer.parseInt(br.readLine());
         marks2[i]=Integer.parseInt(br.readLine());
         marks3[i]=Integer.parseInt(br.readLine());
      }
      System.out.println("RollNumber"+"\tName"+"\tMarks1"+"\tMarks2"+"\tMarks3"+"\
                                             tTotal Marks"+"\tAverage Marks"+"\tRemarks");
      for(int i=0;i<n;i++)
      {
         int total_marks=marks1[i]+marks2[i]+marks3[i];
         double avg=Math.round((total_marks)/3);
         if(avg>=85&& avg<=100)
            System.out.println(rollNo[i]+"\t\t"+name[i]+"\t"+marks1[i]+"\t "+
              marks2[i]+"\t"+marks3[i]+"\t"+total_marks+"\t\t"+avg+"\t\t" +"EXCELLENT");
         else if(avg>=75 && avg<=84)
            System.out.println(rollNo[i]+"\t\t"+name[i]+"\t"+marks1[i]+"\t"+
                          marks2[i]+"\t"+marks3[i]+"\t"+total_marks+"\t\t"+avg+"\t\t"
                                                                   +"DISTINCTION");
         else if(avg>=60 &&avg <=74)
            System.out.println(rollNo[i]+"\t\t"+name[i]+"\t"+marks1[i]+"\t"+
                   marks2[i]+"\t"+marks3[i]+"\t"+total_marks+"\t\t"+avg+"\t\t"+ "FIRST
                                                                        CLASS");
         else if(avg>=40 && avg<=59)
            System.out.println(rollNo[i]+"\t\t"+name[i]+"\t"+marks1[i]+"\t"+
                marks2[i]+"\t"+marks3[i]+"\t"+total_marks+"\t\t"+avg+"\t\t"+ "PASS  ");
         else
            System.out.println(rollNo[i]+"\t\t"+name[i]+"\t"+marks1[i]+"\t"+
                  marks2[i]+"\t"+marks3[i]+"\t"+total_marks+"\t\t"+avg+"\t\t"+ "POOR");
      }
   }
}
```

15. Write a program to input twenty names in an array. Arrange these names in descending order of alphabets, using the bubble sort technique. ***ICSE 2015***

Ans
```
import java.io.*;
class Main
{
   public static void main(String[] args) throws IOException
   {
      InputStreamReader IR=new InputStreamReader(System.in);
      BufferedReader br=new BufferedReader(IR);
      String a[]=new String[20];
      String s;
      System.out.println("Enter name one by one and press enter after every name");
```

```
            for(int i=0;i<20;i++)
            {
               a[i]=br.readLine();
            }
            for(int i=0;i<20;i++)
            {
               for(int j=0;j<20-i-1;j++)
               {
                  if(a[j].compareToIgnoreCase(a[j+1])<0)
                  {
                     s=a[j];
                     a[j]=a[j+1];
                     a[j+1]=s;
                  }
               }
            }
            System.out.println("Names in descending order");
            for(int i=0;i<20;i++)
            {
               System.out.println(a[i]);
            }
         }
      }
```

16. Write a program to accept the year of graduation from school as an integer value from the user. Using the binary search technique on the sorted array of integers given below

Output the message "Record exist". If the value input is located in the array. If not, output the message "Record does not exist".

{1982, 1987, 1993, 1996, 1999, 2003, 2006, 2007, 2009, 2010} ***ICSE 2014***

Ans

```
import java.io.*;
class Search
{
   public static void main(String[] args) throws IOException
   {
      int [] y={1982, 1987, 1993, 1996, 1999, 2003, 2006, 2007, 2009, 2010};
      InputStreamReader r=new InputStreamReader(System.in);
      BufferedReader b=new BufferedReader(r);
      System.out.println("Enter the year of Graduation:");
      int n = Integer.parseInt(b.readLine());
      int L = 0, U = 9, P = -1, mid;
      while(L <= U && P == -1)
      {
         mid = (L + U)/2;
         if(y[mid] == n)
         {
            P = mid;
            break;
         }
         else
         {
            if(y[mid] < n)
               L = mid + 1 ;
            else
               U = mid - 1;
         }
      }
      if(P != -1 )
         System.out.println("Record exists");
      else
         System.out.println("Record does not exist");
   }
}
```

17. Write a program to input 10 integer elements in an array and sort them in descending order using the bubble sort technique. ***ICSE 2013***

Ans
```
import java.io.*;
class Arrange
{
   public static void main(String args[]) throws IOException
   {
      InputStreamReader read = new InputStreamReader(System.in);
      BufferedReader b = new BufferedReader(read);
      int i, j, t;
      int m[] = new int[10];
      System.out.println("Enter numbers");
      for(i=0; i< 10; i++)
      {
         m[i] = Integer.parseInt(b.readLine( ));
      }
      for(i = 0;i< 9;i++)
      {
         for(j = 0;j< (9-i);j++)
         {
            if(m[j] < m[j+1])
            {
               t = m[j];
               m[j] = m[j+1];
               m[j+1] = t;
            }
         }
      }
      System.out.println("The numbers are arranged in descending order are");
      for(i=0 ; i< 10;i++)
         System.out.println(m[i]);
   }
}
```

18. Write a program to accept the names of 10 cities in a single dimensional String array and their STD (Subscribers Trunk Dialing) codes in another single dimensional integer array. Search for a name of a city input by the user in the list. If found, display "Search successful" and print the Name of the city along with its STD Code, or else display the message "Search Unsuccessful, no such city in the list". ***ICSE 2012***

Ans
```
import java.io.*;
class Search
{
   public static void main(String[] args) throws IOException
   {
      String C[] = {"Agra", "Delhi", "Kanpur", "Bombay", "Lucknow",
      "Allahabad", "Meerut", "Varanasi", "Mathura", "Aligarh"};
      int co[] = {562, 100, 555, 123, 257, 565, 375, 333, 552, 543};
      System.out.println("Enter the name of city");
      BufferedReader b=new BufferedReader(new InputStreamReader(System.in));
      int f = 0;
      String m = b.readLine();
      for(int i = 0; i < 10; i++)
      {
         if(m.equals(C[i]) == true)
         {
            System.out.println("Search successful");
            System.out.println("Name" +m +" "+ "STD Code" +co[i]);
            f = 1;
         }
      }
      if(f==0)
      {
         System.out.println("Search unsuccessful, no such city in the list");
      }
   }
}
```

19. Write a program to perform binary search on a list of integers given below, to search for an element input by the user, if it is found display the element along with its position otherwise display the message "Search element not found". *ICSE 2010*

5, 7, 9, 11, 15, 20, 30, 45, 89, 97

Ans

```
import java.io.*;
class Search
{
  public static void main(String[] args) throws IOException
  {
    int x[] = {5, 7, 9, 11, 15, 20, 30, 45, 89, 97};
    System.out.println("Enter the element to search in the list");
    InputStreamReader IR = new InputStreamReader(System.in);
    BufferedReader br = new BufferedReader(IR);
    int y = Integer.parseInt(br.readLine( ));
    int LB = 0, UB = 9, mid = 0;
    boolean Flag = false;
    do
    {
      mid = (LB + UB)/2;
      if(y == x[mid])
      {
        System.out.println("Element is :" +y);
        System.out.println("Found at index:" +mid);
        System.out.println("position in list:" +(mid+1));
        Flag = true;
        break;
      }
      else
        if(y < x [mid])
        {
          UB = mid - 1;
        }
        else
          LB = mid + 1;
    }
    while(LB <= UB);
    if(flag==false)
      System.out.println("Search element not found");
  }
}
```

20. Shasha Travels. Pvt. Ltd. gives the following discount to its customers

Ticket amount	Discount
Above Rs. 70000	18%
Rs. 55001 to Rs. 70000	16%
Rs. 35001 to Rs. 55000	12%
Rs. 25001 to Rs. 35000	10%
Less then Rs. 25001	2%

Write a program to input the name and ticket amount for the customer and calculate the discount amount and net amount to be paid. Display the output in the following format for each customer.

SI. No.	Name	Ticket charges	Discount	Net amount
1.	—	—	—	—

(Assume that there are 15 customers, first customer is given the serial no (SI.No.) 1, next customer 2....and so on.) *ICSE 2010*

Ans

```
import java.io.*;
class Travels
{
  public static void main(String[] args) throws IOException
  {
    InputStreamReader R = new InputStreamReader(System.in);
```

```
        BufferedReader br = new BufferedReader(R);
        String n[] = new String[15];
        double net[]=new double[15];
        double a[] = new double[15];
        double d[] = new double[15];
        for(int i = 0; i < 15; i++)
        {
          System.out.println("Enter the Name of Customer");
          n[i] = br.readLine( );
          System.out.println("Enter the Ticket Amount");
          a[i] = Double.parseDouble(br.readLine());
        }
        System.out.println("SI.No.\t Name\t Ticket charges\t Discount\tNet amount\t");
        for(int i = 0; i < 15; i++)
        {
          if(a[i] <=25000)
          {
            d[i] = 0.02 * a[i];
          }
          else if(a[i] <= 35000)
          {
            d[i] = 0.10 * a[i];
          }
          else if(a[i] <= 55000)
          {
            d[i] = 0.12 * a[i];
          }
          else if(a[i] <= 70000)
          {
            d[i] = 0.16 * a[i];
          }
          else
          {
            d[i] = 0.18 * a[i];
          }
          net[i] = a[i] - d[i];
          System.out.println((i + 1) + "\t" +n[i] + "\t" +a[i] + "\t\t" +d[i]+
                                                                      "\t"+net[i]);
        }
      }
    }
```

21. Write a program to store 6 elements in any array P and 4 elements in an array Q and produce a third array R, containing all the elements of array P and Q.
Display the resultant array *ICSE 2010*

EXAMPLE	INPUT	OUTPUT
P[ ]	Q[ ]	R[ ]
4	19	4
6	23	6
1	7	1
2	8	2
3		3
10		10
		19
		23
		7
		8

Ans
```
import java.io.*;
class Join
{
   public static void main(String args[]) throws IOException
   {
      int p[] = new int[6];
      int Q[] = new int[4];
      int R[] = new int[10];
      InputStreamReader IR = new InputStreamReader(System.in);
      BufferedReader br = new BufferedReader(IR);
      System.out.println("Enter the element of P");
      for(int i = 0; i < 6; i++)
      {
         p[i] = Integer.parseInt(br.readLine());
      }
      System.out.println("Enter the elements of Q");
      for(int i = 0; i < 4; i++)
      {
         Q[i] = Integer.parseInt(br.readLine( ));
      }
      int k, m = 0;
      for(k = 0; k < 6; k++)
      {
         R[k] = p[k];
         m++;
      }
      for(k = 0; k < 4; k++)
      {
         R[m] = Q[k];
         m++;
      }
      System.out.println("The elements of r are:");
      for(int i = 0; i < 10 ; i++)
      {
         System.out.println(R[i]);
      }
   }
}
```

22. The annual examination results of 50 students in a class is tabulated as follows

Roll. No.	Subject A	Subject B	Subject C
....	....	....	....

Write a program to read the data, calculate and display the followings

(i) Average marks obtained by each students.

(ii) Print the roll number and average marks of the students whose average mark is above 80.

(iii) Print the roll number and average marks of the students whose average mark is below 40.

ICSE 2009

Ans
```
import java.io.*;
class Result
{
   public static void main(String args[]) throws IOException
   {
      InputStreamReader ir = new InputStreamReader(System.in);
      BufferedReader bf = new BufferedReader(ir);
      int roll[] = new int[50];
      int subA[] = new int[50];
      int subB[] = new int[50];
```

```
        int subC[] = new int[50];
        int avg[] = new int[50];
        for(int i = 0; i <= 49; i++)
        {
          System.out.println("Enter the roll number");
          roll[i] = Integer.parseInt(bf.readLine());
          System.out.println("Enter the marks for subject A");
          subA[i] = Integer.parseInt(bf.readLine());
          System.out.println("Enter the marks for subject B");
          subB[i] = Integer.parseInt(bf.readLine());
          System.out.println("Enter the Marks for subject C");
          subC[i] = Integer.parseInt(bf.readLine());
          avg[i] = (subA[i] + subB[i] + subC[i])/3;
        }
        System.out.println("Average Marks obtained by each student");
        System.out.println("Roll No.\tsubject A\tsubject B\t subject C\tAverage Marks");
        for(int i = 0; i <= 49; i++)
        {
          System.out.println(roll[i] +"\t"+subA[i]+"\t"+subB[i]+"\t"+subC[i]+"\t"+avg[i]);
        }
        System.out.println("Average Marks obtained by student whose average is above 80");
        System.out.println("Roll No.\tsubject A\tsubject B\tsubject C\tAverage");
        for(int i = 0;  i <= 49; i++)
        {
          if(avg[i] > 80)
             System.out.println(roll[i]+"\t"+sub A[i]+"\t" subB[i]+"\t"+subC[i]+"\t"+avg[i]);
        }
        System.out.println("Average marks obtained by student whose average is below 40");
        System.out.println("Roll No.\tsubject A\tsubject B\t subject C\tAverage");
        for(int i = 0; i <= 49; i++)
        {
          if(avg[i] < 40)
             System.out.println(roll[i]+"\t"subA[i]+"\t" subB[i]+"\t"+subC[i]+"\t"+avg[i]);
        }
    }
}
```

23. Define a class and store the given city names in a single dimensional array. Sort these names in alphabetical order using the Bubble Sort technique only.

INPUT : Delhi, Bangalore, Agra, Mumbai, Calcutta.

OUTPUT : Agra, Bangalore, Calcutta, Delhi, Mumbai. ***ICSE 2008***

Ans

```
import java.io.*;
class Name
{
  public static void main(String args[]) throws IOException
  {
    String city[] = {"Delhi", "Bangalore", "Agra", "Mumbai", "Kolkata"};
    String temp;
    int i, j, n = 5;
    for(i= 1; i< n-1; i++)
    {
      for(j= 0; j<=n-i-1; j++)
      {
        if((city[j].compareTo(city[j+1])) > 0)
```

```
            {
               temp = city[j];
               city[j] = city[j+1];
               city[j + 1] = temp;
            }
         }
      }
      for(int K = 0; K <  n; K++)
      {
         System.out.println(city[K]);
      }
   }
}
```

24. Write a program to initialize the given data in an array and find the minimum and maximum values alongwith the sum of the given elements. ***ICSE 2007***

Number : 2 5 4 1 3

Output : Minimum value : 1
Maximum value : 5
Sum of the elements : 15

Ans

```
import java.io.*;
class Array
{
   public static void main(String[] args)
   {
      int a[] = {2, 5, 4, 1, 3};
      int i, max = a[0], min = a[0], sum = 0;
      for(i = 0; i < a.length; i++)
      {
         if(a[i] > max)
            max = a[i];
         if(a[i] < min)
            min = a[i];
         sum = sum + a[i];
      }
      System.out.println("The minimum element is" +min);
      System.out.println("The maximum element is" +max);
      System.out.println("The sum of all the element is" +sum);
   }
}
```

25. The marks obtained by 50 students in a subject are tabulated as follows

Name	Marks
*	*
*	*
*	*

Write a program to input the names and marks of the students in the subjects. Calculate the display

(i) The subject average marks $\left(\text{subject average marks} = \dfrac{\text{subject total}}{50}\right)$.

(ii) The highest marks in the subject and the name of the student. (The maximum marks in the subject are 100). ***ICSE 2006***

Ans
```
import java.io.*;
class Students
{
   public static void main(String[] args) throws IOException
   {
      int marks[] = new int[50];
      String names[] = new String[50];
      BufferedReader br = new BufferedReader(new InputStreamReader(System.in));
      for(int i = 0; i < 50; i++)
      {
         System.out.println("Enter name of student");
         names[i] = br.readLine();
         System.out.println("Enter his marks");
         marks[i] = Integer.parseInt(br.readLine());
      }
      double avg;
      int high =  marks[0], pos = 0, sum = 0;
      for(int i = 0; i < 50; i++)
      {
         sum += marks[i];
         if(marks[i] > high)
         {
            high = marks[i];
            pos = i;
         }
      }
      avg = sum/50;
      System.out.println("Average marks of the class =" +avg);
      System.out.println("Highest marks =" +high);
      System.out.println("Student who got highest =" +names[pos]);
   }
}
```

26. Write a program to bubble sort, the following set of values in ascending order
5, 3, 8, 4, 9, 2, 1, 12, 98, 16

Output

```
1
2
3
4
5
8
9
12
16
98
```

ICSE 2005

Ans
```
import java.io.*;
class Arrange
{
   public static void main(String args[]) throws IOException
   {
      int Arr[] ={5, 3, 8, 4, 9, 2, 1, 12, 98, 16}, i, j, t;
      for(i = 0; i < 10; i++ )
      {
         for(j = 0; j < (9 - i); j++)
```

```
            {
               if (Arr[j] > Arr[j + 1])
               {
                  t = Arr[j];
                  Arr[j] = Arr[j + 1];
                  Arr[j + 1] = t;
               }
            }
         }
         System.out.println("The numbers are arranged in ascending order are");
         for(i = 0; i < 10; i++)
         {
            System.out.println(Arr[i]);
         }
      }
   }
```

27. Write a program to initialize an array of 5 names and initialize another array with their respective telephone numbers. Search for a name input by the user, in the list. If found, display "search successful" and print the name along with the telephone number, otherwise display "Search unsuccessful: Name not enlisted". ***ICSE 2005***

Ans

```
import java.io.*;
class Search
{
   public static void main(String args[]) throws IOException
   {
      String n[] = {"Anubhav", "Ravi", "Latika", "Rahat", "Anmol"};
      long ph[] = {43457410, 44039181, 46825311, 47411941, 46854341};
      boolean flag = false;
      System.out.println("Enter the name whose phone no. is to be searched");
      InputStreamReader IR = new InputStreamReader(System.in);
      BufferedReader br = new BufferedReader(IR);
      String m = br.readLine();
      for(int i = 0; i < 5; i++)
      {
         if(n[i].compareTo(m)==0)
         {
            flag = true;
            System.out.println(n[i] + " " +ph[i]);
            break;
         }
      }
      if(flag==false)
         System.out.println("Search unsuccessful: Name not enlisted");
   }
}
```

CHAPTER TEST

1 Mark Questions

1. The integer subscript that is used with the array name to access the values of the individual elements is called
(a) data (b) position (c) element (d) index

2. The element at index 0 can be called as
(a) Index element (b) First element (c) Base element (d) All of these

3. The algorithm in which the middle index is found and the array is divided into 2 halves to search for an element is called
(a) Linear search (b) Data Search (c) Long search (d) Binary search

4. Given array int x[]= {11, 22, 33, 44}; the value of x[-1] is
(a) 11 (b) 22 (c) 33 (d) Invalid statement

5. If an array "arr" exists to store 50 in its index 5 the statement will be..................
(a) `arr[50]=5;` (b) `arr.index[5]=50;` (c) `arr[5]=50;` (d) None of these

6. For an array m[]={12.5,15.6,22.7,99.8}
The statement m.length will return
(a) 1 (b) 2 (c) 3 (d) 4

2 Marks Questions

7. Give the output of the following code
```
int m[]= {2, 4, 6, 8} ;
System.out.println(m[1] + " " + m[2]);
```

8. Array is a composite data type. Explain this statement.

9. Define the double dimensional array with their constructs.

10. Differentiate between linear search and binary search.

15 Marks Questions

11. Write a program to search an element in an array using linear search.

12. Write a program to reverse the array without using temporary variable.

08

String Handling

TREND ANALYSIS 3 YEARS

Average No. of Questions Across all Sets

	Types of Questions	2023	2019	2018
String Handling	1 Mark	2	–	–
	2 Marks	1	3	3
	15 Marks	1	1	1

A **string** is a term that refers to set of characters. Java provides a class String in java.lang package whose objects can be treated as variables of type String.

String represents a sequence of characters. The easiest way to represent string in Java is by using a character array. e.g.

```
char charArray [] = new char[4];
charArray [0] = 'J';
charArray [1] = 'a';
charArray [2] = 'v';
charArray [3] = 'a';
```

Strings are class objects and implemented by using two classes, that is **String** and **StringBuffer**. A Java string is an instantiated object of the String class. It is not a character array and not NULL terminated. Strings may be declared and created as follows:

```
String stringName;
stringName = new String("string");
```

e.g. Java offers three classes to work with character data:

1. **Character Class** can hold single character data.
2. **String Class** can hold unchanging string, i.e. once initialised, its contents cannot be modified.
3. **StringBuffer Class** can hold mutable strings, i.e. can be changed or modified.

Declaring and Allocating Strings

To create a String through assignment, we do not require the use of new operator. The most direct way to create a string is to write:

```
String greeting = "Hello world!";
```

The String class supports several constructors. To create an empty string, we call a default constructor.

e.g.

```
String s = new String();
```

This will create an instance of String with no character in it.

To create a String initialised by an array of characters, use the constructor shown here:

```
String(char Chars[ ])
```

e.g.

```
char Chars[ ] = {'a', 'b', 'c'};
String s = new Str+-ing(Chars);
```

Here, this constructor initialises s with the string "abc".

Methods of String Class

Function	Format	Description	Example
charAt( )	a.charAt(n);	Returns the character at the specified index (n^{th} position as it starts counting from 0th position).	a = "computer"; a.charAt(5); Output : t
compareTo( )	a1.compareTo(a2);	Compare two strings lexicographically. It returns negative if a1 < a2 positive if a1 > a2 zero if a1 = a2	a1 = "Computer Application"; a2 = "Computer Application"; a1. compareTo (a2); Output : 0
concat( )	a1.concat(a2);	Concatenates the specified string to the end of the current string object.	a1 = "good"; a2 = "bye"; a1.concat(a2); Output : goodbye
endsWith( )	p.endsWith (b);	Returns True if the string p contains a suffix specified by string b.	p = "COMPUTER"; b = "FUN"; boolean x = p.endsWith(b); Output : False
equals( )	a1.equals(a2);	Check whether contents of two strings are equal or not.	a1 = "Rajendra"; a2 = "Rajendra"; a1. equals(a2); Output : True
equals IgnoreCase( )	a1.equalsIgnoreCase(a2);	Returns True, if a1 and a2 are equal after ignoring cases of the strings and otherwise False, if they are unequal.	a1 = "Computer"; a2 = "COMPUTER"; a1. equalsIgnoreCase(a2); Output : True
indexOf( )	a.indexOf('m');	Returns the position of the first occurrence of 'm' in the string a.	a = "Computer"; a.indexOf('m'); Output : 2
	Or	*Or*	*Or*
	a.indexOf('m', n);	Returns the position of 'm' in the string from n^{th} position.	a = "prime number"; a.indexOf('m', 5); Output : 8 (The next occurrence of 'm' in the string from 5th position is at 8th location).
lastIndexOf( )	int n = s.lastIndexOf('A');	Returns position of last occurrence of letter.	String s = "MALAYALAM"; int n = s.lastIndexOf('A'); Output : 7
length( )	s.length( );	Returns the length of character present in the string.	String s = "MALAYALAM"; s.length( ); Output : 9
replace( )	a.replace('m', 'n');	Replaces all the occurrences of one character or string with other character or string.	a = "Computer"; a.replace ('m', 'n'); Output : Conputer

Function	Format	Description	Example
startsWith( )	p.startsWith(b);	Returns True if the string p starts with specified string b.	p = "Arihant Publication"; b = "Arihant"; boolean x = p.startsWith(b); Output : True
int compare ToIgnoreCase (String str)	s1.compareToIgnore Case (s2);	Compares two strings lexicographically, ignoring case differences	s1="HELLO"; s2="hello"; s1.compareToIgnoreCase(s2); **Output** zero
substring( )	a.substring(m, n);	Returns a substring, out of n −1 characters leaving first m character of the string.	a = "Vidyalaya"; a.substring (3, 8); Output : yalay
toLowerCase( )	a.toLowerCase( );	Converts all the characters of the string in lowercase.	a = "ARIHANT"; a.toLowerCase ( ); Output : arihant
toUpperCase( )	a.toUpperCase( );	Converts all the characters of the string in uppercase.	a = "arihant"; a.toUpperCase( ); Output : ARIHANT
valueOf( )	String.valueOf(b);	Returns string represented by the value of the passed argument.	b = true; String.valueOf(b); Output : true

trim( )	a.trim( );	Removes the whitespaces from the beginning and ending of the current or this string.	a = "# arihant #" //here, # denotes whitespace
			a.trim( );
			Output : arihant

String Array

A Java string array is an object that holds a fixed number of string values. It is a very useful and important data structure that can help and solve many types of problems.

String Array Declaration

Square brackets is used to declare a string array. There are two ways of using it.

e.g.
```
string[]  stringArray;
```
Or
```
string   stringArray[];
```

String Array Initialization

There are multiple ways to initialize a string array. Initialization can also be done at the same time as the declaration.

e.g. `string[] stringArray ={"AA", "BB", "CC", "DD"};`

Another syntax to declare and initialize a string array together is by using the new operator.

e.g. `string []  stringArray=new string [] {"AA", "BB", "CC", "DD"};`

PYQs Previous Years Questions

1 Mark Questions

1. The String class method to join two strings is **ICSE 2023**

   (a) concat(String) (b) <string>.joint(string)
   (c) concat(char) (d) Concat()

Ans (a) concat(String)

2. The output of the function "COMPOSITION". substring (3, 6) **ICSE 2023**

   (a) POSI (b) POS (c) MPO (d) MPOS

Ans (b) POS

3. The method to convert a string to upper case is **ICSE SQP 2023**

   (a) toUpperCase(char) (b) toUPPERCASE(String)
   (c) toUpperCase(String) (d) touppercase(String)

Ans (c) toUpperCase(String)

4. The output of the method "DETERMINATION". substring(2, 6) is **ICSE SQP 2023**

   (a) "TERM" (b) term
   (c) "Term" (d) "TERMI"

Ans (a) "TERM"

5. Give the output of the following String methods.
   `"SUCESS" indexOf('S')+ "SUCESS".lastIndexOf('S')` **ICSE 2022 (Sem II)**

   (a) 0 (b) 5 (c) 6 (d) – 5

Ans (b) **Output** 5

6. Give the output of the following code.
   `System.out.println("Good". concat("Day"));` **ICSE 2022 (Sem II)**

   (a) GoodDay (b) Good Day
   (c) Goodday (d) goodDay

Ans (a) **Output** GoodDay

7. What will be the output of the following code?
   `System.out.println("Lucknow".substring(0 ,4));` **ICSE 2022 (Sem II)**

   (a) Lucknow (b) Luckn
   (c) Luck (d) luck

Ans (c) **Output** Luck

8. Give the output of the following string methods. **ICSE SQP 2022 (Sem II)**
   `"MISSISSIPPI".indexOf('S')+"MISSISSIPPI" .lastIndexOf('I')`

   (a) 10 (b) 12 (c) 20 (d) 11

Ans (b) 12

9. Name a string function which removes the blank spaces provided in the prefix and suffix of a string. **ICSE 2015**

Ans String.trim() is used to remove blank spaces provided in prefix and suffix of a string.

e.g.
```
String S= " ABCD ";
System.out.print(S.trim());
```
Output `ABCD`

10. What is the data type that the following library functions return?
    `isWhitespace(char)` **ICSE 2013**

Ans isWhitespace(char ch) method returns a boolean data type.

2 Marks Questions

1. Give the output of the following String class methods. **ICSE 2023**

   (i) "COMMENCEMENT".lastIndexOf('M')
   (ii) "devote".compareTo("DEVOTE")

Ans (i) 8
(ii) 32

2. Give the output of the following String class method. **ICSE SQP 2023**

   "MISSISSIPPI".replace('S', 't').toLowerCase()

Ans mitittippi

3. Give the output of the following String class method.
   "REDUCE".compareTo("REVOLT") + "ANTARTICA".lastIndexOf('A') **ICSE SQP 2023**

Ans – 10

4. Write a Java statement for each to perform the following task. **ICSE SQP 2020**

   (i) Find and display the position of the last space in a string str.
   (ii) Extract the second character of the string str.

Ans (i) `System.out.println(str.lastIndexOf(' '));`
(ii) `System.out.println(str.charAt(1));`

5. Give the output of the following Java statements. **ICSE SQP 2020**

   (i) "TRANSPARENT".toLowerCase()
   (ii) "TRANSPARENT" .compareTo("TRANSITION")

Ans (i) transparent
(ii) 7

6. Write the return data type of the following functions. *ICSE 2019*

(i) startsWith( ) (ii) random( )

Ans (i) boolean (ii) double

7. Write the output for the following:

```
String s1 = "phoenix"; String s2
                                = "island";
System.out.println(s1.substring (0).
                  concat (s2.substring(2)));
System.out.println(s2.toUpperCase( ));
```

ICSE 2019

Ans phoenixland

ISLAND

8.
```
String x[ ] = {"Artificial
intelligence", "IOT", "Machine
learning", "Big data"};
```

Give the output of the following statements: *ICSE 2019*

(i) `System.out.println(x[3]);`

(ii) `System.out.println(x.length);`

Ans (i) Big Data

(ii) 4

9. What will be the output of the following program segments? *ICSE SQP 2017*

```
String s = "application";
int p = s.indexOf('a');
System.out.println(p);
System.out.println(p+s);
```

Ans 0

0application

10. What will be the output of the following program segments? *ICSE SQP 2017*

```
String st = "PROGRAM";
System.out.println(st.indexOf(st.charAt(4)));
```

Ans 1

11. Write the return data type of the following functions. *ICSE 2018*

(i) endsWith() (ii) log()

Ans (i) Return data type of function endsWith() is boolean.

(ii) Return data type of function log() is double.

12. Give the output of the following string functions. *ICSE 2018*

(i) "ACHIEVEMENT".replace('E', 'A')

(ii) "DEDICATE".compareTo("DEVOTE")

Ans **Output**

(i) ACHIAVAMANT (ii) –18

13. Consider the following String array and give the output. *ICSE 2018*

```
String arr[ ]= {"DELHI", "CHENNAI",
                "MUMBAI", "LUCKNOW", "JAIPUR"};
System.out.println(arr[0].length()>
                              arr[3].length());
System.out.print(arr[4].substring(0,3));
```

Ans **Output**

False

JAI

14. `String x[] = {"SAMSUNG", "NOKIA", "SONY", "MICROMAX", "BLACKBERRY"};` *ICSE 2017*

Give the output of the following statements.

(i) `System.out.println(x[1]);`

(ii) `System.out.println(x[3].length());`

Ans (i) **Output** NOKIA (ii) **Output** 8

15. Write the output for the following *ICSE 2017*

```
String s="Today is Test";
System.out.println(s.indexOf('T'));
System.out.println(s.substring(0,7)+"
"+"Holiday");
```

Ans **Output**

0

Today is Holiday

16. Give the output of the following code. *ICSE 2017*

```
String A="26", B="100";
String D=A+B+"200";
int x=Integer.parseInt(A);
int y=Integer.parseInt(B);
int d=x+y;
System.out.println("Result 1 = "+D);
System.out.println("Result 2 = "+d);
```

Ans **Output**

Result 1 = 26100200

Result 2 = 126

17. Give the output of the following string functions. *ICSE 2016*

(i) "MISSISSIPPI".indexOf('S')+"MISSISSIPPI".lastIndexOf('I')

(ii) "CABLE".compareTo("CADET")

Ans **Output**

(i) 12 (ii) – 2

18. What is the value stored in variable res given below? *ICSE 2015*

```
double res = Math.pow
("345".indexOf('5'), 3);
```

Ans Value stored in variable res is 8.0

19. State the output when the following program segment is executed. *ICSE 2015*

```
String a = "Smartphone", b = "Graphic Art";
String h = a. substring(2,5);
String k = b. substring(8).toUpperCase();
System.out.println(h);
System.out.println(k.equalsIgnoreCase(h));
```

Ans art

True

20. What is the data type returned by the library functions? *ICSE 2014*

(i) compareTo( ) (ii) equals( )

Ans (i) compareTo( ) returns an int data type.

(ii) equals( ) returns boolean data type.

21. State the output of the following program segment. *ICSE 2014*

```
String str1= "great";
String str2 = "minds";
System.out.println(str1.substring(0,2).concat(str2.substring(1)));
System.out.println("WH" + (str1.substring(2).toUpperCase()));
```

Ans The output will be

grinds

WHEAT

22. State the value of characteristic and mantissa when the following code is executed. *ICSE 2014*

```
String s = "4.3756";
int n = s.indexOf('.');
int characteristic = Integer.parseInt(s.substring (0, n));
int mantissa = Integer.valueOf(s.substring (n + 1));
```

Ans characteristic = 4

mantissa = 3756

23. State the values stored in the variable str1 and str2. *ICSE 2013*

```
String s1 = "good"; String s2 = "world/matters";
String str1 = s2.substring(5).replace('t','n');
String str2 = s1.concat(str1);
```

Ans str1 = /manners

str2 = good/manners

24. State the output of the following program segment. *ICSE 2012*

```
String s = "Examination";
int n = s.length();
System.out.println(s.startsWith(s.substring(5, n)));
System.out.println(s.charAt(2) == s.charAt(6));
```

Ans The output will be

False

True

25. State the method that *ICSE 2012*

(i) converts a string to a primitive float data type.

(ii) determines if the specified character is an uppercase character.

Ans (i) `Float.parseFloat( );`

(ii) `Character.isUpperCase(char);`

26. State the data type and values of a and b after the following segment is executed. *ICSE 2012*

```
String s1 = "Computer", s2 = "Applications";
a = (s1.compareTo(s2));
b = (s1.equals(s2));
```

Ans a = (s1.compareTo(s2));

compareTo method returns int value

a = 2 [because C = 3, A = 1,

So, difference = 3 – 1 = 2]

b = s1.equals(s2);

equals method returns boolean value

Both strings are not equal.

So, b = False

27. What will be following code output? *ICSE 2012*

```
String s = "malayalam";
System.out.println(s.indexOf('m'));
System.out.println(s.lastIndexOf('m'));
```

Ans The output will be

0

8

28. Give the output of the following *ICSE 2011*

```
String n = "Computer Knowledge";
String m = "Computer Applications";
System.out.println(n.substring(0,8).concat(m.substring(9)));
System.out.println(n.endsWith("e"));
```

Ans The output will be

Computer Applications

True

29. Write the output of the following statements. *ICSE 2011*

(i) `System.out.println(Character.isUpperCase('R'));`

(ii) `System.out.println(Character.toUpperCase('j'));`

Ans The output will be

(i) true (ii) J

30. Write a statement each to perform the following task on a string *ICSE 2011*

(i) Find and display the position of the last space in a string.

(ii) Convert a number stored in a string variable x to double data type.

Ans (i) `i = s.lastIndexOf(' ');`

(ii) `Double.parseDouble(s);`

31. State the purpose and return data type of the following string functions. *ICSE 2010*

(i) `indexOf()` (ii) `compareTo()`

Ans (i) **indexOf( )** This function returns the index of the character presented in a string.

Syntax `int variable = String.indexOf(character);`

This function returns an integer value.

(ii) **compareTo( )** It is also a type of function which compares two strings. It is not only checks the equality of the strings but also checks whether a string is bigger or smaller than other or not.

Syntax `int variable = String1.compareTo(String2);`

This function can return an integer value depending upon the condition you want to check.

32. Write a statement each to perform the following task on a string *ICSE 2010*

(i) Extract the second last character of a word stored in the variable wd.

(ii) Check if the second character of a string str is in uppercase.

Ans (i) `char c = wd.charAt(wd.length() - 2)`

(ii)
```
if(character.isUpperCase (s.charAt(1)))
{
  ......
}
```

33. If, `String x = "Computer";` *ICSE 2008*

`String y = "Applications";`

What do the following return for

(i) `System.out.print(x.substring(1, 5));`

(ii) `System.out.print(x.indexOf(x.charAt(4)));`

(iii) `System.out.print(y+x.substring(5));`

(iv) `System.out.print(x.equals(y));`

Ans (i) omput (ii) 4 (iii) Applicationster (iv) False

34. Write a Java statement to input/read the following from the user using the keyboard.

(i) Character (ii) String *ICSE 2008*

Ans (i) `char c=(char)object.read();` (ii) `String s=object.readLine();`

35. What is the output of the following *ICSE 2007*

```
String S1 = "Hi";
String S2 = "Hi";
String S3 = "three";
String S4 = "HI";
System.out.println(S1 + "equals" + S2 + "→" + S1.equals(S2));
System.out.println(S1 + "equals" + S3 + "→" + S1.equals(S3));
System.out.println(S1 + "equals" + S4 + "→" + S1.equals(S4));
System.out.println(S1 + "equalsIgnoreCase" + S4 + "→" +
S1.equalsIgnoreCase(S4));
```

Ans HiequalsHi → True

Hiequalsthree → False

HiequalsHI → False

HiequalsIgnoreCaseHI → true

36. Differentiate between compareTo( ) and equals( ) methods. *ICSE 2006*

Ans **compareTo( )** This function is used to compare two strings. It also checks whether a string is bigger or smaller than other or not. It returns integer type.

```
n = s1.compareTo(s2);
if s1 = s2, then n = 0
   s1 > s2, then n > 0
   s1 < s2, then n < 0
```

It checks the ASCII code of character present in the string.

equals( ) This function is used to compare two strings together to check whether they are identical or not. It returns a boolean type value true if both are same, false otherwise.

boolean result = s1.equals(s2);

37. What will be the output for the following program segment? *ICSE 2006*

```
String s = new String("abc");
System.out.println(s.toUpperCase());
```

Ans **Output**

ABC

38. What do the following functions return for **ICSE 2005**

```
String x = "hello";
String y = "world";
```

(i) `System.out.println(x+y);`

(ii) `System.out.println(x.length());`

(iii) `System.out.println(x.charAt(3));`

(iv) `System.out.println(x.equals(y));`

Ans(i) helloworld (ii) 5 (iii) l (iv) False

39. How can you declare string array in Java? **ICSE 2005**

Ans Square brackets is used to declare a string array. There are two ways of using it:

e.g. `string[ ] stringArray;`

Or

`string stringArray[ ];`

10 Marks Questions

1. Define a class to accept a string and print the characters with the uppercase and lowercase reversed, but all the other characters should remain the same as before.

Example : Input : WelCoMe_2022

Output : wELcOmE_2022 **ICSE 2022 (Sem II)**

Ans

```
import java.util.*;
public class UpperLowert
{
    public static void main(String[] args)
    {
        String str="", newstr="";
        Scanner sc=new Scanner(System.in);
        char c;
        int i;
        System.out.println("Enter a string:");
        str=sc.nextLine();
        for(i=0;i<str.length();i++)
        {
            c=str.charAt(i);
            if(Character.isLetter(c) && Character.isUpperCase(c))
                newstr+=Character.toLowerCase(c);
            else if (Character.isLetter(c) && Character.isLowerCase(c))
                newstr+=Character.toUpperCase(c);
            else
                newstr+=c;
        }
            Systerm.out.println("Converted String :"+newstr);
    }
}
```

2. Define a class to accept two strings of same length and form a new word in such a way that, the first character of the first word is followed by the first character of the second word and so on.

Example : Input : String 1-BALL

String 2-WORD

Output : BWAOLRLD **ICSE 2022 (Sem II)**

Ans

```
import java.util.*;
public class Alternate
```

```
{
   public static void main(String[] args)
   {
      String s1="",s2="",newstr="";
      s1=sc.nextLine()+"";
      if(s1.length()!=s2.length())
      {
         System.out.println("Strings should be of same length!!!");
         return;
      }
      else
      {
         for(int i=0;i<s1.length();i++)
         {
            c1=s1.char At(i);
            c2=s2.char At(i);
            newstr+=c1;
            newstr+=c2;
         }
         System.out.println("New string:"+newstr);
      }
   }
}
```

3. Define a class to declare an array to accept and store ten words. Display only those words which begin with the letter 'A' or 'a' and also end with the letter 'A' or 'a'. ***ICSE 2022 (Sem II)***

Example:

Input : Hari, Anita, Akash, Amrita, Alina, Devi, Rishab, John, Farha, AMITHA

Output : Anita
Amrita
Alina
AMITHA

Ans

```
import java.util.*;
public class Words
{
   public static void main(String[] args)
   {
      String s="",str="";
      Scanner sc=new Scanner(System.in);
      System.out.println("Enter the string");
      s=sc.nextLine()+"";
      char cb,ce;
      int l=s.length();
      for(int i=0; i<s.length();i++)
      {
         char c=s.charAt(i);
         if(c!='')
         {
            str+=s.charAt(i);
         }
         else
         {
            cb=str.charAt(0);
```

```
                ce=str.charAt(str.length()-1);
                if ((cb=='a' || cb =='A')&&(ce=='a' || ce=='A'))
                System.out.println(str);
                str="";
            }
        }
    }
}
```

4. Define a class to accept and store 10 strings into the array and print the strings with even number of characters. ***ICSE SQP 2022 (Sem II)***

Ans

```
import java.util.Scanner;
public class StringArray
{
   public static void main(String[] args)
   {
      String[] strings = new String[10];
      Scanner scanner = new Scanner(System.in);
      System.out.println("Enter 10 strings:");
      for (int i = 0; i < strings.length; i++)
      {
         strings[i] = scanner.nextLine();
      }
      System.out.println("Strings with even number of characters:");
      for (String s : strings)
      {
         if (s.length() % 2 == 0)
         {
            System.out.println(s);
         }
      }
   }
}
```

Output

Enter 10 strings:

suman

bhavana

sapna

adishree

farah

gautam

harsha

rakesh

shivani

supriya

Strings with even number of characters:

adishree

5. Define a class to accept two strings, convert them into uppercase, check and display whether two strings are equal or not, if the two strings are not equal, print the string with the highest length or print the message both the strings are of equal length. ***ICSE SQP 2022 (Sem II)***

Ans

```
import java.util.*;
public class StringComparer
{
   public static void compareStrings(String str1, String str2)
```

```
    {
        String upperStr1 = str1.toUpperCase();
        String upperStr2 = str2.toUpperCase();
        if (upperStr1.equals(upperStr2))
        {
            System.out.println("The two strings are equal.");
        }
        else
        {
            int length1 = upperStr1.length();
            int length2 = upperStr2.length();
            String longerString = (length1 > length2) ? upperStr1 : upperStr2;
            System.out.println("The two strings are not equal.");
            System.out.println("The longer string is: " + longerString);
        }
    }
    public static void main(String[] args)
    {
        String str1 = "Hello";
        String str2 = "World";
        compareStrings(str1, str2);
    }
}
```

Output

The two strings are not equal.

The longer string is: WORLD

Concept Enhancer In Java, you can convert a string to uppercase using the toUpperCase() method. To check if two strings are equal in Java, you should use the equals() method rather than the == operator. To find the length of a string, you can use the length() method. To compare the lengths of two strings, you can use the compareTo() method, which returns a positive number if the first string is longer, a negative number if the second string is longer, and zero if they are of equal length.

6. Define a class to accept a string, convert it into lowercase and check whether the string is a palindrome or not.

A palindrome is a word which reads the same backward as forward.

Example:

madam, racecar etc. ***ICSE SQP 2022 (Sem II)***

Ans

```
import java.util.Scanner;
public class PalindromeChecker
{
    public static void main(String[] args)
    {
        Scanner scanner = new Scanner(System.in);
        System.out.print("Enter a string: ");
        String input = scanner.nextLine().toLowerCase();
        if (isPalindrome(input))
        {
            System.out.println("The string is a palindrome.");
        }
        else
        {
            System.out.println("The string is not a palindrome.");
        }
    }
```

```
        private static boolean isPalindrome(String str)
        {
            int length = str.length();
            for (int i = 0; i < length / 2; i++)
            {
                if (str.charAt(i) != str.charAt(length - 1 - i))
                {
                    return false;
                }
            }
            return true;
        }
    }
```

Output 1

Enter a string: madam

The string is a palindrome.

Output 2

Enter a string: world

The string is not a palindrome.

15 Marks Questions

1. Define a class to accept a String and print the number of digits, alphabets and special characters in the string. ***ICSE 2023***

Example : S = "KAPILDEV@83"

Output : Number of digits–2
Number of alphabets–8
Number of special characters–1

Ans

```
import java.util.Scanner;
public class Example
{
    public static void main(String[] args)
    {
        Scanner sc = new Scanner(System.in);
        System.out.println("Enter a string:");
        String str = sc.nextLine();
        int specialCharCount = 0;
        int digitCount = 0;
        int alphabetCount = 0;
        for (int i = 0; i < str.length(); i++)
        {
            char c = str.charAt(i);
            if (Character.isDigit(c))
            {
                digitCount++;
            }
            else if (Character.isLetter(c))
            {
                alphabetCount++;
            }
            else
            {
                specialCharCount++;
            }
        }
        System.out.println("Number of digits: " + digitCount);
```

```
        System.out.println("Number of alphabets: " + alphabetCount);
        System.out.println("Number of special characters: " + specialCharCount);
    }
}
```

Concept Enhancer To count the number of digits, alphabets, and special characters in a string, we can loop through each character in the string and use conditional statements to identify the category of each character. We can use the Character class in Java to check whether a character is a digit or an alphabet. Special characters can be identified by checking if a character is not a digit or an alphabet.

2. Define a class to accept a string and print the same in reverse, also print the number of vowels in the string.

Example : S = "BEAUTIFUL"

Output – "LUFITUAEB"

No. of vowels = 5 ***ICSE SQP 2023***

Ans

```
import java.util.Scanner;
class reverse
{
    public static void main (String[] args)
    {
        Scanner in = new Scanner (System.in);
        System.out.print("Enter the string = ");
        String s = in.nextLine();
        int j = 0;
        String r = "";
        for (int i = s.length() - 1; i >= 0; i--)
        {
            char ch = s.charAt(i);
            r += ch;
            if ("AEIOUaeiou".indexOf(ch) >= 0)
                j++;
        }
        System.out.println(("Reverse of the string = "+ r);
        System.out.println("No. of vowels = " + j);
    }
}
```

3. Write a program to input a string and convert it into uppercase and print the pair of vowels and number of pair of vowels occurring in the string. ***ICSE SQP 2020***

Example:

Input:

"BEAUTIFUL BEAUTIES"

Output:

Pair of vowels: EA, AU, EA, AU, IE

No. of pair of vowels: 5

Ans

```
import java.util.Scanner;
public class KboatVowelPair
{
    static boolean isVowel(char ch)
    {
        ch = Character.toUpperCase(ch);
```

```
        if (ch == 'A' ||ch == 'E' ||ch == 'I' || ch == 'O' ||ch == 'U')
            return true;
        return false;
    }
    public static void main(String args[])
    {
        Scanner in = new Scanner(System.in);
        System.out.println("Enter the sentence : ");
        String str = in.nextLine();
        str = str.toUpperCase();
        int count = 0;
        System.out.print("Pair of vowels: ");
        for (int i = 0; i < str.length() - 1; i++)
        {
            if (isVowel(str.charAt(i)) && isVowel(str.charAt(i + 1)))
            {
                count++;
                System.out.print(str.charAt(i));
                System.out.print(str.charAt(i+1) + " ");
            }
        }
        System.out.print("\nNo. of pair of vowels: " + count);
    }
}
```

Concept Enhancer To enhance your understanding of this problem, it's important to remember that vowels are the letters 'a', 'e', 'i', 'o', 'u', and 'y' in English language. You can use nested loops to find pairs of vowels in the given string. Moreover, to convert a string to uppercase in Java, you can use the toUpperCase() method of the String class.

4. Write a program to input a sentence and convert it into uppercase and count and display the total number of words starting with a letter 'A'.

Example:

Sample Input : ADVANCEMENT AND APPLICATION OF INFORMATION TECHNOLOGY ARE EVER CHANGING.

Sample Output : Total number of words starting with letter 'A' = 4. ***ICSE 2019***

Ans

```
import java.util.*;
class Print_Vowel
{
    public static void main(String args[])
    {
        Scanner sc=new Scanner(System.in);
        System.out.print("Enter any sentence: ");
        String s=sc.nextLine();
        s = s+" ";
        int l=s.length();
        s=s.toUpperCase();
        int pos=0,count=0;
        char ch1, ch2;
        String w;
        for(int i=0; i<l; i++)
        {
            ch1 = s.charAt(i);
            if(ch1 == ' ')
            {
                w = s.substring(pos,i); // extracting words one by one
                ch2 = w.charAt(0);
```

```
            if(ch2=='A' )
            {
               count++;
            }
            pos = i+1;
         }
      }
      System.out.print("No. of words starting with A :"+count);
   }
}
```

5. Write a program in Java to accept a string in lower case and change the first letter of every word to upper case. Display the new string. ***ICSE 2018***

Sample input: we are in cyber world

Sample output: We Are In Cyber World

Ans

```
import java.util.*;
class Convert
{
   public static void main(String args[])
   {
      Scanner sc=new Scanner(System.in);
      System.out.println("Enter any String ");
      String str=sc.nextLine();
      String s1="";
      s1=s1+(Character.toUpperCase(str.charAt(0)));
      for(int i=1;i<str.length();i++)
      {
         if(str.charAt(i)==' ')
         {
            s1=s1+str.charAt(i)+(Character.toUpperCase(str.charAt(i+1)));
            i++;
         }
         else
         s1=s1+(Character.toLowerCase(str.charAt(i)));
      }
      System.out.println(s1);
   }
}
```

6. Design a class to overload a function check() as follows ***ICSE 2017***

(i) void check (String str, char ch)- to find and print the frequency of a character in a string.

Example:

Input:	Output:
str = "success"	number of s present is = 3
ch = 's'	

(ii) void check(String s1)- to display only vowels from string s1, after converting it to lower case.

Example:

Input:

s1 = "computer"

Output : o u e

Ans

```
class Overload
{
```

```
    void check(String str, char ch)
    {
        int l=str.length();
        int count=0;
        for(int i=0;i<l;i++)
        {
            char c=str.charAt(i);
            if(c==ch)
            {
                count++;
            }
        }
        System.out.println("Number of "+ch+" present is = "+count);
    }
    void check(String s1)
    {
        int l=s1.length();
        for(int i=0;i<l;i++)
        {
            char c=Character.toLowerCase(SL.charAt(i));
            if(c=='a'||c=='e'||c=='i'||c=='o'||c=='u')
            {
                System.out.print(c+" ");
            }
        }
    }
}
```

7. Write a program to accept a sentence and print only the first letter of each word of the sentence in capital letters separated by a full stop. ***ICSE SQP 2017***

Example:

INPUT SENTENCE : "This is a cat"

OUTPUT : T.I.A.C.

KEY idea

To achieve the desired output, we need to split the input sentence into words and then capitalize the first letter of each word before concatenating them with a full stop.

Ans

```
import java.util.Scanner;
public class CapitalizeFirstLetter
{
    public static void main(String[] args)
    {
        Scanner scanner = new Scanner(System.in);
        System.out.print("Enter a sentence: ");
        String sentence = scanner.nextLine();
            // Split the sentence into words
        String[] words = sentence.split(" ");
            // Create a StringBuilder to store the capitalized letters
        StringBuilder capitalizedLetters = new StringBuilder();
            // Loop through each word in the sentence
        for (String word : words)
        {
            // Get the first letter of the word and capitalize it
                char firstLetter = Character.toUpperCase(word.charAt(0));
            // Append the capitalized letter to the StringBuilder
                capitalizedLetters.append(firstLetter).append(".");
        }
```

```
        // Print the capitalized letters, removing the last full stop
        System.out.println(capitalizedLetters.deleteCharAt(capitalizedLetters.
                                                       length() - 1).toString());
    }
}
```

8. Special words are those words which start and end with the same letter. ***ICSE 2016***

Examples:
EXISTENCE
COMIC
WINDOW

Palindrome words are those words which read the same from left to right and *vice-versa.*

Examples:
MALAYALAM
MADAM
LEVEL
ROTATOR
CIVIC

All palindromes are special words, but all special words are not palindromes.

Write a program to accept a word check and print whether the word is a palindrome or only special word or none of them.

Ans

```
import java.io.*;
public class SpecPalin
{
    public static void main(String args[]) throws IOException
    {
        String word,rev = " ";
        InputStreamReader IR=new InputStreamReader(System.in);
        BufferedReader br = new BufferedReader(IR);
        System.out.println("Enter any word");
        word=br.readLine();
        int len=word.length();
        word = word.toUpperCase();
        char c1 = word.charAt(0);
        char c2 = word.charAt(len-1);
        for (int i = len - 1; i >= 0; i--)
        rev = rev + word.charAt(i);
        if (word.equals(rev))
           System.out.println("Entered word is a palindrome as well as
                                                              special");
        else if(c1 == c2)
           System.out.println("Entered word is a special");
        else
           System.out.println("Entered word is not a palindrome as well
                                                       as not a special");
    }
}
```

9. Write a program to initialise the seven Wonders of the World alongwith their locations in two different arrays. Search for a name of the country input by the user. If found, display the name of the country alongwith its Wonder, otherwise display "Sorry Not Found!". ***ICSE 2016***

Seven wonders - CHICHEN ITZA, CHRIST THE REDEEMER, TAJMAHAL, GREAT WALL OF CHINA, MACHU PICCHU, PETRA, COLOSSEUM

Locations - MEXICO, BRAZIL, INDIA, CHINA, PERU, JORDAN, ITALY

Example - Country Name : INDIA Output : INDIA - TAJMAHAL
Country Name : USA Output : Sorry Not Found!

Ans
```
import java.io.*;
public class Wonders
{
  public static void main(String args[]) throws IOException
  {
    String[] won={"CHICHEN ITZA","CHRIST THE  REDEEMER","TAJMAHAL",
                        "GREAT WALL OF CHINA", "MACHU PICCHU","PETRA" , "COLOSSEUM"};
    String[] loc={"MEXICO","BRAZIL","INDIA","CHINA","PERU","JORDAN", "ITALY"};
    InputStreamReader IR=new InputStreamReader(System.in);
    BufferedReader br = new BufferedReader(IR);
    System.out.print("Country Name :"};
    String s=br.readLine();
    int f=0;
    for(int i=0;i<7;i++)
      if(s.equals(loc[i]))
      {
        System.out.println(loc[i]+"-"+won[i]);
        f=1;
        break;
      }
      if (f= =0)
        System.out.println("Sorry Not Found!");
  }
}
```

10. Write a program to assign a full path and file name as given below. Using library functions, extract and output the file path, file name and file extension separately as shown.

Input: `C:/Users/admin/pictures/flower.jpg`

Output:
```
Path: C:/Users/admin/pictures
File name : flower
Extension : jpg
```
ICSE 2014

Ans
```
import java.io.*;
class FA
{
  public static void main(String[] args) throws IOException
  {
    String pn, fn, cx, p;
    InputStreamReader ir = new InputStreamReader(System.in);
    BufferedReader b = new BufferedReader(ir);
    System.out.println("Enter the path with filename and extension");
    pn = b.readLine();
    int i = pn.lastIndexOf("/");
    int j = pn.indexOf(".");
    fn = pn.substring(i + 1, j);
    cx = pn.substring(j + 1);
    p = pn.substring(0, i + 1);
    System.out.println("Path : " +p);
    System.out.println("File name : " +fn);
    System.out.println("Extension : " +cx);
  }
}
```

11. Write a program that encodes a word into Piglatin. To translate word into a Piglatin word, convert the word into uppercase and then place the first vowel of the original word as the start of the new word along with the remaining alphabets. The alphabets present before the vowel being shifted towards the end followed by "AY".

Sample input (1) : London, Sample output (1) : ONDONLAY

Sample input (2) : Olympics, Sample output (2) : OLYMPICSAY *ICSE 2013*

Ans

```
import java.io.*;
class Piglatin
{
  public static void main(String[] args) throws IOException
  {
    String str, c, d;
    int x, y;
    char b = 0;
    InputStreamReader ir = new InputStreamReader(System.in);
    BufferedReader ba = new BufferedReader(ir);
    System.out.println("Enter the word");
    str = ba.readLine();
    x = str.length();
    str = str.toUpperCase();
    for(y = 0; y < x; y++)
    {
      b = str.charAt(y);
      if(b=='A' || b=='E' || b=='I' || b=='O' || b=='U')
      break;
    }
    c = str.substring(y, x);
    d = str.substring(0, y);
    System.out.println("The piglatin word is");
    System.out.println(c + d + "AY");
  }
}
```

12. Write a program to accept a string. Convert the string to uppercase count and output the number of double letter sequences that exist in the string.

Sample Input : "SHE WAS FEEDING THE LITTLE RABBIT WITH AN APPLE

Sample Output : 4 *ICSE 2012*

Ans

```
import java.io.*;
class String
{
  public static void main(String[] args) throws IOException
  {
    BufferedReader br=new BufferedReader(new InputStreamReader(System.in));
    System.out.println("Enter any String");
    String str=br.readLine();
    String str1=str.toUpperCase()+" ";
    int c=0;
    int l=str.length();
    for(int i=0;i<l;i++)
    {
      char ch1=str1.charAt(i);
      if(i==l-1)
        break;
      char ch2=str1.charAt(i+1);
      if(ch1==ch2)
        c++;
    }
```

```
        System.out.println("Total number of double letter :"+c);
    }
}
```

13. Write a program to accept a word and convert it into lowercase, if it is in uppercase and display the new word by replacing only the vowels with the character following it.

Example:

Sample Input : Computer

Sample Output : cpmpvtfr **ICSE 2011**

Ans

```
import java.io.*;
class Vowel
{
    public static void main(String[] args) throws IOException
    {
        InputStreamReader r = new InputStreamReader(System.in);
        BufferedReader bf = new BufferedReader(r);
        System.out.println("Enter a string");
        String s = bf.readLine();
        String s1 = s.toLowerCase();
        String n = " ";
        for(int i = 0; i < s1.length(); i++)
        {
            int a = s1.charAt(i);
            if(a=='a' || a=='e' || a=='i' || a=='o' || a=='u')
            {
                a = a + 1;
                n = n + (char)a;
            }
            else
                n = n + (char)a;
        }
        System.out.println("New string is :" + n);
    }
}
```

14. Write a program to input a sentence and print the number of characters found in the longest word of the given sentence.

Example: if s = "India is my country" then the output should be 7. **ICSE 2009**

Ans

```
import java.io.*;
class Myclass
{
    public static void main(String[] args) throws IOException
    {
        InputStreamReader IR=new InputStreamReader(System.in);
        BufferedReader br=new BufferedReader(IR);
        System.out.println("Enter a sentence");
        String sentence = br.readLine();
        int longest = 0;
        int currentWordLength = 0;
        for(int i=0; i<sentence.length();i++)
        {
            char ch = sentence.charAt(i);
            if(ch==' ')
            {
                if(currentWordLength>longest)
                {
                    longest = currentWordLength;
                }
                currentWordLength = 0;
            }
            else
```

```
            {
               currentWordLength++;
            }
         }
         if(currentWordLength>longest)
         {
            longest = currentWordLength;
         }
         System.out.println("The longest word has "+longest+" characters");
      }
   }
```

15. Write a program to enter a sentence from the keyboard and count the number of times a particular word occurs in it. Display the frequency of the search word.

Example

Input: Enter a sentence : the quick brown fox jumps over the lazy dog

Enter a word to be searched : the

Output: Searched word occurs : 2 times. ***ICSE 2007***

Ans

```
import java.io.*;
class Myclass
{
   public static void main(String[] args) throws IOException
   {
      InputStreamReader ir = new InputStreamReader(System.in);
      BufferedReader b = new BufferedReader(ir);
      System.out.println("Enter the sentence");
      String str = b.readLine( );
      int l = str.length();
      System.out.println("Enter the word");
      String w = b.readLine();
      int l1 = w.length();
      int c = 0;
      for(int i = 0; i<l-l1+1; i++)
      {
         if(str.substring(i, i + l1).equals(w))
         {
            c++;
         }
      }
      if(c > 0)
      {
         System.out.println("Searched word occurs "+c+" times");
      }
      else
      {
         System.out.println("Word is not present");
      }
   }
}
```

16. Write a program using a method Palin(), to check whether a string is a Palindrome or not. A Palindrome is a string that reads the same from left to right and *vice-versa*. e.g. MADAM, ARORA, ABBA, etc. ***ICSE 2007***

Ans

```
import java.io.*;
class Myclass
{
```

```
    public void Palin() throws IOException
    {
      InputStreamReader IR = new InputStreamReader(System.in);
      BufferedReader br = new BufferedReader(IR);
      String reverse = " ";
      System.out.println("Enter a string to check if it is a palindrome");
      String original = br.readLine();
      int length = original.length();
      for(int i = length-1; i>=0; i--)
        reverse = reverse + original.charAt(i);
      if(original.equals(reverse))
        System.out.println("Entered string is a palindrome");
      else
        System.out.println("Entered string is not a palindrome");
    }
    public static void main(String args[]) throws IOException
    {
      Myclass m = new Myclass();
      m.Palin();
    }
}
```

17. Consider the following statement.
"January 26 is celebrated as the Republic Day of India".
Write a program to change 26 to 15, January to August, Republic to Independence and finally print "August 15 is celebrated as the Independence Day of India". **ICSE 2006**

Ans

```
import java.io.*;
class Rep
{
    public static void main(String args[])
    {
      String s = "January 26 is celebrated as the Republic Day of India";
      String h = "August 15";
      String str = "Independence";
      System.out.println("Original string");
      System.out.println(s);
      s = h + s.substring(10,32) + str + s.substring(40);
      System.out.println("After replacements string is");
      System.out.println(s);
    }
}
```

18. Write a program to input any given string to calculate the total number of characters and vowels present in the string and also reverse the string
Example
Input: Enter string : SNOWY
Output: Total number of characters : 05
Number of vowels : 01
Reverse string : YWONS **ICSE 2005**

Ans

```
import java.io.*;
class Len
{
```

```
public static void main(String args[]) throws IOException
{
   int v = 0;
   InputStreamReader ir = new InputStreamReader(System.in);
   BufferedReader b = new BufferedReader(ir);
   System.out.println("Enter a string");
   String str = b.readLine();
   int l = str.length();
   char ch;
   String reverse = "";
   for(int i = 0; i < l; i++)
   {
      ch = str.charAt(i);
      reverse = ch + reverse;
      if(ch =='A'||ch =='E'||ch =='I'||ch =='O'||ch =='U')
         v++;
   }
   System.out.println("Total no. of characters =" +l);
   System.out.println("No. of vowels =" +v);
   System.out.println("Reverse string =" +reverse);
}
}
```

CHAPTER TEST

1 Mark Questions

1. Given the code

```
public class Flowers
{
    public static void main(String[] args)
    {
        String s="Flowersarebeautiful";
        System.out.println(s.length()+s.lastIndexOf('u'));
    }
}
```

What will be the output of the code?

(a) 35 (b) 34 (c) 36 (d) 37

2. Choose the Odd one

(a) charAt() (b) rtrim() (c) trim() (d) substring()

3. Two strings in java can be

(a) Subtracted (b) Added (c) Multiplied (d) Divided

4. String data members of a class can be.................

(a) Private (b) Public (c) Protected (d) All of these

5. The function that extracts a part of a string is called:

(a) indexOf() (b) IndexOF() (c) INDEXOf() (d) None of these

2 Marks Questions

6. How can we make string upper case or lower case?
7. How can equivalence of two Strings checked in Java?
8. Why String objects are immutable in Java?
9. Write the return data type of the following function.
   (i) endsWith()
   (ii) log ()

15 Marks Questions

10. Write a program to input a sentence and print the number of characters found in the longest word of the given sentence. For example, if S "Health is = the most important thing in life", then the output should be 9.
11. Write a program in Java to read a string from console and replace all occurrences of the fifth character of the string by the digit 5.
12. Write a program to accept a sentence and print only the first letter of each word of the sentence in capital letters separated by a full stop. Example :

Input: "I love to learn Java"

Output: I.L.T.L.J.

ICSE

CHAPTERWISE SOLVED PAPERS

Sample Question Papers (1-3)

ICSE

SAMPLE QUESTION PAPER 01

Fully Solved

COMPUTER APPLICATIONS-X

Time : 2 hrs | Max. Marks : 100

General Instructions

1. Answer to this paper must be written on the paper provided separately.
2. You will not be allowed to write during the first 15 minutes. This time is to be spent in reading the question paper.
3. The time given at the head of this paper is the time allowed for writing the answers.
4. This paper is divided into two sections. Attempt all questions from Section A and any four questions from Section B.
5. The intended marks for questions or parts of questions are given in brackets [ ].

Section A

(Attempt all Questions from this Section)

1. Choose the correct answers to the questions from the given options. (Do not copy the question, write the correct answers only.) *[20]*

(i) The process of binding the data and method together as one unit is called as

(a) encapsulation (b) inheritance
(c) polymorphism (d) dynamic binding

(ii) The operator which acts on one operand is known as ......

(a) binary (b) ternary
(c) unary (d) relational

(iii) Which of the following keyword is used to create symbolic constants in Java?

(a) final (b) Final
(c) Constant (d) Const

(iv) Give the output of the following.

```
int x;
for ( x =1 ; x <=3; x++ );
System.out.print (x);
```

(a) 1 2 3 (b) 1 2 3 4
(c) 4 (d) 1

(v) What is the final value stored in variable x?

```
double x=Math.ceil(Math.abs(-7.3));
```

(a) 7.0 (b) 8.0
(c) 6.0 (d) 9.0

(vi) Consider the below figure. Coloured part is called as

000	1004	1008	1012	1016	1020	1024	1028
21	45	12	11	3	27	9	18
0	1	2	3	4	5	6	7

(a) Array address (b) Elements
(c) Index (d) None

(vii) Choose the odd one:

(a) >= (b) %
(c) / (d) *

(viii) Parameters used in the method call statement are

(a) actual parameters (b) informal parameters
(c) formal parameters (d) void parameters

(ix) A variable that is bounded to the object itself is called as

(a) instance variable
(b) class variable
(c) local variable
(d) argument variable

(x) The output of Double.parseDouble ("71.25") + (0.75) is

(a) 72 (b) 72.0
(c) 71.0 (d) 71.75

(xi) Give the output of the following statement:

```
"MISSISSIPPI".indexOf('S')+"MISSISSIPPI"
                            .lastIndexOf('I')
```

(a) 10 (b) 12
(c) 20 (d) 11

(xii) Give the output of the following statement:

```
System.out.println("Good".
                    concat("Day"));
```

(a) GoodDay (b) Good Day
(c) Goodday (d) goodDay

(xiii) The jump statement that is used inside a switch case construct to terminate a statement sequence.

(a) continue (b) break
(c) return (d) goto

(xiv) Give the output of the following.

```
int  x = 2, y = 4, z = 1;
int result = (++z) +y + (++x) + (z++);
```

(a) 11 (b) 12
(c) 10 (d) 9

(xv) The ASCII code of B is ....

(a) 67 (b) 66
(c) 98 (d) 99

(xvi) To execute a loop 11 times, which of the following is correct?

(a) for (int i=11;i<=31;i+=2)
(b) for (int i=11;i<=29;i+=2)
(c) for (int i=11;i<=31;i++)
(d) None of the above

(xvii) **Assertion (A)** The factory of object means a factory that produces the objects.

Reason (R) Class is known as object factory, because a single class generates a lot of objects.

(a) Both Assertion (A) and Reason (R) are true and Reason (R) is a correct explanation of Assertion (A).
(b) Both Assertion (A) and Reason (R) are true and Reason (R) is not a correct explanation of Assertion (A).
(c) Assertion (A) is true and Reason (R) is false.
(d) Assertion (A) is false and Reason (R) is true.

(xviii) How many times int i = 0; while (i < 4) System.out.print(i++); executes?

(a) 1 (b) 2
(c) 3 (d) 4

(xix) **Assertion (A)** Array is a data type which can store multiple homogenous variables.

Reason (R) Elements of array are stored in an indexed manner starting with index 0.

(a) Both Assertion (A) and Reason (R) are true and Reason (R) is a correct explanation of Assertion (A).
(b) Both Assertion (A) and Reason (R) are true and Reason (R) is not a correct explanation of Assertion (A).
(c) Assertion (A) is true and Reason (R) is false.
(d) Assertion (A) is false and Reason (R) is true.

(xx)

```
int z = 8;                                  #1
if (z % 2 == 0)
{                                           #2
  System.out.println("z is even");
                                            #3
} else {                                    #4
System.out.println("z is odd,
incremented by 3: " + z);                   #5
z += 3;                                     #6
}                                           #7
```

Choose the correct order to get the proper output:

(a) #1,#2,#3,#4,#6,#5,#7
(b) #1,#4,#2,#3,#5,#6,#7
(c) #1,#2,#4,#5,#3,#6,#7
(d) #1,#4,#5,#2,#3,#6,#7

Ans (i) (a) Binding of data and method in a single unit (i.e. class) is known as encapsulation.

(ii) (c) Unary operator acts on one operand. e.g. ++a;

(iii) (a) final keyword is used to create symbolic constant.

(iv) (c) 4

(v) (b) Math.abs (– 7.3) returns 7.3 and 8.0 is the ceil value of 7.3.

(vi) (a) Array address

(vii) (a) It is a relational operator others are arithmetic operators.

(viii) (a) Parameters used in the method call statement are actual parameters.

(ix) (a) instance variable

(x) (b) 72.0

(xi) (b) 12

(xii) (a) GoodDay

(xiii) (b) break is the jump statement to terminate a case block.

(xiv) (a) 11

(xv) (b) ASCII code of B is 66.

(xvi) (a) for (int i=11;i<=31;i+=2)

(xvii) (a) Both Assertion (A) and Reason (R) are true and Reason (R) is a correct explanation of Assertion (A).

(xviii) (d) 4

(xix) (b) Both Assertion (A) and Reason (R) are true and Reason (R) is not a correct explanation of Assertion (A).

(xx) (a) #1,#2,#3,#4,#6,#5,#7

2. (i) What are the minimum and maximum values that can be accommodated by the following primitive types: *[2]*

(a) float (b) double (c) char

(ii) State the output of the following program segment

```
String str = "HAVE FUN!";
boolean a = str.endsWith("FUN!");
System.out.println(a);
boolean b = str.startsWith("FUN");
System.out.println(b);
```

[2]

(iii) What will be the output of the following code?

```
float x = 7.95f;
System.out.println(Math.ceil(x));
System.out.println(Math.floor(x));
```

[2]

(iv) Consider the following array and answer the questions given below.

```
int b[] = {9, 14, 6, 11, 7, 18, 20};
```

(a) What is the output of System.out.print(b[1] + b[4]);?

(b) What is the index (subscript) of the smallest element in the array b? *[2]*

(v) Rewrite the following code using switch case statement: *[2]*

```
if(value = = 1)
  System.out.println("Computer Books");
else if(value = = 2)
  System.out.println("English Books");
else if(value = = 3)
  System.out.println("GS Books");
else
  System.out.println("Wrong choice");
```

(vi) (a) Write the Java statement to initialize the first 6 even numbers in a 2 × 3 array.

(b) What is the result of y[0][2] + y[1][1] of the above array? *[2]*

(vii) Give the output of the following program segments

```
String str = "PROJECTOR";
System.out.println(str.indexOf
                   (str.charAt(8)));
```

[2]

(viii) The following code has some error(s). Rewrite the correct code and underlining all the corrections made: *[2]*

```
int i;
i=10;
do;
     i=i-4;
     System.out.displayln(i);
}while i>=4;
```

(ix) What does the following statement mean?

```
Student class1 = new Student();
```

[2]

(x) What will be the result of the following code?

```
str1 = "cat";
str2 = "cat";
```

(a) `str1 == str2;`

(b) `str1.equals(str2);` *[2]*

Ans. (i)

Data Type	Minimum Value	Maximum Value
float	3.4×10^{-38}	3.4×10^{38}
double	1.7×10^{-308}	1.7×10^{308}
char	0	65535

(ii) true
false

(iii) 8.0
7.0

(iv) (a) 14 + 7 = 21

(b) The smallest element is 6, and its index is 2.

(v)
```
switch(value)
{
 case 1:
  System.out.println("Computer
                         Books");
    break;
 case 2:
  System.out.println("English
                         Books");
    break;
 case 3: System.out.println("GS
                         Books");
    break;
 default: System.out.println("Wron
                       g choice");
}
```

(vi) (a) int y[][] = {{2, 4, 6},{8, 10, 12}};

(b) y[0][2] = 6, y[1][1] = 10, so the result is 6 + 10 = 16.

(vii) `str.indexOf(str.charAt(8))`
`= str.indexOf('R')[because str = PROJECTOR]`
`= 1`

(viii) The correct code is

```
int i;
i=10;
do
{
  i=i-4;
  System.out.println(i);
 }while (i>=4);
```

(ix) `Student class1 = new Student ();`

In this statement, Student is a class and it creates an object whose name is class1.

(x) (a) false as == operator compares the values of memory addresses of str1 and str2 which are different.

(b) true as the equals () method compares the content of two actual strings.

Section B

(Attempt any Four Questions from this Section)

3. Anshul transport company charges for the parcels of its customers as per the following specifications given below. ***[15]***

Class name	Atransport
Member variables	
String name	to store the name of the customer
int w	to store the weight of the parcel in Kg
int charge	to store the charge of the parcel
Member functions	
void accept ()	to accept the name of the customer, weight of the parcel from the user (using Scanner class)
void calculate()	To calculate the charge as per the weight of the parcel as per the following criteria **Weight in Kg** — **Charge per Kg** Upto 10 Kgs — Rs. 25 per Kg Next 20 Kgs — Rs. 20 per Kg Above 30 Kgs — Rs. 10 per Kg A surcharge of 5 % is charged on the bill.
void print ()	to print the name of the customer, weight of the parcel, total bill inclusive of surcharge in a tabular form in the following format: Name Weight Bill amount ....

Define a class with the above-mentioned specifications, create the main method, create an object and invoke the member methods.

Ans

```
import java.util.Scanner;
public class Atransport
{
   private String name;
   private int w;
   private int charge;
   public void accept()
   {
      Scanner in = new Scanner (System.in);
      System.out.print("Enter Customer Name:");
      name = in.nextLine();
      System.out.print("Enter Parcel Weight:");
      w = in.nextInt();
   }
   public void calculate()
   {
      if (w <= 10)
         charge = w * 25;
      else if (w <= 30)
         charge = 250 + ((w - 10) * 20);
      else
         charge = 250 + 400 + ((w - 30)*10);
      charge += charge * 5 / 100;
   }
   public void print()
   {
      System.out.println("Name\tWeight
                               \tBill amount");
      System.out.println("---\t---\t---");
      System.out.println(name + "\t"
                      + w + "\t" + charge);
   }
   public static void main(String args[])
   {
      Atransport obj = new Atransport();
      obj.accept();
      obj.calculate();
      obj.print();
   }
}
```

4. Define a class to accept values in integer array of size 10. Find sum of one digit number and sum of two digit numbers entered. Display them separately.

e.g. Input

a [] = {2, 12, 4, 9, 18, 25, 3, 32, 20, 1}

Output Sum of one digit numbers

$2+4+9+3+1=19$

Sum of two digit numbers

$12+18+25+32+20=107$ ***[15]***

Ans

```
import java.util.Scanner;
public class Example
{
   public static void main (String[] args)
   {
      Scanner sc = new Scanner (System.in);
      int [] arr = new int[10];
         // Taking input array from user
      System.out.println("Enter
                           10 integer values:");
      for (int i = 0; i < 10; i++)
      {
         arr[i] = sc.nextInt();
      }
      // Calculating sum of one-digit
       and two-digit numbers in the array
      int oneDigitSum = 0;
      int twoDigitSum = 0;
      for (int i = 0; i < 10; i++)
      {
         if (arr[i] >= 0 && arr[i] <= 9)
         {
            oneDigitSum += arr[i];
         } else if (arr[i] >= 10 &&
                              arr[i] <= 99)
```

```
            {
                twoDigitSum += arr[i];
            }
        }
        // Printing sum of one-digit and
            two-digit numbers in the array
        System.out.println("Sum of one-digit
                    numbers in the array: "
                            + oneDigitSum);
        System.out.println("Sum of two-digit
                    numbers in the array: "
                            + twoDigitSum);
    }
}
```

5. Write a program in Java to accept a string and find

(i) the number of blank spaces in the string.

(ii) the number of words in the string.

(iii) the number of characters present in the string. ***[15]***

Ans

```
import java.util.Scanner;
public class Counting
{
    public static void main(String[] args)
    {
        Scanner sc = new Scanner(System.in);
        String name;
        int a, b = 0, w = 0;
        System.out.println("Enter your
                            string:");
        name = sc.nextLine();
        a = name.length();
        for (int i = 0; i < a; i++)
        {
            char chr = name.charAt(i);
            if (chr == ' ')
                b = b + 1;
        }
        w = b + 1;
        System.out.println("The no. of blank
          spaces in the string is " + b);
        System.out.println("The no. of
           words in the string is " + w);
        System.out.println("The no. of
        characters present in the string
                    is " + (a - b));
        sc.close();
    }
}
```

6. Write a program in Java to accept 10 different names in a single dimensional array. Arrange the names in ascending order by using bubble sort method and display them. ***[15]***

Ans

```
import java.util.Scanner;
class Sort
{
    public static void main(String[] args)
    {
        Scanner sc = new Scanner(System.in);
        String[] m = new String[10];
        String t;
        // Input 10 names
        for (int i = 0; i < 10; i++)
        {
            System.out.print("Enter your
                                name: ");
            m[i] = sc.nextLine();
        }
        // Sorting using compareTo
        for (int i = 0; i < 10; i++)
        {
            for (int j = i + 1; j < 10; j++)
            {
                if (m[i].compareTo(m[j]) > 0)
                {
                    t = m[i];
                    m[i] = m[j];
                    m[j] = t;
                }
            }
        }
        // Display sorted names
        System.out.println("\nSorted
                                names:");
        for (int i = 0; i < 10; i++)
        {
            System.out.println(m[i]);
        }
        sc.close();
    }
}
```

7. Define a class to accept a positive integer and check whether it is an Armstrong number or not. An Armstrong number is a number that is equal to the sum of its own digits each raised to the power of the number of digits.

e.g. Input 153

Output "Armstrong number" ***[15]***

Ans

```
import java.util.Scanner;
public class Main
{
    public static void main(String[] args)
    {
        // Accepting input from the user
        Scanner scanner = new Scanner (System.in);
        System.out.print("Enter a positive
                                integer: ");
        int number = scanner.nextInt();
```

```
        // Checking if the number is an
                              Armstrong number
        if (isArmstrongNumber(number))
        {
            System.out.println
                         ("Armstrong number");
        }
        else
        {
            System.out.println
                     ("Not an Armstrong number");
        }
    }
    // Method to check if a number is an
                              Armstrong number
    public static boolean isArmstrongNumber
                                  (int number)
    {
        // Counting the number of digits in
                                    the number
        int originalNumber = number;
        int numberOfDigits = 0;
        while (originalNumber != 0)
        {
            originalNumber /= 10;
            numberOfDigits++;
        }
        // Calculating the sum of digits
           raised to the power of the number
                                     of digits
        int sum = 0;
        originalNumber = number;
        while (originalNumber != 0)
        {
            int digit = originalNumber % 10;
            sum += Math.pow(digit,
                              numberOfDigits);
            originalNumber /= 10;
        }
        // Checking if the sum is equal to
                           the original number
        return sum == number;
    }
}
```

8. Write a menu driven program using the overloaded function 'area' to either calculate the area of a circle or the area of a rectangle or the area of a square depending on the user's choice. ***[15]***

Ans

```
import java.util.Scanner;
public class AreaCalculator
{
    public static void main(String[] args)
    {
        Scanner sc = new Scanner(System.in);
        int choice;
        System.out.println("1. Area of
                             Circle");
        System.out.println("2. Area of
                             Square");
        System.out.println("3. Area of
                          Rectangle");
        System.out.print("Enter your
                           choice: ");
        choice = sc.nextInt();
        switch (choice)
        {
            case 1:
                System.out.print("Enter
                           radius: ");
                double r = sc.nextDouble();
                area(r);
                break;
            case 2:
                System.out.print
                       ("Enter side: ");
                int s = sc.nextInt();
                area(s);
                break;
            case 3:
                System.out.print
                     ("Enter length: ");
                int len = sc.nextInt();
                System.out.print
                    ("Enter breadth: ");
                int b = sc.nextInt();
                area(len, b);
                break;
            default:
                System.out.println
                       ("Wrong choice");
        }
        sc.close();
    }
    static void area(double ra)
    {
        double a = 3.14 * ra * ra;
        System.out.println("Area of
                       circle is " + a);
    }
    static void area(int si)
    {
        int a = si * si;
        System.out.println("Area of
                       square is " + a);
    }
    static void area(int l, int bre)
    {
        int a = l * bre;
        System.out.println("Area of
                    rectangle is " + a);
    }
}
```

ICSE
SAMPLE QUESTION PAPER 02

Unsolved

COMPUTER APPLICATIONS-X

Time : 2 hrs   Max. Marks : 100

General Instructions See Sample Question Paper 01.

Section A
(Attempt all Questions from this Section)

1. Choose the correct answers to the questions from the given options. (Do not copy the question, write the correct answers only.) *[20]*

(i) Consider the below figure. What is first, last index?

11	12	13	14	15	16	17	18	19

(a) 0,9 (b) 0,8
(c) 1,9 (d) None

(ii) How many times int i = 0; while (i < 4) System.out.print(i++); executes?
(a) 1 (b) 2
(c) 3 (d) 4

(iii) A single dimensional array has 100 elements, which of the following is the correct statement to initialize the last element to 99.
(a) x[99]=99 (b) x[98]=99
(c) x[100]=99 (d) x[97]=99

(iv) The number of bytes occupied by the constant 45 are
(a) Four bytes (b) Two bytes
(c) Eight bytes (d) One byte

(v) The program code written in any high-level language to solve a problem is
(a) object code (b) source code
(c) machine code (d) bytecode

(vi) DMRC is an example for .... access specifier.
(a) public (b) local
(c) protected (d) private

(vii) Which of the following is a correct method prototype in Java?
(a) public void myMethod(int a, b);
(b) void myMethod(int a, int b);
(c) public myMethod(int a, int b);
(d) public void myMethod(int a, int b);

(viii) Method which is a part of a class rather than an instance of the class is termed as
(a) static method (b) non-static method
(c) wrapper class (d) string method

(ix) The number of bits occupied by the value 'a' are
(a) 1 bit (b) 2 bits
(c) 4 bits (d) 16 bits

(x) Wrapper classes are available in ...... package.
(a) java. io (b) java.util
(c) java.lang (d) java.awt

(xi) The method to check if a character is an alphabet or not is
(a) isLetter(char) (b) isAlpha(char)
(c) isUppercase(char) (d) isLowercase(char)

(xii) The method to convert a string to upper case is
(a) toUpperCase(char)
(b) toUPPERCASE(String)
(c) toUpperCase(String)
(d) touppercase(String)

(xiii) What is the final value stored in variable x?

```
double a =-8.35;
double x = Math.abs(Math.floor(a));
```

(a) 9.0 (b) 7.0
(c) 6 (d) 7

(xiv) Give the output of the following statement, when x = 5.

x += x++ + ++x + --x + x;

(a) 29 (b) 28
(c) 26 (d) None of these

(xv) A student wants to multiply a variable 'y' by 5. They have written the following statement, which is incorrect:

```
y = y * 5
```

What will be the correct statement?

A. y *= 5;

B. y = 5 * y;

C. y = y * 5;

(a) Only A (b) Only B
(c) A and B (d) All are correct

(xvi) The following lines of code are jumbled. Arrange them in the correct order to form a valid if-else statement that checks if a number is positive or negative.

Jumbled lines:

```
1. System.out.println("The number is
   negative.");  }  }
2. } else {
3. if (number > 0) {
4. public class Main {
5. } else {
6. public static void main(String[] args) {
```

(a) 4, 6, 3, 5, 2, 1 (b) 4, 6, 3, 2, 5, 1
(c) 6, 4, 3, 2, 5, 1 (d) 4, 6, 2, 3, 5, 1

(xvii) **Assertion (A)** Pure functions define a relationship between input and output.

Reason (R) Pure function does not depend on any state beyond its local scope.

(a) Both Assertion (A) and Reason (R) are true and Reason (R) is a correct explanation of Assertion (A).
(b) Both Assertion (A) and Reason (R) are true and Reason (R) is not a correct explanation of Assertion (A).
(c) Assertion (A) is true and Reason (R) is false.
(d) Assertion (A) is false and Reason (R) is true.

(xviii) Which of the following is not control flow Java keyword?

(a) if
(b) else
(c) try
(d) enum

(xix) **Assertion (A)** Jump statements can be used to modify the behaviour of conditional and iterative statements.

Reason (R) When the break statement is encountered, the next iteration starts and the remaining statements in the present iteration are skipped.

(a) Both Assertion (A) and Reason (R) are true and Reason (R) is correct explanation of Assertion (A).
(b) Both Assertion (A) and Reason (R) are true but Reason (R) is not correct explanation of Assertion (A).
(c) Assertion (A) is true and Reason (R) is false.
(d) Assertion (A) is false and Reason (R) is true.

(xx) The element in x[4] of the array {3, 5, 7, 12, 16, 18, 20, 35, 42, 89} is

(a) 16 (b) 12 (c) 7 (d) 18

2. (i) Consider the following array and answer the questions given below: ***[2]***

```
int a[] = {12, 10, 8, 4, 6, 2, 3, 5, 7};
```

(a) What is the output of System.out.print(a[0] + a[5]);?

(b) What is the index (subscript) of the largest element of the array a?

(ii) Find and correct the errors in the following program segment

```
int n[] = (2, 4, 6, 8, 10);
for(int i = 0; i<=5, i++)
System.out.println("n["+i"]=" n[i]);
```
[2]

(iii) What will be the output of following code?

```
class operator
{
   public static void main(String
                              args[])
   {
      int a = -1, b = -2;
      int maxvalue;
      System.out.println("a =" +a);
      System.out.println("b =" +b);
      System.out.println("maxvalue
                =(a>b)?a:b="+(a>b)?a:b);
   }
}
```
[2]

(iv) State the purpose and return datatype of the wrapper class methods

(a) long valueOf(String s)

(b) long parseLong(String s) ***[2]***

(v) (a) Name one String method which results in a character. **[2]**

(b) What will be the output of str.charAt(2) if str = "HELLO"?

(vi) Give the output of the following: **[2]**

(a) `System.out.println("Hello" + 2 + 5);`

(b) `System.out.println("Hello" + (2 + 5));`

(c) `System.out.println("B".compareTo ("A"));`

(d) `System.out.println("Welcome". charAt(2) + "Welcome".charAt(0));`

(vii) (a) Write the Java statement to initialise the first 6 odd numbers in a 3 × 2 array x. **[2]**

(b) What is the result of x[0][1] + x[2][1]?

(viii) What will be the output of the following program segments? **[2]**

(a)
```
double x = 29.31;
System.out.println(Math.ceil(x));
```

(b)
```
float x=7.91, y=21.2;
System.out.println(Math.rint(x));
System.out.println(Math.rint(y));
```

(ix) What will be the result of the following code? **[2]**

```
Str1="Hello";
Str2="hello";
```

(a) `Str1!=Str2;`

(b) `Str1.equals(Str2);`

(x) Rewrite the following code of if-else statements in terms of switch-case statements. **[2]**

```
class Number
{
   public static void
                      main(String[] args)
   {
      int num, calc;
      System.out.println("Enter
                        a Number");
      if(num==5)
      {
         calc = num * 25 - 20;
         System.out.println(num + calc);
      }
      else
         if(num==10)
         {
            calc=num*25-15;
            System.out.println
                        (calc-num);
         }
   }
}
```

Section B

(Answer any Four Questions from this Section)

3. Write a program in Java to enter a number containing three digits or more in an array.
Arrange the digits of the entered number in ascending order and display the result.

Sample Input Enter a number 4972

Sample Output 2, 4, 7, 9, **[15]**

4. Write a program in Java to accept two words and check whether they are Anagram or not.

Anagram A word that is made with the combination of the letters present in the original word. e.g. A word is FLOW and the other word is WOLF, which is formed with the combinations of the letters present in the original word.
Thus, FLOW and WOLF are Anagrams. **[15]**

5. Write a program to input and store roll numbers, names and marks in 3 subjects of n number of students in five single dimensional array and display the remark based on average marks as given below: (The maximum marks in the subject are 100) **[15]**

$$\text{Average marks} = \frac{\text{Total marks}}{3}$$

Average marks	Remark
85-100	EXCELLENT
75-84	DISTINCTION
60-74	FIRST CLASS
40-59	PASS
Less than 40	POOR

6. A company pays commission to its salesman on the sale value according to the following rates:

Sale	Commission
Upto Rs. 1000	5% on sale
Rs. 1001– Rs. 2000	10% on sale
Rs. 2001 and Above	15% on sale

Model a class program with the following specifications:

Class name Salecom

Data members private double sale, com

Member methods

Salecom (double s)	constructor to initialize sale and com with s and o respectively.
void commission()	to find the commission
void display()	to display the commission

[15]

7. Design a class to overload a function polygon() as follows *[15]*

(i) void polygon(int n, char ch)
with one integer argument and one character type argument that draws a filled square of side n using the character stored in ch.

(ii) void polygon(int x, int y)
two integer arguments that draws filled rectangle of length x and breadth y, using the symbol '@'.

(iii) void polygon()
with no argument that draws a filled triangle shown below.

```
*
* *
* * *
```

8. Write a program in Java to accept a word. Arrange all the alphabets of the word in ascending order and display the new word.

Sample Input : BLUEJ

Output : BEJLU *[15]*

Answers

(i) (b)	(ii) (d)	(iii) (a)	(iv) (a)	(v) (b)	(vi) (a)	(vii) (d)	(viii) (a)
(ix) (d)	(x) (c)	(xi) (a)	(xii) (c)	(xiii) (a)	(xiv) (a)	(xv) (c)	(xvi) (b)
(xvii) (b)	(xviii) (d)	(xix) (c)	(xx) (a)				

ICSE
SAMPLE QUESTION PAPER 03

Unsolved

COMPUTER APPLICATIONS-X

Time : 2 hrs | Max. Marks : 100

General Instructions See Sample Question Paper 01.

Section A

(Attempt all Questions from this Section)

1. Choose the correct answers to the questions from the given options. (Do not copy the question, write the correct answers only.) ***[20]***

(i) Intermediate code obtained after compilation
(a) Source code (b) Byte code
(c) Object code (d) Compile code

(ii) Given the following 2D array:

	Column 0	Column 1	Column 2	Column 3
Row 0	1	2	3	4
Row 1	5	6	7	8
Row2	9	10	11	12

What is the value at array[1][2]?
(a) 5 (b) 6 (c) 7 (d) 8

(iii) How many times int i = 10; while (i > 4) System.out.print(i--); executes?
(a) 5 (b) 6 (c) 3 (d) 4

(iv) State the value of y after the following program is executed.
```
char x = 7;
y = Character.isLetter(x);
```
(a) false (b) 7 (c) true (d) '7'

(v) do while loop is an
(a) entry controlled loop (b) infinite loop
(c) exit controlled loop (d) finite loop

(vi) Govt. office is an example for ____ access specifier.
(a) private (b) local
(c) public (d) protected

(vii) A single dimensional array contains N elements. What will be the last subscript?
(a) N (b) N-1
(c) N-2 (d) N+1

(viii) The output of Math.sqrt(Math.pow(-3,2)) is:
(a) 9.0 (b) -9.0
(c) 3.0 (d) 4.0

(ix) Which of the following keyword is used to create an instance of a class?
(a) new (b) public
(c) class (d) None of these

(x) Method that converts a character to uppercase is ______________.
(a) toUpper( ) (b) ToUpperCase( )
(c) toUppercase( ) (d) toUpperCase(char)

(xi) What will be the output of the following code?
```
System.out.println("Lucknow"
                   .substring(0,4));
```
(a) Lucknow (b) Luckn
(c) Luck (d) luck

(xii) Which of the following is a correct way to initialize an array in Java?
(a) int arr[] = new int[5];
(b) int arr[5] = new int[];
(c) int arr[] = new int[5] {1, 2, 3, 4, 5};
(d) int arr() = new int[5];

(xiii) Give the output of the following code :

```
int  x = 2, y = 4, z = 1;
int result = (++z) +y + (++x) + (z++);
```

(a) 11 (b) 12
(c) 10 (d) 9

(xiv) Give the output of the following code :

```
int x;
for ( x =0 ; x <=3; x++ );
System.out.print (x);
```

(a) 1 2 3 (b) 1 2 3 4
(c) 4 (d) 3

(xv) Give the output of the following code :

```
int f=10,m=9;
String e=(m%f==9)? "YES": "NO";
System.out.print(e);
```

(a) YES (b) NO
(c) YESNO (d) NOYES

(xvi) The following code snippets are part of a Java program to reverse a number. Arrange them in the correct order.

1. `while (n != 0) {`
2. `reversed = reversed * 10 + digit;`
3. `int reversed = 0;`
4. `n /= 10; }`
5. `digit = n % 10;`
6. `int n = 1234;`
7. `System.out.println("Reversed Number: " + reversed);`

(a) 6, 3, 1, 5, 2, 4, 7 (b) 6, 3, 1, 5, 4, 2, 7
(c) 6, 1, 5, 3, 2, 4, 7 (d) 3, 6, 1, 5, 2, 4, 7

(xvii) **Assertion (A)** Wrapper class is used to convert any primitive data type into object.

Reason (R) To achieve call by reference, we use the wrapper class.

(a) Both Assertion (A) and Reason (R) are true and Reason (R) is a correct explanation of Assertion (A).
(b) Both Assertion (A) and Reason (R) are true but Reason (R) is not a correct explanation of Assertion (A).
(c) Assertion (A) is true and Reason (R) is false.
(d) Assertion (A) is false and Reason (R) is true.

(xviii) The output of 9*7/3 is:

(a) 21.0 (b) 21
(c) error (d) 0

(xix) **Assertion (A)** Primitive data types are the data types defined by the language itself.

Reason (R) Class interface and array are the examples of primitive data types.

(a) Both Assertion (A) and Reason (R) are true and Reason (R) is a correct explanation of Assertion (A).
(b) Both Assertion (A) and Reason (R) are true but Reason (R) is not a correct explanation of Assertion (A).
(c) Assertion (A) is true and Reason (R) is false.
(d) Assertion (A) is false and Reason (R) is true.

(xx) Identify the correct array declaration statement.

(a) `int a [10] ;`
(b) `int a [] = new int [10];`
(c) `int arr [i] = 10;`
(d) `int a [10] = new int [];`

2. (i) Find the output.

```
int a=50;
String s1="MAHATMA";
String s2="GANDHI";
```

(a) `System.out.print(a + s1 + s2);`
(b) `System.out.print(s1 + s2);`
(c) `System.out.print(s1.length() + s2.length());`
(d) `System.out.print(s1.charAt(3) + s2.charAt(5));` **[2]**

(ii) Rewrite the following code using while loop. **[2]**

```
int a,b;
for(a=10,b=4;a<=16;a++,b+=2)
{
    System.out.println(" " +a--);
}
```

(iii) Assume the following initialisations and compute the results

```
int j=2;
double x=0.005, y= -0.2;
char c='9';
```

(a) `Math.sqrt(x * x + y * y)`
(b) `Math.abs(j * 2 + y)` **[2]**

(iv) Consider the following code and state the output

```
char c='a';
switch(c)
{
  case 'a':
    System.out.print("A");
  case 'b':
    System.out.print("B");
  default:
    System.out.print("C");
}
```

[2]

(v) (a) Write the java statement to initialize the first 9 even numbers in a 3 × 3 array. *[2]*

(b) What is the result of x[1][2]+[2][2] of the above array?

(vi) Write the output

(a) `char c = "COMPUTER APPLICATIONS".charAt(4);`

(b) `char c = "Hello".indexOf('c');`

(c)
```
int d = 97;
char c = (char)d + 10;
```
(d) `int e = 50/4 * 2;` *[2]*

(vii) (a) What is the index of element 'o' in the array

`char arr[ ] = {'a', 'e', 'i', 'u', 'o'};`

(b) a[16] is the .... element of the array. *[2]*

(viii) State the total size in bytes of the arrays a[4] of char data type and p[4] of float data type. *[2]*

(ix) (a) Name one string method which results in boolean value.

(b) Name one string method which results in a string. *[2]*

(x)
```
double x = Math.floor(-6.8);
double y = Math.ceil (Math.floor(75.2));
int z = Math.Pow(("20".indexOf('2')), 3);
```
Specify the type of the error in the above program, correct and write the program to be error free. *[2]*

Section B

(Answer any Four Questions from this Section)

3. Using the switch statement, write a menu driven program to

(i) Generate and display the first 10 terms of the Fibonacci series 0, 1, 1, 2, 3, 5, ...

The first two Fibonacci numbers are 0 and 1 and each subsequent number is the sum of the previous two.

(ii) Find the sum of the digits of an integer that is input.

Sample Input : 1 5 3 9 0

Sample Output : Sum of the digits = 18

For an incorrect choice, an appropriate error message should be displayed. *[15]*

4. Write a program to input a sentence and convert it into uppercase and count and display the total number of words starting with a letter 'A'.

Example,

Sample Input : Advancement And Application of Information Technology Are Ever Changing. *[15]*

5. Jharkhand State Electricity Board (JSEB) charges their consumers according to the units consumed (per month) as per the given tariff

Units Consumed	Charges
Upto 100 units	80 paise/unit
> 100 and upto 200 unit	Rs. 1/unit
> 200 units	Rs. 1.25/unit

Moreover, every consumer has to pay Rs. 50 as service charge per month. Write a program in Java to calculate the electricity bill. *[15]*

6. Write a program in Java to find the sum of the series, taking the value of 'a' and 'n' from the user.

$$s=\frac{a+1}{2}+\frac{a+3}{4}+\frac{a+5}{6}+\ldots \text{ to n terms}$$ *[15]*

7. Write a program in Java to accept 10 different numbers in a Single Dimensional Array (SDA) and display the maximum and the minimum number of the array elements. *[15]*

8. Write a program in Java by using a class with the following specifications

Class name : Rectangle

Data members/Instance variables : int length, breadth

Member functions :

void inputdata( ) : to accept length and breadth of the rectangle

void calculate( ) : to find area, perimeter and diagonal of the rectangle

void outputdata( ) : to print the results *[15]*

Answers

(i) (b)	(ii) (c)	(iii) (b)	(iv) (a)	(v) (c)	(vi) (c)	(vii) (b)	(viii) (c)
(ix) (a)	(x) (d)	(xi) (c)	(xii) (a)	(xiii) (a)	(xiv) (c)	(xv) (a)	(xvi) (a)
(xvii) (b)	(xviii) (b)	(xix) (c)	(xx) (b)				

ICSE

LATEST SPECIMEN QUESTION PAPER

Fully Solved

COMPUTER APPLICATIONS-X

Time : 2 hrs | Max. Marks : 100

General Instructions

1. Answer to this paper must be written on the paper provided separately.
2. You will not be allowed to write during the first 15 minutes. This time is to be spent in reading the question paper.
3. The time given at the head of this paper is the time allowed for writing the answers.
4. This paper is divided into two sections. Attempt all questions from Section A and any four questions from Section B.
5. The intended marks for questions or parts of questions are given in brackets [ ].

Section A

(Attempt all Questions from this Section)

1. Choose the correct answers to the questions from the given options. **[20]**

(Do not copy the question, write the correct answers only.)

(i)

Name the above structure: • *Analysis*

(a) One dimensional array

(b) Two dimensional array with 4 rows and 5 columns

(c) Three dimensional array

(d) Two dimensional array with 5 rows and 4 columns

(ii) "Java compiled code (byte code) can run on all operating systems" – Name the feature. • *Understanding*

(a) Robust and Secure (b) Object Oriented

(c) Platform Independent (d) Multithreaded

(iii) The size of '\n' is: • *Recall*

(a) 2 bytes (b) 4 bytes

(c) 8 bytes (d) 16 bytes

(iv) Identify the operator that gets the highest precedence while evaluating the given expression: • *Analysis*

$$a + b \% c * d - e$$

(a) + (b) %

(c) – (d) *

(v) Which of the following is a valid Java keyword? • *Understanding*

(a) If (b) BOOLEAN

(c) static (d) Switch

(vi) The output of the following code is: • *Analysis*

```
System.out.println(Math.ceil(6.4)
                  +Math.floor(-1 - 2));
```

(a) 3.0 (b) 4

(c) 3 (d) 4.0

(vii) Which of the following returns a String? • *Understanding*

(a) length() (b) charAt(int)

(c) replace(char, char) (d) indexOf (String)

(viii) Which of the following is not true with regards to a switch statement? • *Understanding*

(a) checks for an equality between the input and the case labels

(b) supports floating point constants

(c) break is used to exit from the switch block

(d) case labels are unique

(ix) Consider the array given below:

```
char ch[]={ 'A','E','I','O', 'U'};
```

Write the output of the following statements. • *Analysis*

```
System.out.println(ch[0]*2);
```

(a) 65 (b) 130 (c) 'A' (d) 0

(x) To execute a loop 10 times, which of the following is correct? • *Analysis*

(a) for (int i=11;i<=30;i+=2)
(b) for (int i=11;i<=30;i+=3)
(c) for (int i=11;i<20;i++)
(d) for (int i=11;i<=21;i++)

(xi) A single dimensional array has 50 elements, which of the following is the correct statement to initialize the last element to 100. • *Analysis*

(a) x[51]=100 (b) x[48]=100
(c) x[49]=100 (d) x[50]=100

(xii) Method prototype for the method compute which accepts two integer arguments and returns true/false. • *Understanding*

(a) void compute (int a, int b)
(b) boolean compute (int a, int b)
(c) Boolean compute (int a,b)
(d) int compute (int a, int b)

(xiii) The statement that brings the control back to the calling method is: • *Recall*

(a) break (b) System.exit(0)
(c) continue (d) return

(xiv) The default value of a boolean variable is: • *Recall*

(a) False (b) 0 (c) false (d) True

(xv) The method to convert a lowercase character to uppercase is: • *Recall*

(a) String.toUpperCase()
(b) Character.isUppercase (char)
(c) Character.toUpperCase(char)
(d) toUpperCase ()

(xvi) **Assertion (A)** Integer class can be used in the program without calling a package.

Reason (R) It belongs to the default package java.lang. • *Application*

(a) Both Assertion (A) and Reason (R) are true and Reason (R) is a correct explanation of Assertion (A)
(b) Both Assertion (A) and Reason (R) are true and Reason (R) is not a correct explanation of Assertion(A)
(c) Assertion (A) is true and Reason (R) is false
(d) Assertion (A) is false and Reason (R) is true

(xvii) A student executes the following code to increase the value of a variable '*x*' by 2.

He has written the following statement, which is incorrect. • *Analysis*

```
x = +2;
```

What will be the correct statement?

A. $x += 2;$
B. $x = 2;$
C. $x = x + 2;$

(a) Only A (b) Only C
(c) All the three (d) Both A and C

(xviii) The statement used to find the total number of Strings present in the string array String s[] is: • *Analysis*

(a) s.length (b) s.length()
(c) length(s) (d) len(s)

(xix) Consider the following program segment in which the statements are jumbled, choose the correct order of statements to swap two variables using the third variable. • *Analysis*

```
void swap(int a, int b)
{
  a = b;  → (1)
  b = t;   → (2)
  int t = 0;  → (3)
  t = a;  → (4)
}
```

(a) (1) (2) (3) (4) (b) (3) (4) (1) (2)
(c) (1) (3) (4) (2) (d) (2) (1) (4) (3)

(xx) **Assertion (A)** An argument is a value that is passed to a method when it is called. • *Application*

Reason (R) Variables which are declared in a method prototype to receive values are called actual parameters.

(a) Both Assertion (A) and Reason (R) are true and Reason (R) is a correct explanation of Assertion (A)
(b) Both Assertion (A) and Reason (R) are true and Reason (R) is not a correct explanation of Assertion(A)
(c) Assertion (A) is true and Reason (R) is false
(d) Assertion (A) is false and Reason (R) is true

2. (i) Rewrite the following code using single if statement. **[2]**
• *Understanding*

```
if (code= = 'g')
  System.out.println ("GREEN");
else if (code=='G')
  System.out.println ("GREEN ");
```

(ii) Evaluate the given expression when the value of a=2 and b=3 **[2]**
• *Analysis*

```
b* = a + + - + + b + + + a;
System.out.println ("a= "+a);
System.out.println ("b= "+b);
```

(iii) A student executes the following program segment and gets an error. Identify the statement which has an error, correct the same to get the output as WIN. **[2]**

• *Analysis*

```
boolean x = true;
switch(x)
{
  case 1: System.out.println("WIN");
  break;
  case 2: System.out.println
                        ("LOOSE");
}
```

(iv) Write the Java expression for $\sqrt[3]{x} + \sqrt{y}$ **[2]**

• *Understanding*

(v) How many times will the following loop execute? Write the output of the code: **[2]**

• *Analysis*

```
int x = 10;
while (true)
{
  System.out.println (x++*2);
  if (x%3==0)
  break;
}
```

(vi) Write the output of the following String methods: • *Analysis*

```
String x = "Galaxy ", y = "Games ";
```

(a) `System.out.println (x.charAt(0)==y.charAt(0));`

(b) `System.out.println (x.compareTo(y));` **[2]**

(vii) Predict the output of the following code snippet: **[2]**

• *Analysis*

```
char ch='B';
char chr= Character.toLowerCase(ch);
int n=(int) chr-10;
System.out.println((char)n+"
                        \t"+chr);
```

(viii) A student is trying to convert the string present in x to a numerical value, so that he can find the square root of the converted value. However the code has an error. Name the error (syntax/logical/ runtime). Correct the code so that it compiles and runs correctly. • *Analysis*

```
String x= "25";
int y=Double.parseDouble (x);
double r=Math.sqrt (y);
System.out.println (r);
```

[2]

(ix) Consider the following program segment and answer the questions below: • *Analysis*

```
class calculate
{
  int a; double b;
  calculate()
  {
    a=0;
    b=0.0;
  }
    calculate(int x, double y)
    {
      a=x;
      b=y;
    }
    void sum()
    {
      System.out.println(a*b);
    }
}
```

Name the type of constructors used in the above program segment? **[2]**

(x) Consider the following program segment and answer the questions given below:

• *Analysis*

```
int x[ ][ ]={{2,4,5,6}, {5,7,8,1},
{34, 1,10, 9}};
```

(a) What is the position of 34?

(b) What is the result of x[2][3] + x[1][2]? **[2]**

Section B

(Answer any Four Questions from this Section)

3. Define a class with the following specifications: **[15]**

• *Understanding/Application*

Class name	Bank
Member variables	
double p	stores the principal amount
double n	stores the time period in years
double r	stores the rate of interest
double a	stores the amount
Member methods	
void accept ()	input values for p and n using Scanner class methods only.
void calculate ()	calculate the amount based on the following conditions:

Time in (Years)	Rate %
Upto ½	9
> ½ to 1 year	10
> 1 to 3 years	11
> 3 years	12

$$a = p\left(1 + \frac{r}{100}\right)^n$$

void display ()	display the details in the given format. Principal Time Rate Amount XXX XXX XXX XXX

Write the main method to create an object and call the above methods.

4. Define a class to search for a value input by the user from the list of values given below. If it is found display the message "Search successful", otherwise display the message "Search element not found" using Binary search technique. **[15]**

   5.6, 11.5, 20.8, 35.4, 43.1, 52.4, 66.6, 78.9, 80.0, 95.5 • *Understanding/Application*

5. Define a class to accept a string and convert the same to uppercase, create and display the new string by replacing each vowel by immediate next character and every consonant by the previous character. The other characters remain the same.
   Example : Input : #IMAGINATION@2024
   Output : #JLBFJMBSJPM@2024 **[15]**
   • *Understanding/Application*

6. Define a class to accept values into 4 × 4 array and find and display the sum of each row.
   • *Understanding/Application*

   Example
   A[][]={1,2,3,4},{5,6,7,8},{1,3,5,7},{2,5,3,1}}
   Output
   sum of row 1 = 10 (1 + 2 + 3 + 4)
   sum of row 2 = 26 (5 + 6 + 7 + 8)
   sum of row 3 = 16 (1 + 3 + 5 + 7)
   sum of row 4 = 11 (2 + 5 + 3 + 1) **[15]**

7. Define a class to accept a number and check whether it is a SUPERSPY number or not. A number is called SUPERSPY if the sum of the digits equals the number of the digits. **[15]**

   Example1:
   Input: 1021
   Output: SUPERSPY number
   [SUM OF THE DIGITS = 1 + 0 + 2 + 1 = 4, NUMBER OF DIGITS = 4]
   Example2:
   Input: 125
   Output: Not an SUPERSPY number [1+2+5 is not equal to 3] • *Understanding/Application*

8. Define a class to overload the method display() as follows: **[15]**

void display()	To print the following format using nested loop. 1 2 1 2 1 1 2 1 2 1 1 2 1 2 1
void display (int n, int m)	To print the quotient of the division of m and n if m is greater than n otherwise print the sum of twice n and thrice m.
double display (double a, double b, double c)	To print the value of z where $z = p \times q$, $p = \frac{a+b}{c}$, $q = a + b + c$

• *Understanding/Application*

Answers

1. (i) (*b*) Two dimensional array with 4 rows and 5 columns
   (ii) (*c*) Platform Independent
   (iii) (*a*) 2 bytes
   (iv) (*b*) %
   (v) (*c*) static
   (vi) (*d*) 4.0
   (vii) (*c*) replace(char, char)
   (viii) (*b*) supports floating point constants
   (ix) (*b*) 130
   (x) (*a*) for (int i=11;i<=30;i+=2)
   (xi) (*c*) x[49]=100
   (xii) (*b*) boolean compute (int a, int b)
   (xiii) (*d*) return
   (xiv) (*c*) false
   (xv) (*c*) Character.toUpperCase(char)
   (xvi) (*a*) Both Assertion (A) and Reason (R) are true and Reason (R) is a correct explanation of Assertion (A)
   (xvii) (*d*) Both A and C
   (xviii) (*a*) s.length
   (xix) (*b*) (3) (4) (1) (2)
   (xx) (*c*) Assertion (A) is true and Reason (R) is false

2. (i)
```
if (code = = 'g'||code = = 'G')
System.out.println("GREEN");
```
   (ii) 4, 6
   (iii) Statement with error – boolean x = true; To get the required output – int x = 1;
   (iv) Math.cbrt(x) + Math.sqrt(y)
   (v) Loop is executed two times
   20
   22
   (vi) (a) true
   (b) –1
   (vii) X b
   (viii) Syntax error, double y = Double.parseDouble(x)
   (ix) Default constructor, Parameterized Constructor
   (x) (a) x[2][0]
   (b) 17

3.
```
import java.util.*;
class Bank
{
  double p, n, r, a;
  Scanner ob = new Scanner(System.in);
  void accept()
  {
    System.out.println ("Enter principal");
    p = ob.nextDouble();
    System.out.println("Enter number of years");
    n = ob.nextDouble();
  }
  void calculate()
  {
    if (n <= 0.5)
      r = 9;
    else if (n > 0.5 && n < 1)
      r = 10;
    else if (n >= 1 && n <= 3)
      r = 11;
      a = p * Math.pow(1 + r / 100, n);
  }
  void display()
  {
    System.out.println("Principal"
                  + "\t" + "Rate" + "\t" + "Time"
                                 + "\t" + "Amount");
    System.out.println(p + "\t" + r +
                              "\t" + n + "\t" + a);
  }
  public static void main(String[] args)
  {
    Bank b = new Bank();
    b.accept();
    b.calculate();
    b.display();
  }
}
```

4.
```
class Binary
{
  double x[] = {5.6, 11.5, 20.8, 35.4, 43.1, 52.4,
                        66.6, 78.9, 80.0, 95.5};
  double n;
  Binary(double z)
  {
    n = z;
  }
  void search()
  {
    int f = 0, l = x.length - 1, m;
    while (f <= l)
    {
      m = (f + l) / 2;
      if (x[m] == n)
      {
        System.out.println("Search Successful");
```

```
            System.exit(0);
          }
          if (x[m] < n)
            f = m + 1;
          else
            l = m - 1;
        }
        System.out.println("Search Unsuccessful");
      }
      public static void main(String[] args)
      {
        Binary binarySearch = new
                        Binary(43.1); // Example search
        binarySearch.search();
      }
    }
```

5.
```
class Convert
{
  String s;
    // Constructor to initialize the string
  Convert(String z)
  {
    s = z;
  }
  // Method to perform the conversion
  void convert()
  {
    int i, l = s.length();
    char ch;

    String ns = "";
    for (i = 0; i < l; i++)
    {
      ch = s.charAt(i);
      if (Character.isLetter(ch))
      {
        if ("AEIOUaeiou".indexOf(ch) >= 0)
          ns = ns + (char) (ch + 1);
        else
          ns = ns + (char) (ch - 1);
      }
      else
      {
        ns = ns + ch;
      }
    }
    System.out.print(ns);
  }
  public static void main(String[] args)
  {
    Convert obj = new Convert("Example");
    obj.convert();  // Call the convert method
  }
}
```

6.
```
class SumRow
{
  int x[][];
    // Correct declaration of the 2D array
    // Constructor to initialize the array
  SumRow(int z[][])
  {
    x = z; // Correctly assigning the parameter
                                 to the class variable
  }
  // Method to calculate and print the sum of
                                          each row
  void calculate()
  {
    int r, c, s;
    for (r = 0; r < x.length; r++)
    { // Use x.length to handle different sizes
                                         of arrays
      s = 0;
        // Initialize sum for each row
      for (c = 0; c < x[r].length; c++)
      { // Use x[r].length to handle different
                                      column sizes
        s += x[r][c]; // Accumulate the sum for
                                   the current row
      }
      System.out.println("Sum of row " + r + "
                 = " + s); // Print the sum of the
                                       current row
    }
  }
  public static void main(String[] args)
  {
    int[][] array =
    {
      {1, 2, 3, 4},
      {5, 6, 7, 8},
      {9, 10, 11, 12},
      {13, 14, 15, 16}
    };
    SumRow sr = new SumRow(array);
    sr.calculate(); // Call the method to
                       calculate and print row sums
  }
}
```

7.
```
class Superspy
{
  int n;
  Superspy(int x)
  {
    n = x;
  }
  boolean isSuperspy()
  {
    int d, s = 0, c = 0;
    int temp = n;  // Use a temporary variable
```

```
                      to keep the original value of n
    while (temp > 0)
    {
      d = temp % 10;
      s = s + d;
      c++;
      temp = temp / 10;
    }
    return s == c;
  }
  public static void main(String[] args)
  {
    Superspy spy = new Superspy(123);
    if (spy.isSuperspy())
    {
      System.out.println("The number is a
                               superspy number.");
    }
    else
    {
      System.out.println("The number is not a
                               superspy number.");
    }
  }
}
```

8.

```
class Overload
{
  // Method to display a pattern of 1s and 2s
    void display()
  {
    int r, c;
    for (r = 1; r <= 3; r++)
    {
      for (c = 1; c <= 5; c++)
      {
        if (c % 2 == 0)
          // Fixed condition to check for
                                 even numbers
          System.out.print(2);
        else
          System.out.print(1);
      }
      System.out.println();
    }
  }
  // Method to display result based on
                          comparison of m and n
  void display(int m, int n)
  {
    if (m > n)
      System.out.println(m / n);
    else
      System.out.println(2 * n + 3 * m);
  }
  // Method to perform calculations with double
                                         values
  void display(double a, double b, double c)
  {
    double z, p, q;
    p = (a + b) / c;
    q = a + b + c;
    z = p * q; // Corrected multiplication
    System.out.println(z);
  }
  // Main method to run the program
  public static void main(String[] args)
  {
    Overload obj = new Overload();
    obj.display();
      // Calls method with no arguments
    obj.display(10, 5);
      // Calls method with int arguments
    obj.display(5.0, 3.0, 2.0);
      // Calls method with double arguments
  }
}
```

ICSE

Examination Paper 2024

COMPUTER APPLICATIONS-X

Time : 2 hrs | Max. Marks : 100

General Instructions

1. Answers to this paper must be written on the paper provided separately.
2. You will not be allowed to write during the first 15 minutes. This time is to be spent in reading the question paper.
3. The time given at the head of this paper is the time allowed for writing the answers.
4. This paper is divided into two sections. Attempt all questions from Section A and any four questions from Section B.
5. The intended marks for questions or parts of questions are given in brackets [ ].

Section A

(Attempt all questions from this Section)

1. Choose the correct answers to the questions from the given options **[20]**

(Do not copy the questions, write the correct answers only)

(i)

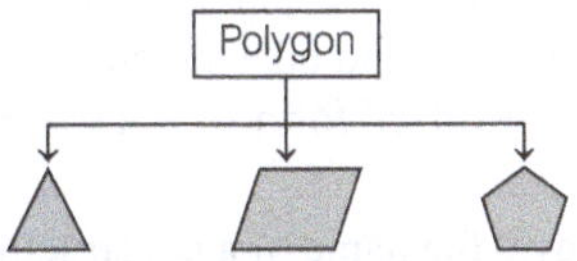

Consider the above picture and choose the correct statement from the following

(a) Polygon is the object and the pictures are classes
(b) Both polygon and the pictures are classes
(c) Polygon is the class and the pictures are objects
(d) Both polygon and the pictures are objects

(ii) `int x = 98 ; char ch = (char) x ;` what is the value in ch?

(a) b (b) A (c) B (d) 97

(iii) The output of the statement "CONCENTRATION". indexOf ('T') is

(a) 9 (b) 7 (c) 6 (d) (–1)

(iv) The access specifier that gives least accessibility is

(a) package (b) public
(c) protected (d) private

(v) The output of the statement "talent''. compare To("genius") is

(a) 11 (b) –11 (c) 0 (d) 13

(vi) Which of the following is an escape sequence character in Java?

(a) /n (b) \t (c) /t (d) //n

(vii) If (a > b & & b > c) then largest number is

(a) b (b) c
(c) a (d) wrong expression

(viii) What is the output of `Math. ceil(5.4)+ Math. ceil (4.5)`?

(a) 10.0 (b) 11.0 (c) 12.0 (d) 9.0

(ix) What is the method to check whether a character is a letter or digit?

(a) `isDigit(char)`
(b) `isLetterOrDigit()`
(c) `isLetterOrDigit(char)`
(d) `isLETTERorDIGIT(char)`

(x) The extension of a Java source code file is

(a) exe (b) obj (c) jvm (d) java

(xi) The number of bytes occupied by a character array of four rows and three columns are

(a) 12 (b) 24 (c) 96 (d) 48

(xii) Which of the following data type cannot be used with switch case construct?

(a) int (b) char
(c) String (d) double

(xiii) Which of the following are entry controlled loops?
1. for 2. while 3. do..while 4. switch
(a) Only 1 (b) 1 and 2
(c) 1 and 3 (d) 3 and 4

(xiv) Method which reverses a given number is
(a) Impure method (b) Pure method
(c) Constructor (d) Destructor

(xv) If the name of the class is "Yellow", what can be the possible name for its constructors?
(a) yellow (b) YELLOW
(c) Yell (d) Yellow

(xvi) Invoking a method by passing the objects of a class is termed as
(a) Call by reference (b) Call by value
(c) Call by method (d) Call by constructor

(xvii) The correct statement to create an object named mango of class fruit
(a) `Fruit Mango = new fruit();`
(b) `fruit mango = new fruit();`
(c) `Mango fruit = new Mango();`
(d) `fruit mango = new mango();`

(xviii) **Assertion (A)** Static method can access static and instance variables.
Reason (R) Static variable can be accessed only by static method.
(a) Assertion and Reason both are correct.
(b) Assertion is true and Reason is false.
(c) Assertion is false and Reason is true.
(d) Assertion and Reason both are false.

(xix) What is the output of the Java code given below?
```
String color [ ] = {"Blue", "Red", "Violet"};
System.out.println(color[2].length());
```
(a) 6 (b) 5
(c) 3 (d) 2

(xx) Which of the following mathematical methods returns only an integer?
(a) `Math.ceil(n)` (b) `Math.sqrt(n)`
(c) `Math.floor(n)` (d) `Math.round(n)`

Ans (i) (c) In the given picture, Polygon is the class and other pictures are objects.

(ii) (a) In the ASCII system, the decimal value 98 corresponds to the character 'b'.
So, the value of ch would be 'b'.

(iii) (c) The output would be: 6
This is because in the String "CONCENTRATION", the character 'T' is located at the 7th position (indexing starts from 0). So, the indexOf() method returns 6.

(iv) (d) The private access specifier achieves the lowest level of accessibility.

(v) (d) `Output: 13`

(vi) (b) \t - Inserts a tab character

(vii) (c) The expression (a > b && b > c) evaluates to true if a is greater than b, and b is greater than c. This essentially means that a is the largest number among a, b, and c.
So, according to the expression, the largest number is a.

(viii) (b) `Math.ceil(5.4)` rounds up 5.4 to 6.0
`Math.ceil(4.5)` rounds up 4.5 to 5.0
Therefore, the result is 11.0

(ix) (c) The `isLetterOrDigit(char)` method in Java is a part of the Character class. It determines whether the specified character is a letter or a digit.

(x) (d) Extension for Java source code file is .java.

(xi) (b) Total number of elements = Number of rows * Number of columns = 4 * 3 = 12
Each element occupies 2 bytes.
Total number of bytes = Total number of elements * Size of each element = 12 * 2 = 24 bytes

(xii) (d) double data type cannot be used with switch case construct.

(xiii) (b) In Java, both the "for" and "while" loops are entry-controlled loops.

(xiv) (b) A pure method is a method that only depends on its input parameters and does not modify any external state. In the context of reversing a number, a pure method would take the number as input and return its reversed form without altering any external state.

(xv) (d) In Java, the name of a constructor must match exactly with the name of the class. Therefore, for a class named "Yellow", the possible name for its constructors would be Yellow.

(xvi) (a) In Java, invoking a method by passing the objects of a class is termed as Call by reference.

(xvii) (b) The correct statement to create an object named mango of class fruit in Java would be
`fruit mango = new fruit();`

(xviii) (c) Assertion is false and Reason is true.

(xix) (a) The code then prints the length of the string at index 2 of the array, which is "Violet". The length of "Violet" is 6 characters.
So, the correct output is: 6

(xx) (d) `Math.round(n)` mathematical methods returns only an integer.

2. (i) Write Java expression for **[2]**

$$\frac{|a+b|}{\sqrt{a^2+b^2}}$$

(ii) Evaluate the expression when x is 4 **[2]**

```
x + = x + + * + + x % 2;
```

(iii) Rewrite the following *do while* program segment using for **[2]**

```
x = 10;  y = 20;
do
{
  x + +;
  y + +;
} while (x < = 20);
System.out.println(x * y) ;
```

(iv) Give the output of the following program segment. How many times is the loop executed? **[2]**

```
for (x = 10; x > 20; x + +)
System.out.println (x);
System.out.println (x * 2);
```

(v)
```
String s1= "45.50";String s2 = "54.50";
double d1 = Double.parseDouble(s1);
double d2 = Double.parseDouble(s2);
int x =(int)(d1+d2);
```
[2]

What is value of x ?

(vi) Consider the following two-dimensional array and answer the questions given below **[2]**

```
int x[][] = {{4,3,2},{7,8,2},{8,3,10},{1,2,9}};
```

(a) What is the order of the array?

(b) What is the value of x[0][0] + x[2][2]?

(vii) Differentiate between boxing and unboxing. **[2]**

(viii) The following code to compare two strings is compiled, the following syntax error was displayed - incompatible types – int cannot be converted to boolean. Identify the statement which has the error and write the correct statement. Give the output of the program segment. **[2]**

```
void calculate()
{
  String a = "KING", b = "KINGDOM";
  boolean  x = a.compareTo(b);
  System.out.println(x);
}
```

(ix) Consider the given program and answer the questions given below **[2]**

```
class temp
{
  int a;
  temp()
  {
    a = 10;
  }
  temp(int z)
  {
    a = z;
  }
  void print()
  {
    System.out.println(a);
  }
  void main()
  {
    temp t = new temp();
    temp x = new temp(30);
    t.print();
    x.print();
  }
}
```

(a) What concept of OOPs is depicted in the above program with two constructors?

(b) What is the output of the method main()?

(x) Primitive data types are built in data types which are a part of the wrapper classes. These wrapper classes are encapsulated in the java.lang package. Non-primitive datatypes like Scanner class are a part of the utility package for which and object needs to be created. **[2]**

(a) To which package the Character and Boolean classes belong?

(b) Write the statement to access the Scanner class in the program.

Ans. (i) The Java expression for:

```
Math.abs(a+b)/Math.sqrt(a*a+b*b);
```

(ii)
```
x+ = x++ * ++x %2;
x = 4 + 4 * 6 % 2
x = 4 + 4 * 0
x = 4 + 0
x = 4
```

(iii)
```
int x = 10;
int y = 20;
for (; x <= 20; x++, y++)
{
}
System.out.println(x * y);
```

(iv) Output of the program will be 20.
The loop is not executed at all.
So, the loop is executed 0 times.

(v) Result in the output is 100.

(vi) (i) The order of the array, it's a 2D array with 4 rows and 3 columns. Each row represents a separate array with 3 elements.

(ii) The program then prints the sum of two elements: x[0][0] and x[2][2].

x[0][0] refers to the element in the first row and first column, which is 4. x[2][2] refers to the element in the third row and third column, which is 10.

So, the sum x[0][0] + x[2][2] is equal to 4 + 10 = 14.

(vii)

Boxing	Unboxing
Boxing is used to store value types in the Garbage-collected Heap.	Unboxing an Interface type of a value type that implements the interface.
Convert the value type to reference type.	Convert to reference type to value type.
Implicit Conversion	Explicit Conversion

(viii) `boolean x = a.compareTo(b);`

This statement has the error because int datatype is used in place of boolean datatype.

In this case:

"KING" is lexicographically less than "KINGDOM".

The difference in lengths of the strings is taken into account.

The length of "KING" is shorter than "KINGDOM" by 3 characters.

So, the output is -3.

(ix) (a) Constructor overloading

(b) 10

30

(x) (a) The Character and Boolean classes belong to the java.lang package.

(b) To access the Scanner class in a Java program, you need to import it from the java.util package using the statement: `import java.util.Scanner;`. Then, create an object of the Scanner class to use its functionalities.

Section B

(Answer any Four questions from this Section)

The answers in this section should consist of the programs in either BlueJ environment or any program environment with Java as the base.

Each program should be written using variable description/mnemonic codes so that the logic of the program is clearly depicted.

Flowcharts and algorithms are not required.

3. DTDC a courier company charges for the courier based on the weight of the parcel. Define a class with the following specifications: **[15]**

Class name	Courier	
Member variables	name—name of the customer	
	weight—weight of the parcel in kilograms	
	address—address of the recipient	
	bill—amount to be paid	
	type—'D'-domestic, 'I'-international	
Member methods:		
`void accept( )`	to accept the details using the methods of the Scanner class only.	
`void calculate( )`	to calculate the bill as per the following criteria:	
	Weight in Kgs	Rate per Kg
	First 5 Kgs	Rs. 800
	Next 5 Kgs	Rs. 700
	Above 10 Kgs	Rs. 500
	An additional amount of Rs. 1500 is charged if the type of the courier is I (International)	
`void print( )`	To print the details	
`void main( )`	to create and object of the class and invoke the methods	

Ans.

```
import java.util.Scanner;
class Courier
{
  String name;
  double weight;
  String address;
  double bill;
  char type;
  void accept()
  {
    Scanner scanner = new Scanner(System.in);
    System.out.println("Enter customer name:");
    name = scanner.nextLine();
    System.out.println("Enter weight of the parcel
                                             in kilograms:");
    weight = scanner.nextDouble();
    scanner.nextLine(); // Consume newline character
    System.out.println("Enter address of the
                                                recipient:");
    address = scanner.nextLine();
    System.out.println("Enter type of courier
         (D for domestic, I for international):");
    type = scanner.nextLine().charAt(0);
```

```
    }
    void calculate()
    {
      if (weight <= 5)
      {
        bill = weight * 800;
      }
      else if (weight <= 10)
      {
        bill = 5 * 800 + (weight - 5) * 700;
      }
      else
      {
        bill = 5 * 800 + 5 * 700 + (weight - 10) * 500;
      }
      if (type == 'I')
      {
        bill += 1500;
      }
    }
    void print()
    {
      System.out.println("\nCustomer Name: " + name);
      System.out.println("Weight of the parcel: "
                                  + weight + " kgs");
      System.out.println("Address of the recipient:
                                        " + address);
      System.out.println("Type of courier: " +
                                             type);
      System.out.println("Bill Amount: Rs. " + bill);
    }
    public static void main(String[] args)
    {
      Courier courier = new Courier();
      courier.accept();
      courier.calculate();
      courier.print();
    }
}
```

Output

Enter customer name:

OM

Enter weight of the parcel in kilograms:

10

Enter address of the recipient:

Noida

Enter type of courier (D for domestic, I for international):

D

Customer Name: OM

Weight of the parcel: 10.0 kgs

Address of the recipient: Noida

Type of courier : D

Bill Amount: Rs. 7500.0

4. Define a class to overload the method perform as follows: **[15]**

`double perform (double r, double h)`	to calculate the return the value of Curved surface area of cone CSA = πrl $l = \sqrt{r^2 + h^2}$
`void perform (int r, int c)`	Use NESTED FOR LOOP to generate the following format r = 4, c = 5 output—1 2 3 4 5 1 2 3 4 5 1 2 3 4 5 1 2 3 4 5
`void perform (int m, int n, char ch)`	to print the quotient of the division of m and n, if ch is Q else print the remainder of the division of m and n if ch is R

Ans.

```
public class OverloadedMethods
{
  // Method to calculate and return the curved
                              surface area of a cone
  double perform(double r, double h)
  {
    double CSA = Math.PI * r * Math.sqrt(r*r + h*h);
    return CSA;
  }
  // Method to print a nested format of numbers
  void perform(int r, int c)
  {
    for (int i = 1; i <= r; i++)
    {
      for (int j = 1; j <= c; j++)
      {
        System.out.print(j);
      }
      System.out.println();
    }
  }
  // Method to print quotient or remainder
                    based on the character provided
  void perform(int m, int n, char ch)
  {
    if (ch == 'Q')
    {
      System.out.println("Quotient: " + (m / n));
    }
    else if (ch == 'R')
    {
```

```
            System.out.println("Remainder: " + (m % n));
        }
        else
        {
            System.out.println("Invalid character
                                        provided.");
        }
    }
    // Main method to test the class
    public static void main(String[] args)
    {
        OverloadedMethods obj = new OverloadedMethods();
        // Testing perform(double r, double h)
        double r = 3.0;
        double h = 4.0;
        System.out.println("Curved Surface Area
                    of Cone: " + obj.perform(r, h));
        // Testing perform(int r, int c)
        int rows = 4;
        int columns = 5;
        System.out.println("Nested Format of Numbers:");
        obj.perform(rows, columns);
        // Testing perform(int m, int n, char ch)
        int m = 10;
        int n = 3;
        char ch = 'Q';
        obj.perform(m, n, ch); // Should print quotient
        ch = 'R';
        obj.perform(m, n, ch); // Should print remainder
    }
}
```

Output

Curved Surface Area of Cone: 47.12388980384689

Nested Format of Numbers:

12345

12345

12345

12345

Quotient : 3

Remainder : 1

5. Define a class to accept a number from user and check if it is an EvenPal number or not. (The number is said to be EvenPal number when number is palindrome number (a number is palindrome if it is equal to its reverse) and sum of its digits is an even number.) **[15]**

Example 121 is a palindrome number

Sum of the digits 1 + 2 + 1 = 4 which is an even number

Ans.

```
import java.util.Scanner;
public class EvenPalNumberChecker
{
    // Function to check if a number is palindrome
    public static boolean isPalindrome(int num)
    {
        int reversedNum = 0;
        int originalNum = num;
        while (num != 0)
        {
            int digit = num % 10;
            reversedNum = reversedNum * 10 + digit;
            num /= 10;
        }
        return originalNum == reversedNum;
    }
    // Function to calculate sum of digits
    public static int sumOfDigits(int num)
    {
        int sum = 0;
        while (num != 0)
        {
            sum += num % 10;
            num /= 10;
        }
        return sum;
    }
    // Main method
    public static void main(String[] args)
    {
        Scanner scanner = new Scanner(System.in);
        // Accepting the number from the user
        System.out.print("Enter a number: ");
        int number = scanner.nextInt();
        // Checking if it's a palindrome and sum
        of digits is even
        if (isPalindrome(number)
                    && sumOfDigits(number) % 2 == 0)
        {
            System.out.println(number + " is an EvenPal
                                            number.");
        }
        else
        {
            System.out.println(number + " is not an
                                    EvenPal number.");
        }
        scanner.close();
    }
}
```

Output

Enter a number: 231

231 is not an EvenPal number.

Enter a number: 121

121 is an EvenPal number.

6. Define a class to accept values into an integer array of order 4 × 4 and check whether it is a DIAGONAL array or not. An array is DIAGONAL if the sum of the left diagonal elements equals the sum of the right diagonal elements. Print the appropriate message. **[15]**

Example

3 4 2 5	Sum of the left diagonal elements =
2 5 2 3	3 + 5 + 2 + 1 = 11
5 3 2 7	Sum of the right diagonal elements =
1 3 7 1	5 + 2 + 3 + 1 = 11

Ans.

```
import java.util.Scanner;
public class DiagonalArrayCheck
{
  public static void main(String[] args)
  {
    Scanner scanner = new Scanner(System.in);
    int[][] array = new int[4][4];
    System.out.println("Enter values for a 4x4
                                              array:");
    // Accepting values into the array
    for (int i = 0; i < 4; i++)
    {
      for (int j = 0; j < 4; j++)
      {
        array[i][j] = scanner.nextInt();
      }
    }
    // Checking if it's a diagonal array
    boolean isDiagonal = true;
    int leftDiagonalSum = 0;
    int rightDiagonalSum = 0;
    for (int i = 0; i < 4; i++)
    {
      leftDiagonalSum += array[i][i];
      rightDiagonalSum += array[i][3 - i];
    }
    if (leftDiagonalSum != rightDiagonalSum)
    {
      isDiagonal = false;
    }
    // Printing the appropriate message
    if (isDiagonal)
    {

      System.out.println("The array is a DIAGONAL
                                              array.");
    }
    else
    {
      System.out.println("The array is NOT
                                   a DIAGONAL array.");
    }
  }
}
```

Output

Enter values for a 4x4 array:

3 4 2 5

2 5 2 3

5 3 2 7

1 3 7 1

The array is a DIAGONAL array.

Enter values for a 4x4 array:

3 4 5 3

3 5 1 1

6 3 2 4

1 4 2 5

The array is NOT a DIAGONAL array.

7. Define a class PinCode and store the given pin codes in a single dimensional array. Sort these pin codes in ascending order using the Selection Sort technique only. Display the sorted array. **[15]**

110061, 110001, 110029, 110023, 110055, 110006, 110019, 110033

Ans.

```
public class PinCode
{
  private int[] pinCodes;
  public PinCode(int[] pinCodes)
  {
    this.pinCodes = pinCodes;
  }
  public void selectionSort()
  {
    int n = pinCodes.length;
    for (int i = 0; i < n - 1; i++)
    {
      int minIndex = i;
      for (int j = i + 1; j < n; j++)
      {
        if (pinCodes[j] < pinCodes[minIndex])
        {
          minIndex = j;
        }
      }
      if (minIndex != i)
      {
        int temp = pinCodes[minIndex];
        pinCodes[minIndex] = pinCodes[i];
        pinCodes[i] = temp;
```

```
            }
        }
    }
    public void displaySortedPinCodes()
    {
        System.out.println("Sorted Pin Codes:");
        for (int pinCode : pinCodes)
        {
            System.out.print(pinCode + " ");
        }
        System.out.println();
    }
    public static void main(String[] args)
    {
        int[] pinCodes = {110061, 110001, 110029,
            110023, 110055, 110006, 110019, 110033};
        PinCode pinCodeObj = new PinCode(pinCodes);
        System.out.println("Original Pin Codes:");
        for (int pinCode : pinCodes)
        {
            System.out.print(pinCode + " ");
        }
        System.out.println();
        pinCodeObj.selectionSort();
        pinCodeObj.displaySortedPinCodes();
    }
}
```

Output

Original Pin Codes:

110061 110001 110029 110023 110055 110006 110019 110033

Sorted Pin Codes:

110001 110006 110019 110023 110029 110033 110055 110061

8. Define a class to accept the gmail id and check for its validity. **[15]**

A gmail id is valid only if it has:

→@

→.(dot)

→gmail

→com

Example icse2024@gmail.com is a valid gmail id.

Ans.

```
import java.util.Scanner;
public class GmailValidator
{
    private String gmailId;
    public GmailValidator(String gmailId)
    {
        this.gmailId = gmailId;
    }
    public boolean isValid()
    {
        // Checking if the gmailId contains '@', '.',
                                     and 'gmail.com'
        if (gmailId.contains("@") && gmailId.contains
            (".") && gmailId.endsWith("gmail.com"))
        {
            int atIndex = gmailId.indexOf("@");
            int dotIndex = gmailId.indexOf(".", atIndex);
            // Checking if '.' comes after '@'
            if (dotIndex > atIndex)
            {
                return true;
            }
        }
        return false;
    }
    public static void main(String[] args)
    {
        Scanner scanner = new Scanner(System.in);
        System.out.println("Enter your Gmail ID:");
        String gmailId = scanner.nextLine();
        GmailValidator validator = new
                              GmailValidator(gmailId);
        if (validator.isValid())
        {
            System.out.println(gmailId + " is a
                                  valid gmail id.");
        }
        else
        {
            System.out.println(gmailId + " is not
                                a valid gmail id.");
        }
        scanner.close();
    }
}
```

Output

Enter your Gmail ID:

icse2024@gmail.com

icse2024@gmail.com is a valid gmail id.

Enter your Gmail ID:

jointeamgmail.com

jointeamgmail.com is not a valid gmail id.

ICSE

EXAMINATION PAPER 2025

Fully Solved

COMPUTER APPLICATIONS-X

Time : 2 hrs | Max. Marks : 100

General Instructions

1. Answer to this paper must be written on the paper provided separately.
2. You will not be allowed to write during the first 15 minutes. This time is to be spent in reading the question paper.
3. The time given at the head of this paper is the time allowed for writing the answers.
4. This paper is divided into two sections. Attempt all questions from Section A and any four questions from Section B.
5. The intended marks for questions or parts of questions are given in brackets [ ].

Section A

(Attempt all Questions from this Section)

1. Choose the correct answers to the questions from the given options. (Do not copy the questions, write only the correct answers) **[20]**

(i) Character class methods are found in the package called

(a) java.util (b) java.lang
(c) java.awt (d) java.io

(ii) `System.out.println('Z' + 32);` will display

(a) *z* (b) *Z*
(c) 122 (d) 154

(iii) double *x* [] = {2.5, 4.5, 5.5, 6.4}; occupies .... bytes.

(a) 16 (b) 4
(c) 8 (d) 32

(iv) The output 42/6% 2 is:

(a) 1 (b) 10
(c) 2 (d) 0

(v)

Consider the two dimensional array P[2][3], of peripherals (input/output devices) given above, state the index of the device Barcode Scanner.

(a) P[1][1] (b) P[0][1]
(c) P[1][2] (d) P[0][0]

(vi) Which of the following is user defined data type?

1. array	3. class
2. double	4. boolean

(a) only 1
(b) 1 and 3
(c) only 2
(d) only 4

(vii) Select the infinite loop:

(a) for(int i = 1; i< = 10; i + +)
(b) for(int i = 2; i! = 0; i – = 3)
(c) for(int i = 5; i< = 5; i + +)
(d) for(int i = 1; i > = 1; i – –)

(viii) The output of Math.max(– 7, Math.min(–5, – 4)) is

(a) – 5 (b) – 4
(c) – 7 (d) error

(ix) Which of the following is true for the given object creation statement?

```
Game cricket = new Game( );
```

(a) Game is an object of cricket class
(b) New keyword creates object Game
(c) Game is a class and cricket is an object
(d) Game and cricket are objects

(x) Post office is an example for .... access specifier.

(a) public (b) local
(c) protected (d) private

(xi) **Assertion (A)** In switch case break statement avoids fall through.

Reason (R) break statement helps to execute only one case at a time.

(a) Both (A) and (R) are true and (R) is a correct explanation of (A).
(b) Both (A) and (R) are true and (R) is not a correct explanation of (A).
(c) (A) is true and (R) is false.
(d) (A) is false and (R) is true.

(xii) A physical education teacher asks the students to do the side stretch as shown below, 10 times. Which programming construct the teacher uses?

(a) if (b) switch
(c) for (d) if else if

(xiii) The index (subscript) of the last element of an array ar[ ] is:

(a) ar.length( ) (b) ar[ ].length
(c) ar.length( ) – 1 (d) ar.length – 1

(xiv) **Assertion (A)** A clock is a real-life example of nested loops.

Reason (R) The hour hand moves through 12 positions, while the minute hand moves through 60 positions within each hour.

(a) Both (A) and (R) are true and (R) is a correct explanation of (A).
(b) Both (A) and (R) are true and (R) is not a correct explanation of (A).
(c) (A) is true and (R) is false.
(d) (A) is false and (R) is true

(xv) Which of the following pairs of methods will cause a compile-time error due to incorrect method overloading?

(a) void test(int a, int b) and void test(double a, double b)
(b) void test(int a, double b) and void test(double a, int b)
(c) void test(int a, double b) and void test(int a)
(d) void test(int a) and int test(int a)

(xvi) Which of the following converts "25" to 25.0?

(a) Double.Parsedouble("25")
(b) Double.parse("25")
(c) Double.parseDouble("25")
(d) Double.parseDouble(25)

(xvii) Consider the program segment:

```
int p=0;
for(p=4;p>0;p- =2);
System.out.print(p);
System.out.println(p);
```

The above statements will display:

(a) 42 (b) 4200
(c) 0
0 (d) 00

(xviii) `System.out.println("I said,\ "It\'s wise to obey elders.\"");`

The output of the above statement is:

(a) I said,'It is wise to obey elders'.
(b) I said, "It's wise to obey elders."
(c) I said, It's wise to elders.
(d) "'It's wise to obey elders."'

(xix) What is the output of the statement given below?

```
"ANGER".compareTo("ANGEL")
```

(a) 3 (b) – 6
(c) 6 (d) 0

(xx) Consider the following program segment in which the statements are jumbled.

Choose the correct order of statements to calculate and return the factorial of 4.

```
for (k=1;k<=4;k+ +) ——→ 1
return fa; ——→ 2
long fa=1, k; ——→ 3
fa*=k; ——→ 4
```

(a) 1, 2, 3, 4 (b) 3, 1, 4, 2
(c) 3, 1, 2, 4 (d) 1, 3, 2, 4

2. (i) Write the java expression to find the product of square root of *P* and the square root of *Q* using the methods of Math class. **[2]**

(ii) Write the output of the following String method:

```
String x=" talent"; String y="matrix";
System.out.print(x.substring(3).concat
(y.substring(3));
```
[2]

(iii) Write the Java statement for creating an object named 'sifra' of the class 'Robot', which takes three double parameters. **[2]**

(iv) Convert the given loop into exit controlled loop. **[2]**

```
int a,b;
for (a=10,b=1; a>=1;a- =2)
{
 b+ =a;
```

```
  b+ +;
}
System.out.print(b);
```

(v) Consider and give the output of the following program: **[2]**

```
class report
{
 int a,b;
 report( )
 {
   a=10;
   b=15;
 }
 report(int x, int y)
 {
   a=x;
   b=y;
 }
 void print( )
 {
   System.out.println(a*b);
 }
 static void main( )
 {
   report r = new report( );
   r.print( );
   report p = new report(4, 5);
   p.print( );
 }
}
```

(vi) (a) Name one String method which results in positive integer only. **[2]**

(b) Name one String method which results in a character.

(vii) John was asked to write a Java code to calculate the surface area of a cone, the following code was written by him: **[2]**

Surface area of cone is $A = \pi rl$

$$l = \sqrt{r^2 + h^2}$$

```
class area
{
 double area (double r, double h)
 {
   double l, a;
   a=22.0/7*r*l;
   l=Math.sqrt(r*r+h*h);
   return a;
 }
}
```

Specify the type of the error in the above program, correct and write the program to be error free.

(viii) Consider the following array and answer the questions given below: **[2]**

```
int a[ ] = {12, 10, 8, 4, 6, 2, 3, 5, 7}
```

(a) What is the output of System.out.print(a[0]+a[5]);?

(b) What is the index (subscript) of the largest element of the array a[ ]?

(ix) (a) Write the Java statement to initialise the first 6 odd numbers in a 3×2 array. **[2]**

(b) What is the result of x[0][1] + x[2][1] of the above array?

(x) Give the output of the following program segment and specify how many times the loop is executed.

```
String s = "JAVA";
for(i=0;i<s.length();i+ =2)
System.out.println(s.substring(i));
```
[2]

Section B

(Answer any Four Questions from this Section)

3. Define a class named CloudStorage with the following specifications **[15]**

Member Variables	
int acno	stores the user's account number
int space	stores the amount of storage space in GB purchased by the user.
double bill	stores the total price to be paid by the user
Member Methods	
void accept()	prompts the user to input their account number and storage space using Scanner class methods only.
void calculate()	calculates the bill total price based on the storage space purchased using the pricing table provided:
	Storage range — Price per GB (Rs)
	First 15 GB — 15
	Next 15 GB — 13
	Above 30 GB — 11
void display()	displays the account number, storage space and bill to be paid

Write a main method to create an object of the class and invoke the methods of the class with respect to the object.

4. Define a class to accept values into a 4 × 4 integer array. Calculate and print the NORM of the array. **[15]**

NORM is the square root of sum of squares of all elements.

1	2	1	3
5	2	1	6
3	6	1	2
3	4	6	3

Sum of squares of elements $= 1 + 4 + 1 + 9 + 25$
$+ 4 + 1 + 36 + 9 + 36 + 1 + 4 + 9 + 16 + 36 + 9 = 201$

NORM = Squareroot of 201
$= 14.177446878757825$

5. Define a class to accept a String and Print if it is a Super string or not. A String is Super if the number of uppercase letters are equal to the number of lower case letters. **[15]**

[Use Character & String methods only]

Example: "COmmITmeNt"

Number of Uppercase letters -5

Number of Lowercase letters-5

String is a Super String

6. Define a class to initialise the following data in an array.

Search for a given character input by the user, using the Binary Search technique. **[15]**

Print "Search Successful" if the character is found otherwise print "Search is not Successful"

'A', 'H', 'N', 'P', 'S', 'U', 'W','Y', 'Z', 'b', 'd'

7. Define a class to overload the method print( ) as follows: **[15]**

void print( )	To print the given format using nested loops. @#@#@ @#@#@ @#@#@ @#@#@
double print(double a, double b)	To display the sum of numbers between a and b with difference of 0.5 eg. if a = 1.0, b = 4.0 output is: 1.0 + 1.5 + 2.0 + 2.5 + ... + 4.0
int print(char ch1, char ch2)	compare the two characters and return the ASCII code of the largest character.

8. Define a class to accept a number. Check if the sum of the largest digit and the smallest digit is an even number or an odd number. Print appropriate messages. **[15]**

Sample Input:	6425	3748
Largest digit:	6	8
Smallest digit:	2	3
Sample Output:	Sum is even	Sum is odd

Answers

1. (i) (b) java.lang
   (ii) (c) 122
   (iii) (d) 32
   (iv) (a) 1
   (v) (a) P[1][1]
   (vi) (b) 1 and 3
   (vii) (b) for(int i = 2; i! = 0; i – = 3)
   (viii) (a) – 5
   (ix) (c) Game is a class and cricket is an object
   (x) (a) public
   (xi) (a) Both (A) and (R) are true and (R) is a correct explanation of (A).
   (xii) (c) for
   (xiii) (d) ar.length – 1
   (xiv) (a) Both (A) and (R) are true and (R) is a correct explanation of (A).
   (xv) (d) void test(int a) and int test(int a)
   (xvi) (c) Double.parseDouble("25")
   (xvii) (d) 00
   (xviii) (b) I said, "It's wise to obey elders."
   (xix) (c) 6
   (xx) (b) 3, 1, 4, 2

2. (i) `Math.sqrt(P)*Math.sqrt(Q)`
   (ii) **Output** endrix
   (iii) `Robot sifra = new Robot (1.0,2.0,3.0);`
   (iv)

```
int a, b;
a = 10;
b = 1;
do{
    b = b + a;
    b++;
    a -= 2;
} while (a >= 1);
System.out.println(b);
```

   (v) **Output**
   150
   20
   (vi) (a) length()
   (b) charAt(int index)
   (vii)

```
class area
{
   double surfaceArea(double r, double h)
   {
      double l = Math.sqrt(r * r + h * h);
      // Correct slant height calculation
      return Math.PI * r * (r + l);
      // Correct total surface area formula
   }
}
```

   (viii) (a) 12 + 7 = 19
   (b) 0
   (ix) (a) int[][] oddNumbers = {{1, 3}, {5, 7}, {9, 11}};
   (b) 1 + 3 + 5 = 9
   (x) **Output**
   J
   JA
   JAV
   JAVA
   Number of times the loop is executed: 4

3.

```
import java.util.Scanner;
class CloudStorage
{
   // Member Variables
    int acno;
    int space; // in GB
    double bill;
    // Method to accept user input
    void accept()
     {
        Scanner sc = new Scanner(System.in);
        System.out.print("Enter account number: ");
        acno = sc.nextInt();
        System.out.print("Enter storage space
                                   purchased (in GB): ");
        space = sc.nextInt();
        sc.close();
    }
    // Method to calculate bill
    void calculate()
    {
        int remaining = space;
        bill = 0;
        if (remaining > 30)
        {
            bill += (remaining - 30) * 11;
            remaining = 30;
        }
        if (remaining > 15)
        {
            bill += (remaining - 15) * 13;
            remaining = 15;
        }
        if (remaining > 0)
        {
            bill += remaining * 15;
        }
    }
    // Method to display results
```

```java
    void display()
    {
        System.out.println("\nAccount No: " + acno);
        System.out.println("Storage Space (GB): "
                                          + space);
        System.out.println("Total Bill (Rs): " + bill);
    }
    // Main method to test the class
    public static void main(String[] args)
    {
        CloudStorage cs = new CloudStorage();
        cs.accept();
        cs.calculate();
        cs.display();
    }
}
```

4.
```java
import java.util.Scanner;
class NormCalculator
{
   int[][] arr = new int[4][4];
   // Method to accept values using Scanner
   public void acceptValues()
   {
     Scanner sc = new Scanner(System.in);
     System.out.println("Enter 16 integers for the
                                    4x4 array:");
     for (int i = 0; i < 4; i++)
     {
       for (int j = 0; j < 4; j++)
       {
         arr[i][j] = sc.nextInt();
       }
     }
   }
   // Method to calculate and print NORM
   public void calculateNorm()
   {
     int sum = 0;
     for (int i = 0; i < 4; i++)
     {
       for (int j = 0; j < 4; j++)
       {
         sum += arr[i][j] * arr[i][j];
           // square of each element
       }
     }
     double norm = Math.sqrt(sum);
     System.out.println("NORM = " + norm);
   }
   // Main method
   public static void main(String[] args)
   {
     NormCalculator obj = new NormCalculator();
     obj.acceptValues();
     obj.calculateNorm();
   }
}
```

Output

Enter 16 integers for the 4 × 4 array:
2 3 4 5
6 7 8 9
2 3 4 5
6 2 1 5
NORM = 20.09975124224178

5.
```java
import java.util.Scanner;
class SuperStringChecker
{
   // Method to accept a string and check if it is a
                                       Super String
   public void checkSuperString()
   {
     Scanner sc = new Scanner(System.in);
     System.out.print("Enter a string: ");
     String input = sc.nextLine();
     int upperCount = 0;
     int lowerCount = 0;
     // Count uppercase and lowercase characters
     for (int i = 0; i < input.length(); i++)
     {
       char ch = input.charAt(i);
       if (Character.isUpperCase(ch))
       {
         upperCount++;
       }
       else if (Character.isLowerCase(ch))
       {
         lowerCount++;
       }
     }
     // Display results
     System.out.println("Number of Uppercase letters
                               = " + upperCount);
       System.out.println("Number of Lowercase
                           letters = " + lowerCount);
       if (upperCount == lowerCount)
       {
         System.out.println("String is a Super
                                        String");
       }
       else
       {
         System.out.println("String is NOT a
                                   Super String");
       }
     }
     // Main method
     public static void main(String[] args)
     {
       SuperStringChecker obj = new
                            SuperStringChecker();
```

```
        obj.checkSuperString();
    }
}
```

Output

Enter a string: COmmiTMENT

Number of Uppercase letters = 7

Number of Lowercase letters = 3

String is NOT a Super String

6.
```
import java.util.Arrays;
import java.util.Scanner;
class BinarySearchChar
{
    char[] arr = {'A', 'H', 'N', 'P', 'S', 'U', 'W',
                                          'Y', 'Z', 'b', 'd'};
    // Method to perform binary search
    public void searchChar()
    {
        Scanner sc = new Scanner(System.in);
        System.out.print("Enter a character to search: ");
        char key = sc.next().charAt(0);
        // Sort the array before binary search
        Arrays.sort(arr);
        int left = 0, right = arr.length - 1;
        boolean found = false;
        while (left <= right)
        {
            int mid = (left + right) / 2;
            if (arr[mid] == key)
            {
                found = true;
                    break;
            }
            else if (arr[mid] < key)
            {
                left = mid + 1;

            }
            else
            {
                right = mid - 1;
            }
        }
        // Output result
        if (found)
        {
            System.out.println("Search Successful");
        }
        else
        {
            System.out.println("Search is not Successful");
        }
    }
    // Main method
    public static void main(String[] args)
    {
        BinarySearchChar obj = new BinarySearchChar();
        obj.searchChar();
    }
}
```

Output

Enter a character to search: B

Search is not Successful

7.
```
import java.util.Scanner;
class Printer
{
    public void print()
    {
        for (int i = 0; i < 5; i++)
        {
            for (int j = 0; j < 5; j++)
            {
                System.out.print("@");
            }
            System.out.println();
        }
    }
    public void print(double a, double b)
    {
        if (a > b)
        {
            double temp = a;
                a = b;
                b = temp;
        }
        for (double i = a; i <= b; i += 0.5)
        {
            System.out.print(i);
            if (i + 0.5 <= b)
            {
                System.out.print(" + ");

            }
        }
        System.out.println();
    }
    public int print(char ch1, char ch2)
    {
        if (ch1 > ch2)
        {
            return (int) ch1;
        }
        else
        {
            return (int) ch2;
        }
    }
    public static void main(String[] args)
    {
        Scanner scanner = new Scanner(System.in);
```

```
        Printer printer = new Printer();
        System.out.println("Calling print() with no
                                              arguments:");
        printer.print();
        System.out.println();
        System.out.println("Calling print(double a,
                                              double b):");
        System.out.print("Enter the value of a: ");
        double a = scanner.nextDouble();
        System.out.print("Enter the value of b: ");
        double b = scanner.nextDouble();
        printer.print(a, b);
        System.out.println();
        System.out.println("Calling print(char ch1,
                                              char ch2):");
        System.out.print("Enter the first character: ");
        char char1 = scanner.next().charAt(0);
        System.out.print("Enter the second character: ");
        char char2 = scanner.next().charAt(0);
        int largestASCII = printer.print(char1, char2);
        System.out.println("ASCII code of the largest
                            character: " + largestASCII);
        scanner.close();
    }
}
```

Output

Calling print() with no arguments:

@@@@@
@@@@@
@@@@@
@@@@@
@@@@@

Calling print(double a, double b):

Enter the value of a: 1.0

Enter the value of b: 4.0

1.0 + 1.5 + 2.0 + 2.5 + 3.0 + 3.5 + 4.0

Calling print(char ch1, char ch2):

Enter the first character: a

Enter the second character: c

ASCII code of the largest character: 99

8.
```
import java.util.Scanner;
class DigitSumCheck
{
    int num;
    // Method to accept input
    void accept()
    {
        Scanner sc = new Scanner(System.in);
        System.out.print("Enter a number: ");
        num = sc.nextInt();
        sc.close();
    }
    // Method to find largest and smallest digit
                                          and check the sum
    void checkSumEvenOdd()
    {
        int temp = num;
        int largest = 0;
        int smallest = 9;
        while (temp > 0)
        {
            int digit = temp % 10;
            if (digit > largest)
            {
                largest = digit;
            }
            if (digit < smallest)
            {
                smallest = digit;
            }
            temp /= 10;
        }
        int sum = largest + smallest;
        System.out.println("Largest digit: " + largest);
        System.out.println("Smallest digit: " + smallest);
        if (sum % 2 == 0)
        {
            System.out.println("Sum is even");
        }
        else
        {
            System.out.println("Sum is odd");
        }
    }
    // Main method
    public static void main(String[] args)
    {
        DigitSumCheck obj = new DigitSumCheck();
        obj.accept();
        obj.checkSumEvenOdd();
    }
}
```